BULLERS ARMS

A Baby Boomer's Quest for the Simple Life at the Beginning of the 21st Century

Mark R. Horowitz

Writers Club Press

San Jose New York Lincoln Shanghai

Bullers Arms
A Baby Boomer's Quest for the Simple Life at
the Beginning of the 21st Century

Published by Writers Club Press
an imprint of iUniverse.com, Inc.

For information address:
iUniverse.com, Inc.
5220 S 16th, Ste. 200
Lincoln, NE 68512
www.iuniverse.com

ISBN: 0-595-01238-8

Printed in the United States of America

To

Jerry Brauer who hoped to embark on this journey
and
Julie who graciously allowed me to take it

Contents

List of Illustrations

Photographs:

The Bar, Bullers Arms, Chagford
General Buller, Bullers Arms, Chagford
Spinsters' Rock, Drewsteignton, Dartmoor
Saxon Well (pre-1066), Widecombe, Dartmoor
One of 24 Bronze Age stone huts, Grimspound, Dartmoor
Cover: *Stonehenge to Star Wars*
Market House, Chagford
Three Crowns Inn, Chagford
Prouz coat of arms, St. Michael's church, Chagford
Bullers Arms, 7 Mill Street, Chagford
The Servery, Bullers Arms, Chagford
Buller Memorial, Winchester Cathedral
Flag at Rorke's Drift, 22 Jan 1879, Brecon Museum, Wales
Downes Manor, Devon—Home of General Buller
Trethevy Quoit, St. Cleer, Cornwall
"My" table, Bullers Arms
Bell Tower, St. Michael's, Chagford
Statue of General Buller, Exeter, Devon
"The bench" on one side of Market House, Chagford
Grave of Gen. Redvers Buller, VC, Crediton churchyard, Devon

Drawings:

Map of Chagford
Map of Colonies
Cover: *Time Magazine*, April 8, 1991. Reprinted with permission of Time Warner, Inc.

Foreword

Initially, I believed my first contact with Chagford [England] was actually a view of the proverbial *simple life*...the true yearning for the American Baby Boom group, all 77 million of us strong. But then I was to discover links from past to present to future in this small village on the moor: from Adolph Hitler and concentration camps and "ethnic cleansing" in Bosnia-Herzegovina and a very young, cocky Winston Churchill to Vietnam, racism, the power of the media, real "family values" (not the McCarthy-baiting stuff from the 1992 presidential campaign) and what it means to fulfill a life. I would also learn that Chagford had its own terrible ghost, a ghost similar to the one shared by Baby Boomers.

At the same time, the simple life that I personally fantasized about since early adulthood was to have its definition altered. For as I probed deeper into the *story* of Chagford and its people, I was to stumble upon parallels with my own experiences—situations and occurrences not unlike what my generation had witnessed or absorbed over the course of the last three decades.

All this from a half-forgotten village, its unforgettable cast of characters—including a most fascinating woman and a tragic Victorian general—and a pub called Bullers Arms....

I did find the Simple Life, you see. But it wasn't all that simple.

Bullers Arms

"The Simple Life": A Prologue

IN APRIL OF 1991, ONE OF TIME MAGAZINE'S weekly cover stories was entitled "The Simple Life," with the subtitle 'Rejecting the rat race, Americans get back to basics.' It showed a picture of the front wheel of a bicycle and a half-laced pair of worn hiking boots. No doubt many millions of Americans gave a heavy sigh as they viewed this cover. They could regard it as a representation of the yearning and calling of all those in the land of the free and the home of the brave who toiled, day after day, until the realization hit home that there must be something better than all that toiling. A bicycle tire and a pair of hiking boots? Well, clearly the suggestive title in tandem with the picture gave hope to the eager reader that, indeed, something better than their current lives could be found within the pages.

Upon opening the magazine it did get better. The Table of Contents on page three continued the alluring theme with another teaser: 'Goodbye to having it all. Americans are embracing the simple life.' See page 58. It sounded good to me. At this point, I had been "working away, doin' just what they all say"—a brief paraphrasing of the late-1960s Cat Stevens song, *But I might die tonight*, from the movie Deep End. Only gentle, peace-and-love Cat didn't die but went on to become a religious fanatic and hatemonger. Things change.

Anyway, I remember fervently turning to page 58, as millions of tired, burned out Americans with convoluted lives did, to learn about that "simple life" and where to find it. And no Americans were more desirous to locate this glimmer of light amid the dark caverns of their existence than the 77 million Baby Boomers populating the place, especially that first crop born in the late-1940s that would begin to turn 50 in 1996 at the disconcerting rate of *10,000 per day* with little ceremony and lots of aches and pains. Indeed, I could not name a single representative of the male category known to me who didn't long for a simpler life. And the desire was starting to spread to the female side of the aisle.

(For a somber perspective of America in the last decade of the 20th century, or what I label the *Bankrupt 90s*, and why it is less than simple, see the APPENDIX.)

The "simple life" *was* on page 58, in a way. The page subheading announced 'Tired of trendiness and materialism, Americans are discovering the joys of home life, basic values and things that last.' Things that last? A gut feeling told me I wasn't necessarily going to read about VCRs or room deodorants. Nevertheless, I liked the pictures on the pages that followed: a Manhattan male executive, presumably with big bucks, chucking it all for an apple winery and cider mill in Vermont ("the old corporate chase doesn't mean anything to me anymore," quoth he); a well-traveled female business professional who gave it up for a food market in her neighborhood in St. Paul, Minnesota ("I'm tired at night, but it's a healthy tired," saith she, with fruit and nut basket in hand to prove it); and four other formerly have-it-all people who have-it-not at present because they found alternative, "simple" lifestyles that joyfully replaced the acquisitions, the glitter, the workaholism, the corporate titles and, naturally, the money.

'Uh oh,' thoughteth I. A wary reader of *Time* since early college days, I was not a little concerned that 'six people a national trend did not make,' especially if THE SIX bagged a few coins on their way to making "the transition." *Time* was always pontificating on the latest trends and fads in a land of more than a quarter billion people, and it invariably had a statistically meaningless five or six *living examples* to show just how fast that locomotive was traveling downhill. Translation: *Time* often identified trends by creating them. Worse, this cover story also had THE SURVEY—a few numbers showing that people, in fact, were willing to give it all up for something that had nothing to give up at all. (?)

And yet…another gut feeling told me that Americans—millions of them—were in fact tiring of the 1980s *me* mentality that had "No problem" presidents amid fundamental problems, fundamental greed and a true loss of meaning for the words *living* and *caring*. People were not happy with their lives as they began heading into the 21st century. When the *Time* article on the simple life came out, friends and acquaintances of mine—the "I'm-into-my-40s-and-it's-not-entirely-my-fault" group—were haplessly searching for something besides money and materialism, especially those who contributed to their company's *downsizing* by losing their jobs and paychecks. The little cabin near the lake, the corner grocery store—hell, the pro shop at the country club. My peers were feeling *my* feelings about the need to find something a bit more simple, less stressful, more rewarding, more friendly. Perhaps more pure. Their lives seemed cursed to live out an existence of complexity and unhappiness.

So the *Time* piece hit a raw nerve, but it didn't expose it or explain it or attempt to get into the psyche of a generation lost at sea and in search of a safe port they could call home.

Worse, that initial crop of Baby Boomers carried a second curse besides enduring a stressful, unrewarding life—an albatross about its neck the later Boomers were too young to acquire first-hand: the 1960s, with its tragedy of Vietnam, its questioning of truth, justice and the

American way (even Superman was killed off at one point!), its search for simplicity and caring in a perplexing, often cruel, rarely judicious world. Yes, the Early Boomers had been "searching" since high school and college; *Time* didn't remember that when it came out with its story in 1991.

The 1960s were a time of unbridled emotion among a numerically prodigious group of young people wanting a simple life—a life where people would finally begin to care about the environment, world stability, racial and gender equality, feeding the poor, cleaning up government...and for each other. Long memories and the traumas and failures of the 1960s have made for painful presents and often hopeless futures. When self-proclaimed problem solver Abigail Van Buren asked her problem-laden readers not long ago to send her postcards telling where they were the day President John F. Kennedy was killed in 1963, she was shocked when she received 300,000 responses, mostly in letter form. Long memories; hurt feelings that still throb.

Kennedy's death may have been a quick dose of lost innocence to a post-World War II Superpower, but it did not stop a broad generation from hoping for a better, more simpler life. Moreover, his death should remind us all that Boomers have etched-in-stone memories. They are not so much products of their own past as living memorials to it.

But clearly the most painful memory of this curse of the 1960s acquired by a generation was *Vietnam*, which, far from fading as a national wound—remember the Gulf War being referred to as a panacea for the "Vietnam Syndrome?"—actually became a presidential campaign issue in 1992. Unbelievable. Four years after *Time's* "Simple" cover, another of its covers led with the headline "Vietnam: twenty years later, it haunts us still." And surveys continue to show that a majority of Americans think the Vietnam War was a mistake—more than two decades after it was ignominiously ended. Even one of its architects—former Secretary of State Robert S. McNamara—belatedly saw the errors of his ways, although one wonders what else he sees when he visits the somber black marble Vietnam Memorial for the dead.

Vietnam was more than a tragedy. It has survived as a ghost—a dark, everlasting memory because it touched so many lives. Moreover, it can never go away for the Boomers. It has become a reference point of tragedy by which all that is sad and potentially wrong will be measured—a national guilt trip that will always keep a Boomer's life *far from simple.* Indeed, the U.S. government continues to spend $100 million a year looking for the remains or possible whereabouts of American soldiers still missing in foreign wars, including some 2,000 in Vietnam.

Even as I began writing this little journey, Vietnam surfaced as the ubiquitous evil spirit. A cover of *Time* read "Anguish Over Bosnia: Will it be Clinton's Vietnam?"[*] And as I completed it, former POW and U. S. Senator John McCain was lambasting the Vietnamese government—in Vietnam—on the 25th anniversary of the fall of Saigon (30 April 1975).

It just won't go away for Baby Boomers. Ever.

I carry a hurt from the 1960s and I suspect many other early Boomers do as well: that ache of trying to swim upstream, of hoping to bring about change without a map or a guide and, quite often, without a prayer. I lost friends to a foreign war that was fought but never declared, and I lost friends to an overabundance of drugs upon which war was declared but never seriously fought.

If the early Boomers could sigh collectively, the resulting cloud of despair and loss could plug the hole in the expanding ozone layer. Maybe part of that sigh was electing a Boomer president in 1992.

And yet..."The Simple Life" article came in the middle of my own personal journey that, ironically, I was unaware of, although it surfaced in November of 1989 and slammed into that elusive port in May, 1992. Only it didn't involve six living examples of a national longing. This unintentional quest encompassed the life of one person—yours truly—and the people and past of a landlocked village in the middle of

---

[*] A Chicago Tribune article dated 9 April 1999 had the headline "Vietnam mistakes live on in White House's Kosovo policy, critics say."

a desolate, spooky moor across the Atlantic Ocean that I never knew existed, nor did I seek it out. Perhaps it sought *me* out—stranger things happened during the unfolding of this tale.

I did find the Simple Life, you see. But it wasn't all that simple.

Mark R. Horowitz

Parallels: An Introduction

IN NOVEMBER OF 1989, JUST BEFORE THE DAWN of the last decade of the 20th century, I found myself in Chagford, a very old village in western England tucked inside the many folds of hills and valleys that comprise the famous—and infamous—Dartmoor. Emerging from the forests and rolling terrain that flow westward into this part of the island, Dartmoor is a broken granite, 300 square mile region of marshes, moors, valleys, stone circles, brooks and streams, standing monoliths, old villages and farms, medieval crosses, ancient slab bridges and craggy rock formations. I have always been enamored with this sometimes dreary, often spectacular part of county Devon, mostly for its stark beauty and harsh stone remnants of a mystical past that has largely faded into legend and conjecture. Although relatively small as a national park—some 23 miles from north to south and 10–12 miles east to west—it is one of the few inhabited places on earth where you can wander for a period of time without hearing or seeing a reminder of current civilization, with virtual silence broken only by the baying of a wild moor pony or a cry from a newborn lamb unsure of its footing.

Sounds pretty idyllic, yes? And notice that nary an adjective has been spared, although the intent is to paint a pellucid picture, not position the prose for a Pulitzer Prize. (Besides, I have come to loathe filling out contest forms.) Beginnings of *anything* are hard to get into, but if you survive this Introduction I'll lay you odds that you might allow yourself to fall into this story, much as I did—quite by accident, and with far-reaching personal consequences. But I digress....

Dartmoor was the home of ancient peoples who constructed stone huts and lived a rough, moorswept life. These same tenacious humans

set up enormous stones (monoliths), often for burial mounds or
religious ceremony. Their grandest achievements were accomplished
further east by the cousins and relations who built Stonehenge and
Avebury. But Dartmoor remained mostly a rugged landscape of
scattered settlements, wedged between the summer country (Somerset)
to the east and the horn of land (Cornwall) to the west that terminates
at Land's End.

The moor witnessed the steady formation of perhaps the best-
known country in history: The invasion and conquest by, and later
departure of, the Romans (c. 405 A.D.); the defiance of the indigenous
Celts—perhaps led by a late-5th century Romano-Celtic warrior
named Arthur—against immigrant Anglo-Saxons; the Saxon's conquest
of *Angle-land* and their subsequent battles with invading Vikings (c. 9th
to 11th centuries) ; the Saxon's own subjugation by the Norman French
(1066 and all that), who were the last invaders of Britain—the Germans
of World War II "flew over"; raids from Ireland and Scotland
(intermittent); piracy and adventure by the western seafarers of Devon
and Cornwall (16th to 19th centuries); civil war between king and
parliament (mid-17th c.); and, a century ago, the creation of a legend
amid Dartmoor's treacherous mires and craggy granite citadels: Sir
Arthur Conan Doyle's *Hound of the Baskervilles*.

Quaint little national park.

The English historian part of me knew much of this; in fact, enjoyed
reliving it in my mind as I trekked up to the natural granite *tors*
(medieval contraction for 'towers') piled high atop gradually-rising
mountain paths, or I walked into an ancient oak forest. But on this
entry into Dartmoor in November of 1989, I was to confront my present and future in some very unexpected ways because of a place called
Chagford. Although it was but one of numerous sleepy villages dotting
Dartmoor, this encounter in Chagford, and another some 30 months
into the future, was to bring up feelings and fears about my life as it
might, I suspected, for the rest of my numerically-broad generation—

fears that cast long shadows over what I thought was a fairly defined 'plan' for my personal future.

Initially, I believed my first contact with Chagford was actually a view of the proverbial *simple life*—the life briefly related in the aforementioned *Time* magazine article as the true yearning for the American Baby Boom group, all 77 million of us strong. But then I was to discover links from past to present to future in this small village on the moor: from Adolph Hitler and concentration camps and 'ethnic cleansing' in Bosnia-Herzegovina and a very young, cocky Winston Churchill, to Vietnam, racism, the power of the media, *real* "family values" (not the McCarthy-baiting stuff from the 1992 presidential campaign) and what it means to fulfill a life. I would also learn that Chagford had its own terrible ghost, a ghost similar to the one shared by Baby Boomers.

At the same time, the simple life that I personally fantasized about since early adulthood was to have its definition altered. For as I probed deeper into the *story* of Chagford and its people, I was to stumble upon parallels with my own experiences: situations and occurrences not unlike what my generation had witnessed or absorbed over the course of the last three decades.

All this from a half-forgotten village, its unforgettable cast of characters—including a most fascinating woman and a tragic Victorian general—and a pub called Bullers Arms.

Chapter 1

November 1989

AFTER WANDERING THE MOOR on a chilly November day in 1989 it was time to reenter my rental car and find a place to stay for the night during a brief vacation to England. My goal was to locate a Bed-and-Breakfast inside Dartmoor that I could use as a base of exploration for two days. Imagine driving along a narrow road in the early evening, sun slowly setting, with no barriers to your vision, no fences or buildings or anything remotely "civilized." Just a road, with the treeless hills rising up on one side of it and falling into a valley on the other side. Only at a crossroad are you reminded that habitation exists, for there is usually a white wooden post with white wooden signs attached, all pointing in different directions, each with the name of one or more villages and their distances from the post. The only thing missing was a Cheshire cat, perched on top.

One of these small signs said *Chagford*, so I followed a lane that took me around narrow curves and high hedges, barely allowing one car to fit without scraping the doors against protruding branches. Much of the shrubbery in the area was of a prickly nature, usually referred to as gorse. (This would have greater significance later on, believe it or not.) Soon, I entered the village.

It was like emerging from a confusing maze onto a neatly-arranged Monopoly board of the medieval variety. The main street began at the large parish church and carried on some 200 yards to the village square. This area, literally a square, consisted of an octagonal building in the center of an open area and stood on the spot of the medieval market place. The road encircled it and buildings and shops surrounded it on four sides—we will take a 'walking tour' in a later chapter. It still served as the market center today, sloping slightly downwards on the Northeast and Northwest ends with roads running on either side of it perpendicular to the main street. These roads curved downhill and converged out of sight, swallowed up by more shops and buildings.

It took less than three minutes to follow each street flowing in and out of the market square. After stopping at Bed-and-Breakfast establishments, it soon became apparent that getting a room was going to be difficult. November, I knew, was not open season for tourists. But given tough economic times—especially in the west country—I felt that a few B&B's would be receptive to a former Colonist on holiday with a couple of English pounds to lose. Most, however, were not, and the few that were open had filled their rooms for the night.

When first entering Chagford I had made a mental note of the Three Crowns Inn, across the street from the raised cemetery that stood on the church grounds several feet above street level. The inn was built of stone and looked very old, although everything looked old to me after leaving London for the countryside. I now went inside and discovered that rooms were available at about $32.00 per night per single, full English breakfast included. This was above my self-imposed limit, but the quest of this trip was Dartmoor exploration within a narrow time frame, so the die was cast and I took the room for two nights.

After unloading my small suitcase and camera bag, I went downstairs and stood in front of the roaring fireplace. It was a chilly, humid night and my sweater and light jacket weren't doing the trick. The bartender asked me if I would like something, and I resorted to a drink introduced to me by a colleague when I spent a year in London conducting historical research: Rum and Black. This consisted of a small glass of black currant liqueur mixed with rum, frequently of the dark genus, and an ice cube if requested. Although sweet, it went down this night with nary a smack of the lips, and I felt like I had just plugged into a wall socket as my internal coils started glowing hot.

I looked around the large room. The lobby was actually like a pub, with the expected wall paraphernalia, wooden tables and chairs, large bar and previously-mentioned fire. There were only a few people in the lobby although it was about 7:00 in the evening, and I asked where I might get a meal in the village. The bartender suggested Bullers Arms, a pub just up the street past the market square...I couldn't miss it. I finished the drink, left a tip and entered the chilling air.

Now it should be understood that I am not necessarily the loner type, although I have traveled alone before. Usually I like traveling with others, to offer what I know about a country's history or to share experiences as they come along, especially if it is in England, Scotland or Wales. My wife, Barb, and I once traveled with another couple into the Scottish Highlands. John and Anne Dumas, from Birmingham, Alabama, were neighbors of ours during Queen Elizabeth II's Jubilee year, 1977, when we spent the year in a London establishment for foreign and commonwealth graduate students and professionals. (John was "the doctor." I was the "historian.") John and I temporarily abandoned our wives in a small hotel in Inverness—they were pooped out from a day of exploration—and we began a freezing April night playing dominos in a crowded, smoky pub before driving along Loch Ness in search of its elusive monster. We ended up slinking around Urquhart Castle, the monster's favorite place for photo ops. As it turned out, John and I ran into a suspicious-looking character of the human-monster variety—he had shotguns in the back seat of his car—and we never did find Nessie, although I thought we handled the disappointment well. Our spouses thought we were nuts. Probably.

No, I'm not always the solitary type. But as a child of the 1960s who watched personal sacrifice and introspection succumb to the greed and materialism of the 1980s, I liked occasional solo sojourns to ponder where the world was headed and what path I should be taking on the

Slippery Sidewalk of Life. A walk down Chagford's main street to
Bullers Arms fit the bill well, and as I zipped up my jacket and mean-
dered up the sidewalk fronting the graveyard, I wondered why the other
77 million Boomers didn't take a stab at such soul-searching solitude.
Too busy, I supposed. Or perhaps too frightened.

So I did it *for* them, with interesting consequences.

Chapter 2

Bullers Arms

The Bar, Bullers Arms, Chagford

IT WAS STILL LIGHT OUT when I entered Bullers Arms. Now new initiates to a true English pub—as opposed to the "lobby pub" I had just left at the Three Crowns Inn—might be in awe of what lies before them as they push through the doors during a busy evening. Most of the patrons in the pub are there because it's their pub, and they view it as a quid pro quo. They visit regularly to support the pub by buying the beer, the sherry, the snacks and meals and other oral-intake offerings; the pub supports their way of life by providing a warm atmosphere and a home away from home.

A home. From my perspective, this *is* their home—the place they reside after work and before sleep ends the day. They meet their other "family" of friends, acquaintances and passerby relatives to review the events of the day, solve the woes of tomorrow and generally validate their lives as worth living, worth relating and worth more than the material world has to offer. This is especially true in a remote village where "things" are often beyond imagining, let alone purchasing. It was a lesson I was to learn two-and-one-half years later.

But for now, I entered the pub, found a table, sat down and looked around with curious eyes. It was a good-sized pub. Upon entering, I had seen tables to the far left and a dart board on the wall. The bar was ahead and to the left, surrounded by barstools. Directly in front of me and to the right were more tables, and there was another dart board on the wall at the end of the room opposite the front door. A small hallway past the dart board on the far right presumably led to the rest rooms: an integral part of any establishment catering to the rapid acceleration of kidney functions.

The pub had many pictures and pub trappings on the walls, and the bar was replete with glasses, brass pots and numerous inverted bottles waiting to be measured out for drinks. Several large handles drew beer, stout, ale and lager on draft, and the bartender—actually the proprietor—was busy distributing pints to thirsty patrons. The steady din of conversation was rising as others entered the pub, and space went at a premium. I thought it time to rise and approach the bar, so to speak. I carefully reviewed the menu and politely waited to be recognized.

The proprietor soon acknowledged me. He was a medium-sized, slightly rounded man with a closely-trimmed beard, neatly-groomed graying hair, immaculately-styled jacket and a large smile. In fact, he was so properly attired that my mind referred to him as Mr. Properly Attired, or simply Mr. P.A. He asked me what I would like and I ordered an apple cider. In return, I asked to review the menu a few moments longer.

A two-paragraph digression—one of numerous sidesteps coming up, to say nothing of myriad parenthetical prosaics and breath-robbing overlong sentences. These will be on food and cider.

Paragraph One: Historically, to the American palate English food is only slightly above what animals far down on the food chain consume as a matter of survival. The bland beef, slippery mutton, post-Apocalypse-looking vegetables and runny 'tomato sauce' (read *ketchup*) are rarely preceded with the adjective "appetizing." Some of that has changed in England, thanks in part to the need to cater to more discriminating tastes of the 'tourist' kind; in part to the influx of Third World people well-versed in spices and culinary capabilities. No longer must the tourist order the butter-and-cucumber sandwich on white bread sliced as thin as the most advanced laser technology can accomplish. Many hot and cold dishes have taste, substance and variety. Moreover, a word is popping up on the island that should bring smiles to the American tourist more concerned about what to eat than what to see: *deli.*

Paragraph Two: On a more personal level there is apple cider, which is distributed in bottles nationally and on-tap locally through nearby distilleries or farms. There is dry, medium and sweet cider, and also the thermonuclear variety known as farm cider, which can run from pale yellow to outright green and serves as a ready substitute for the firing fuel of Space Shuttle booster rockets. Apple cider has alcoholic content of varying percentages and the trial user should set up a buddy system before imbibing. Since I have never been greatly fond of beer— although I will try it occasionally in England, but usually in lager or real ale form—I have developed a taste for cider. But usually just one. Otherwise, the eyesight quickly fails and the day of consumption might as well be written off as having never occurred at all.

I ordered a hot meal from Mr. P.A. and then he asked me if I was from America. We went through the "From Chicago—actually a sub-urb/Love to visit England/Dartmoor is one of my favorite places/Sure is chillier than I expected" banter that is always required and brief. Then he moved on to the next desert-worn mouth while I settled back into my chair and sipped the cider.

And as I sipped I noticed the portrait of a military-looking person on the wall among all the other paintings and wall-hangings. He was bull-ish-looking, much as how John Bull (the British version of our 'Uncle

Sam') was supposed to look. Only the expression, while forceful, was more serene than the British representation of Imperial Power. I stood up with my cider and wandered over to it.

General Buller, Bullers Arms, Chagford

The gentleman in question was one General Sir Redvers Buller, with several sets of letters after his name. The only set I recognized was *V.C.*, for Victoria Cross. Since this was the equivalent of America's Congressional Medal of Honor, I figured Sir Redvers—what a strange forename!—must have done something heroic during a war or battle, any of hundreds since this was England and he looked like he flourished during the British Empire when Her Majesty's government were busy exporting wars and battles at an alarming rate.

While I had no idea that this visit to the wall picture was only the beginning of a series of mysteries and revelations I would encounter in Chagford, I now at least solved one obvious puzzle: the pub was named after Sir Redvers Buller, himself.

Chapter 3

A Quick View of Dartmoor

ALTHOUGH THIS JOURNEY IS NOT about Dartmoor per se, I think it useful to describe a few sites and sights to provide a sketch of the environment within which Chagford and its people are found. After all, part of the simple life revolves around the setting one finds oneself in. Moreover, that environment is a contributing factor to what the simple life is all about. Selling fruit from a tiny stand may sound quaint and simple and therapeutic and rewarding, but it isn't if you are on the corner of Sixth Avenue and 48th Street in mid-town Manhattan round about lunchtime on a steamy, hot Monday in August!

I originally came to Dartmoor to view the ancient stone remains and snoop around the moor villages, seeking out interesting legends and stories that cling to the moor like the bracken, the gorse and the fallen granite boulders. I suppose this was the journalist and the romantic in me more than the historian, since proper historians don't engage in such non-essential wanderings—Where are the documents? But it was me nonetheless so there you have it. It would be no different on this trip.

After a good dinner at Bullers Arms and a quiet night's sleep in the Three Crowns Inn—which has a ghost who took the night off and I shall talk about later—I consumed the traditional egg-bacon-toast-tea-sausage English breakfast, avoided the fried toast and overheated tomato and drove on the "wrong side of the road" through Dartmoor. There is much to see, with or without an Ordinance Survey map. For example, near Chagford outside Drewsteignton stands Spinsters' Rock, three large upright stones each weighing many tons and capped by a fourth one. The green plaque at the entrance to the field where the rocks reside says it all:

> *A Neolithic burial chamber erected around 3500–2500 B.C. The chamber probably contained many burials and would originally have been covered by a long earthen mound. The stones fell down in 1862 and were re-erected in the same year.*
>
> *Traditionally the monument was erected by three spinsters one morning before breakfast.*

One can only surmise what grandiose features the structure might have acquired had the ladies approached their task after the benefit of a full-course English breakfast.

Spinsters' Rock, Drewsteignton, Dartmoor

I was mightily impressed upon first viewing this ancient site, especially after learning that the "quoit," as these tomb-like structures are called, measured two feet thick by fifteen in length and ten in breadth. But later on, a note I discovered in R. N. Worth's *A History of Devonshire* (1886) let me know that modern-day novices shouldn't marvel at such marvels too much. Worth stated that, after the stones collapsed in January, 1862, "a builder and a carpenter of Chagford, by the aid of pulleys and a screw-jack, replaced it at a cost of £20; and thus very much reduced the vague wonder that commonly attaches to the erection of such structures." Next we will learn that Stonehenge was put up by a farmer and his two daughters during Spring Break. Can't people leave wonderment alone without injecting harmful doses of reality?

The day took me to ancient—or medieval, depending on your guide-book—*clapper bridges*, which were gigantic slabs of granite laid across piled-up columns of rocks upon which travelers forded a river. Building bridges and fording rivers was a millennial pastime in England. Indeed, it has helped name whole towns that bridged a river (*Cambridge* has a bridge over the Cam River) or afforded people a place to ford one (*Oxford* has a place where Saxon *ox*-drovers forded the river Thames). Clapper bridges mainly survive today in Dartmoor. There is a complete one at Postbridge, a smaller one over the Dart River, a tiny one at Powder Mills and a large one missing a center slab at Bellever.

Dartmoor places and villages abound with eerie sensations and intriguing stories. You can walk deep into Wistman's Wood, said to be the last primeval forest in Britain with 2,000-year-old stunted oak trees, and ponder what the world was like before people started diddling with it. Or you can visit the churchyard of the parish church in Moretonhampstead, where several French soldiers from the Napoleonic Wars were buried after spending their last days as prisoners in Dartmoor. A few of the gravestones found in the cemetery or hung in the church porch are written in French as reminders of this interesting fluke in Napoleonic history.

Saxon Well (pre-1066), Widecombe, Dartmoor

Then there is the village of Widecombe-in-the-Moor, with its towering parish church steeple, an old Saxon well (pre-1066 A.D.) that still dribbles out water, and a 14th century inn—called the Old Inn to make the point stick—that is associated with the Widecombe Fair and Tom Cobley and his six friends.

Good time for a digression.

If I may digress a paragraph: While visiting the Old Inn, I decided to interview Carol Webb for a weekly syndicated column I wrote for United Press International. According to one of her local fans, Carol was the "best barmaid in the business." I couldn't disagree. She was an indomitable woman who served up the brew and much of the social-izing…and not a few stories. "It was the old Widecombe Fair, on the second Tuesday of September, that brought in the farmers, the tinners, the chickens and the pigs," Carol told me. "Some of the men would get drunk on cider and race horses against each other. Then, of course, there's the story of Tom Cobley."

Apparently it will take *two* paragraphs! According to legend, Tom Cobley came down the hill to Widecombe to visit the fair on a white mare he borrowed from Tom Pearce, or as the very old poem goes, *Tom Pearce, Tom Pearce, lend me your grey mare; All along, down along, out along lee; For I want to go to Widecombe Fair*. Old Tom Cobley gathered up Bill Brewer, Jan Stewer, Peter Gurney, Peter Davy, Daniel Whiddon, and Harry Hawk—all plastered on cider and riding the mare to Widecombe Fair. Unfortunately, the mare died in mid-stride—an overload in steerage, perhaps?—to the owner's great distress. Tom Cobley and crew, although Driving Under the Influence, were also devastated, and they purportedly sat down and cried. "It was later said that sometimes on the moor at night you can see the skeleton of the old mare with Tom Cobley and his friends," Carol concluded. "You can even hear the bones of the horse rattling in the wind." She smiled at me and it was difficult to tell how much of all this she swallowed. But one or two of Tom Cobley's friends may be related to the history of Chagford, which we will get to later. (I realize I promise lots of *laters*, but I am keeping a list.)

A few miles from Widecombe stands Warren House Inn, literally in the middle of nowhere within the moor. It boasts a fireplace that has kept burning for over 150 years non-stop, or so the proprietor and the tourist bureaus will tell you. (I had hoped to stop in after hours to check up on the flame, but it gets pitch black on the moor and you never know when Tom Cobley and company might show up.) There are numerous other tales and quaint discoveries, and small booklets for tourist review, enticingly labeled *The Devil on Dartmoor* or *The Mysterious Moor*, relate places and stories that could keep the adventurer and the romantic wandering around Dartmoor a lifetime and more. For me, I probably hadn't spent 10 days total in Dartmoor despite several trips to England. No complaints. In fact, I knew how lucky I was to see a part of the planet most will miss. But where was I going to get 'a lifetime and more?'

Nevertheless, I did make the most of this day after my arrival in Chagford the previous night, ending with a climb up the side of a steep hill leading to Grimspound, a Bronze Age settlement of 24 ruined stone huts surrounded by a stone wall and entered through what was once an impressive stone gateway. (The word 'grimm' is Old English for *savage*, but Grim was also the mythological Saxon leader of the hunt.) This place was the end—and the eventual beginning—of a personal journey for Sir Arthur Conan Doyle.

One of 24 Bronze Age stone huts, Grimspound, Dartmoor

That journey may have commenced when, more than a century ago, he visited the 13th century Holy Trinity Church in Buckfastleigh high up on a hill just inside the moor. In the cemetery is the large, 17th century tomb of Sir Richard Cabell of Brooke Manor, a baddy if there ever was one. Cabell hunted

black hounds on the moor, which eventually became wild and even
nastier than he did. Conan Doyle learned about Cabell and, after viewing the tomb, asked his coachman to take him into the moor, perhaps
to Grimspound.

The coachman's name was Baskerville, Conan Doyle got to thinking…and the ruins of Grimspound that would impress him so greatly
became the "Grimpen Mire" in his famous Sherlock Holmes novel, the
Hound of the Baskervilles. In such ways are stories grown, twisted and
turned into legend.

Chapter 4

A Cast of Characters

THERE WAS NO QUESTION that my second dinner in Dartmoor would be at Bullers Arms in Chagford. I enjoy looking at people's faces in a pub while trying to pick up snippets of conversation. My first night there was convivial, although no faces or words stood out, except for the pleasantries of the assiduous proprietor, Mr. Properly Attired, who kept the pints flowing as quickly as the conversations. But this night would be very different, especially since there was a dart tournament.

I could spend many paragraphs talking about the English and their darts, and the abilities of those Chagford folk involved in the sport. Since that is best left for my return to Chagford and Bullers Arms described on pages ahead, suffice it to note that World War II would have lasted only a fortnight if either side had the pinpoint accuracy of the dart players I saw practicing their art in this pub. Hitler and Roosevelt clearly distracted themselves needlessly with heavy water, plutonium, V-2's and radar instead of darts; Churchill should have known better. His War Cabinet might have consulted with the dart players in Chagford.

After a quick wash to remove some of the ancient moor from my hands and face and a change of clothes, I left the Three Crowns Inn and walked up the street. It was not as cold this evening, although it didn't take long to realize that a warm fireplace was being demanded by my nerve endings. I entered Bullers Arms, marched up to the bar, greeted Mr. P.A.—who cheerfully recognized "the American"—and ordered my

cider and another hot meal. I then found the same table, saluted
General Sir Redvers Buller (not yet knowing the story behind the "John
Bull" face), and soaked in the warm smells and the noise from conver-
sation and laughter.

Soon I began to focus on certain faces and voices, since they seemed
to stand out from the collective cacophony of sounds. This was a grad-
ual process because people were slowly coming into the pub after eating at home or stopping off from work to have a drink or meal with
friends. The cast of characters came out this way in my mind on this
November night in 1989:

Mr. Properly Attired—the proprietor/bartender. His impeccable
dress complements his grooming habits. Enjoys his job—at least outwardly—and seems to have everything under control.

Mrs. Properly Attired—the proprietor/bartender's wife, who now
was in view during my second night. It didn't take long to sort her out
and place her in the correct "Hierarchy of Bullers Arms." Mrs. P.A. likes
to laugh and on occasion it proves to be contagious.

Mr. Crafty Cool—a looker. He enjoys eyeing female posteriors, but
only if the ladies in question notice that he's noticing. A cigarette box
fits snugly into his left jeans rear pocket, and his sweater and shirt are
arranged to look as if they haven't been arranged. CC would have given
James Dean a run for his money…maybe not.

Mr. Pipe & Pits—relaxed, at ease and *trés* content. By chewing an
unlit pipe with arms folded so each hand fitted neatly under an armpit,
Mr. P&P held his own (Freud would've had a field day with all this!)
while listening to Mr. Crafty Cool. Female anatomy flowing across the
room didn't seem to concern him.

Mr. Sloppy—third member of the Triumvirate along with CC and
P&P. With tousled hair and undesigner clothing, he makes self-important
statements that seem to lose meaning as they cross over to the ears of

Crafty Cool and Pipe & Pits. I see in him a slight throwback to the 1960s search for non-descriptfullness, if such a word could be concocted.

Miss Short Blonde—thick, tinted blonde hair cut above the shoulders, which works well against a backdrop of black clothing. She is very secure about herself and would be one of the first to break through the corporate *glass ceiling* to the Executive Suite, just for laughs, on a Tuesday.

"Hugh Griffith"—I swear it's him! If you don't remember him, rent the video *Tom Jones*, Albert Finney's first great movie, and check out the squire with the bushy eyebrows, squinty eyes, gruff voice and red nose. This pub version of "Hugh" wore a cap (perhaps Andy's Capp?) and it's hard not to walk up and ask him how "Tom" was getting on. He looks like he spent a century sweeping chimneys in several Dickens' novels.

"Chirpy"—I'm cheating here. That whole evening my mind referred to him as Mr. Rosy Cheeks, because they shone red as a tomato as he gulped pints and told stories that made his eyes grow large. I was to find out in 1992 that Mr. Rosy Cheeks was in fact called "Chirpy" by the locals, so I'll give a sneak preview of what is to come.

My meal arrived, I dug in as if half-starved—Conan Doyle had a walking stick and a coachman when climbing up to Grimspound, I didn't!—and I continued to listen and watch as the pub filled up. Soon the conversations by all parties concerned turned to darts, mainly because numerous people began practicing at the dart board to the left of the entrance while the scoreboard was being cleaned off near the dart board opposite the entrance. I could tell that something important was going to happen.

Then, quite unexpectedly, it happened. Two teams, forming out of what seemed to be an amorphous crowd of people, began playing darts against each other.

I watched in utter fascination at the method to their madness of whipping darts at a complicated disk of metal numbers, concentric circles and alternating black and white segments separated by thin circles comprised of very small red and green segments. One person caught my attention immediately: an intriguing woman in tight jeans with incredibly thick, straight grayish hair streaked with black—it's hard to describe—cut evenly above the shoulder with thick bangs barely above the eyebrows. She was so obviously the captain of one team that I was amazed that a person in a crowd could boldly stand out and announce her station in life without issuing a word. Captain, who was perhaps in the 36-to-40 age range, had a smile that was broad and infectious, lighting up her entire face and accented by glowing cat eyes that truly enjoyed watching each recipient's reactions to her actions. I strained to observe her as she flicked her three darts in rapid succession, followed by cheers or 'awws' depending on the final destination of the darts. Mostly they were cheers.

In between throws, players and patrons alike drank and drank and smoked and drank—the Hollywood stars of the 1930s would have felt at home on this "set." I looked around to see how others were reacting to the play in a pub that was now completely stuffed with the residents of Chagford. Mr. Crafty Cool was talking to Mr. Properly Attired, and occasionally to Mrs. P.A., as both proprietors continued serving drinks as quickly as the dart players could call out their orders. CC would occasionally let his eyes wander to a passing *bum* (that's "bottom" in Cockney), but his conversation never missed a beat. Messrs. Pipe & Pits and Sloppy continued their talking, intermittently looking over to see how the teams were doing. Miss Short Blonde seemed to have ducked out as the contest began in earnest, but I caught Hugh Griffith slurping away and raising and lowering his pushbroom eyebrows. Chirpy, I could now see, wore a dark blazer with some kind of shield or insignia on it, perhaps suggesting that the red cheeks were acquired in the Royal

Navy at sea serving with a prince or something. He was rooting on the players, especially the Captain in the Tight Jeans.

The conversations varied and changed speed and pitch at will. There was talk of local happenings, including several stories related to farms. There was gossip about certain people—probably found in Bullers Arms at this moment. There was mention of the government, of the economy, of football (*aka* soccer), of an upcoming event in a neighboring village, of some tourists last summer, of someone's boss, of a young person doing well on one of the dart teams. My mind was taking it all in and going into overload, trying to sort out the various story lines while assessing what it all meant, how speaker and listener felt about it, where it fit into the overall lives that were lived in Chagford.

And then a glow began to surge inside me, and not from the cider. I could see that these people were enjoying themselves *in earnest*, and not for the benefit of others, least of all me, who pretty much went unnoticed. Words began to appear on an imaginary list of descriptions in my mind that assigned meaning to the scene in the pub: contentment, warmth, joviality, comfort, reliance, empathy, camaraderie, acceptance, peace. Peace. No one was trying to prove anything, or display the inner turmoil I have often seen in such gatherings of people trying to achieve *something* before the night was over, at the very least the triumph of being liked. No, despite the various personalities and idiosyncrasies of these residents of Chagford (and if CC looked at one more fanny I felt sure his tongue would fall out of his mouth), there was an aura of comfortable warmth and simplicity enveloping Bullers Arms. I wasn't part of it, but I could feel it.

As the evening wore on and I became totally lost as to who was winning or even why, I found myself staring unabashedly at Captain. Through it all, she kept her smile and her glow, and she seemed to have fun with whomever she was talking to at a given moment. At one point I thought she looked over at me, and I tried to hold my eyes long enough to confirm whether she spotted a foreign apple among the

Chagford barrel. But her eyes looked past me, and soon she was flicking away at the dart board between cigarettes and sips from a small glass. I would find out much later what was in that glass, and perhaps why.

A sharp neurological response helped me discover the reason why certain people would suddenly disappear from the room and reappear minutes later: my bladder now sent a message to my brain that the time had arrived for either relief or embarrassment for the American in the pub. I stood up slowly and wondered how I was going to get through the crowds and around the two dart teams to walk the long hall to the rest rooms, known to the natives as *The Loo*. Since lower muscles only work for so long before they quit, the point became moot as I 'Excuse me'-d through the crowds toward the dart board for a quick swing to the right and down the narrow passageway some 39 paces from Pub Central to the Gents. (Hitchcock should have worked this into his *39 Steps* masterpiece, but perhaps he didn't know.)

And then the gods played a little joke—remember, I was in western England where ancient Celts and their gods never quite departed and never took kindly to outsiders. As I maneuvered sideways past the area of dart play, the Captain forcefully walked up to the throwing position, aimed a dart…and almost stuck the back of it into my eye en route to my brain. She gazed at me in wide-eyed surprise and said 'Oh excuse me!' at the same time I did. We then lost each other's eye contact quickly and went about our business, hers for the glory of Bullers Arms, mine for the relief of a traveler in renal distress.

When I returned from what seemed like the passing of an era, the game was over and people were beginning to file out of the pub. Miss Short Blonde made a quick entrance, chatted up the Properly Attireds with frequent bobbings of her head for emphasis and left for the evening. The trio of Crafty Cool, Pipe & Pits and Sloppy revved up their conversations for the final lap, downed their glasses as if an afterthought and then pushed off the bar from their barstools in perfect World Class backstroke form to head for the exit. The other characters of my evening couldn't be located, but as I went back to my table to finish the last of the cider I saw Captain, her back to me, in animated talk with several others while taking something out of her purse and puffing on a cigarette. Her hair was bouncing with each laughing moment, and I could see by the faces of her audience that they thoroughly enjoyed whatever she was relating.

I knew it was time to depart since I had to get up early and head back to London. But some odd feelings arose in me that kept me frozen in front of my table watching the woman in the tight jeans go about her life in the pub. For a moment I wanted to be part of that conversation, which I thought odd since I usually disdained parties where little grouplets of people chatted this-and-that in between hand waves to passing faces. Yet I felt that *this* conversation taking place, like so many others I had only caught fragments of during the evening, was important. This was not social wordsmithing or first-impression showcasing. Captain was just being Captain, and it was important to her and to her listeners. Maybe it was watching the *belonging* of these people to each other— something I had never seen in an American bar or pickup joint, crowded but cold places where coupling or cohabitation were the usual objectives of the evening.

Most of all, I had a longing to learn what was on Captain's mind, what she thought of the world—her world—and of the other characters in Bullers Arms. I wondered where she was coming from, where she was going, amid an ancient moor that had no place to go but into the mists of a forgotten past with little relevance for the present and future, or so I thought. But at that moment, it was very clear the voyager from a suburb of Chicago was light-years from that conversation, a conversation among friends from an age-old village that was many centuries in the making.

So I put down my glass and left the pub.

And then I realized that one thing was missing as I walked the 50 or so paces from the pub to the market square: the destination of these

participants in what appeared to be a warm, fulfilling, "simple" life.
What exactly happened to them when they emerged from Bullers Arms?
I stood for a few moments in front of the octagonal Market House and
watched as the people from the pub entered the dark main street of
Chagford, talking in two's and three's before bidding goodnight and
walking down the various lanes angling away from the square. A few got
into small cars. After turning on their fog lights, the drivers zipped out
of the village, their tiny car engines sounding like so many lawnmowers
going up and back.

It all came together so nicely. The patrons of Bullers Arms—their
home away from home—returning to their farms or their village flats
or cottages, surrounded by peace and tranquillity. I stood there and
watched it—an American who grew up in the heart of Chicago where
today, depending on the neighborhood, a walk at night with less than a
detachment of U. S. Marines was considered a death wish.

'How comfortable they must feel here,' I thought as I walked past the
Market House toward the Three Crowns Inn. 'And yet they probably
don't realize that, having never known the *discomfort* of other places,
especially of the urban variety. After all, what could have changed in a
sleepy village over the centuries? Was not tonight like every other night
in Chagford? And what would it be like to wake up without the anxiety
of having to enter the stressful, shark-infested world of corporate life?'

I stood still just outside the Inn and let myself feel the cool air and
calming silence, broken only by an occasional "lawnmower" headed
out of town. I was waxing all content inside at the contentment I felt
I had witnessed at Bullers Arms. How much more simple could a
simple life get?

Chapter 5

Back to "Reality"

THE NEXT MORNING I CROSSED the street from the Three Crowns Inn toward the market square to go to my car and almost got myself killed by a taxi. Americans may think that being equipped with a similar language and supermarket-tabloid knowledge of the Royal Family's intimate and dysfunctional behavior qualifies them to tour England. Not so. If Americans like to sniff that the English drive on the wrong side of the road, they had better remember that those cars are coming from the wrong side of the road! I forgot that little tidbit upon leaving the Three Crowns, looked the "wrong way"...and almost had tire treads tattooed to my legs as the taxi took a sharp turn 'round the square' and zoomed out of town.

And as I shakily jumped back on the curb, I noticed the back of the driver's head and realized it was Captain. 'Amazing,' I thought. 'Not only would she outperform a cruise missile on its way to a dart board, she was also a Formula One driver who could race rings around Indy 500 qualifiers!' Lots of raw talent there, and I was the discoverer. But that's all I was. For as I saw her drive off and I squinted to see her rearview mirror to confirm it was indeed the face of Captain, I understood that, like Brigadoon, this would all disappear as I drove off for London, Heathrow Airport, boarded a jumbo jet and arrived at O'Hare Field in Chicago for a return to the life I continued to live. It was then, standing on the curb watching the taxi round a bend out of sight, that I felt a little hurt form inside, one that suggested I had had a wonderful time in the pub without uttering a word besides ordering food and drink and muttering 'Excuse me' to an unusual woman who now twice almost killed me without taking much notice.

Strange feelings for a husband with two kids—but had I not partaken of the *simple* life, the one I had always dreamed about and *Time* magazine was later to write about, if only as an outsider peeking in?

The year 1990 was a *transitional* one for me—that overused word that was once shoved back into my face during Ph.D. oral exams at the University of Chicago. Having proclaimed 15th century England to be "transitional," my medieval examiner wryly replied 'So when, may I ask, was there a period of history that wasn't in transition?'

Oh.

Nonetheless, 1990 was a year of changes, if not transitions, both in thinking and in planning. My book, with the ominous title *Stonehenge to Star Wars: Discovering the Present by Exploring the Past*, was coming out in the late Spring, and I wondered how it would be received...or if anyone would receive it at all! I continued writing my weekly column for *United Press International*—including one on Tom Cobley and company—as well as giving weekly commentaries on a radio station in Chicago, entitled "Taking A Step Back." I also penned occasional articles as a Guest Columnist for USA TODAY, plus pieces for other papers.

All of this literary output involved a *historical perspective* that related what was happening today and tomorrow from the vantage point of the last 5,000 years of history. How that came about remains both strange and unexpected to me. Although I had been in the pre-medical program at Tulane University with the thought of being a doctor since birth—a clearly "Baby Boomer" goal—I majored in Ancient and Medieval history and became hooked on English history my senior year. I was always the hopeless romantic—King Arthur, castles, cathedrals, valleys and mountains and monasteries and hidden caves—the whole lot. I also wanted to be a writer, but didn't think my parents would relish the thought of supporting me until well past age 70. I also had an interest in business.

Typical college student—all over the map! Here's what happened to one Boomer, in three paragraphs:

During my last year at Tulane, I met with the dean of Arts and Sciences and told him that a Ford Foundation study had just been published claiming that a 4-year college education was *irrelevant.* I then asked him what I should tell my father now that he had spent all that money on my 4-year college education. (Remember, this was the early-1970s when university administrations were still afraid of students, and students were absurdly outspoken.) The dean was adroitly equipped to respond. He looked me in the eye and said "So what are you going to do about it?" Anxiety attack. I wasn't prepared to go beyond voicing a little anger and frustration at the world I was about to face upon graduation. My surprising response—for the dean *and* me—was "So let me give lectures on things I deem relevant to the present."

The rest is, well, history. I was awarded a fellowship at Tulane to give 'lectures on things I deem *relevant* to the present' using the vehicle of a Western civilization course, beginning to present. Each lecture was to be repeated three times in different sections of a Western Civ class to students only one or two years younger than me. I also enrolled as a graduate student and took courses—part of the deal—and I began writing a novel at night. Several nights a week I demonstrated toys at a department store to supplement my $75/month fellowship stipend. Although the lectures were a moderate success, I declined doing the fellowship a second year, became engaged to be married and visited England and Scotland for the first time with my brother and parents. That trip, along with the "relevancy" experience at Tulane, pretty much sealed my fate.

After getting married and blue-jeaning through Europe, bride in hand, for two adventurous months, I decided to go for a Masters degree in British history at the University of Illinois on a scholarship while starting a 20K gold jewelry manufacturing company for fun and a modest cash flow. Upon completing the M.A. degree, I was accepted to the Ph.D. program at the University of Chicago. In the interim, my wife and I took 50 high school students to Europe as principal/assistant principal for the Foreign Study League. Never a dull moment, and not that dissimilar to other potpourri Baby Boomer lives I have met over the years.

Now I realize that all sounded very self-indulgent as a piece of writing. But the rest of this journey probably won't make much sense unless I show where I'm coming from. Otherwise, you'll never figure out where I'm going. Besides, Baby Boomers have always been accused of practicing self-indulgence, so allow me just a few more paragraphs.

While at the U of C, I did the unthinkable: I "went public" with an article in the *New York Times* comparing the economic woes of the 1970s with those of the 1570s in England.[*] Apparently some readers liked this *relevant* view of history—I got letters—but several U of C faculty members grumbled that THE HISTORIAN does not talk to the rabble, only to the profession. I thought that was bunk and it explained to me why historians won't have to worry about an errant asteroid hit-

---

[*] My original title was "The Rich: Historical Villains." The Times, ever to tweak a beard, retitled it "The Filthy Rich," thereby alienating me from that upper one percent of our population, I suspect.

ting their history departments and making them extinct, like the dinosaurs. They've already got a head start, with no need of assistance from the galaxies.

So I kept on writing *historical perspectives* and haven't been able to stop, believing that we are not only products of our past, but that we cannot understand the present or future—let alone plan for them—if we don't seek out what went on before. The jewelry business experience, along with my writing background, helped me enter the marketing communications field. And I began giving lectures, courses and seminars on a variety of things related to history and writing, either for bucks or for free, usually the latter. In 1990, I found myself doing more writing than ever, but that wasn't the real game.

All the flurry of writing and broadcasting by this time was avocational. My main occupation—the one that paid the rent—was as an executive for a worldwide marketing communications and public relations firm. Since graduate school, I had wanted more time for writing and was getting less of it as I traveled through the years and up the corporate mountain—there *is* no corporate ladder, since ability and accomplishments do not get you as far as politics, mentoring, backstabbing and starting avalanches. I was lucky at first because I only played the mentoring game, but it eventually got nastier the higher up I went.

By the late-1980s, I eventually wearied of corporate life and all the incompetency one discovers upon entering the rarefied stratosphere that is senior management. Worse, it was becoming disconcerting to see the beancounters at corporate headquarters conclude with their fellow American Corporations that "downsizing" could make the bottom line look better. Not a few of my colleagues of the Senior VP-and-above species were handed pink slips and summary farewells. It was time for a change.

And, of course, I had wandered into a *place* in November of 1989 that seemed to suggest a different kind of life, one where happiness could be found without the hope or need of success, whatever *success* meant. Indeed, I couldn't get the images of Bullers Arms and its occupants out of my mind—people who seemed enormously content and at ease with their lives. Maybe that was my problem, one shared by all Boomers. We are not at ease. We are nervous, insecure and we don't know what we want…but we're damn sure we think we know what we *don't* want, which is everything we have. Confusing, isn't it? The people in Bullers Arms were not confused.

Back to 1990. The book came out in June and I had already decided that I was leaving Corporate America in early 1991, hopefully to strike out on my own as a senior marketing communications consultant so I could find more time to write, spend time with the kids, maybe travel. When 1991 was underway I found myself half-way to my goal, cutting the corporate cord but not quite set up in anything solid enough to bring in consistent dollars for mortgage and mouth-feedings. Yet it was an interesting year that saw me solidify my business, write more than ever before…and think about a trip back to England some day, hopefully with my family. I now had a simpler life of sorts, with more control over my time, if not my finances. That clearly was part of the simple life the Boomers pondered—having more time to call their own. Question was, what would they do with it?

As 1992 arrived, I was getting that itch for travel again—hopeless romantics must always travel or they will turn to dust and get unceremoniously swept off that Slippery Sidewalk of Life. And, of course, the *Time* article had come out earlier and all my friends and acquaintances were champing at the bit to do what I had done—hop off the treadmill and strike out toward newer, apparently *simpler* horizons—although there was nothing simple about wondering where your next dollar was coming from. I didn't even have a pair of those worn hiking boots propped on the cover of *Time*!

Fortuitously, one of my clients had a facility in England and agreed to let me bill some time to meet with a senior manager in their

London office should I "cross the pond" any time soon. It got even better when my wife recognized my restless state and, despite our recent observation that the kids were still too young for England, felt I needed a week there *Real Bad*. The target date was mid-May, and as it came closer and faxes crossed the ocean to set up my meeting in London, I could hardly contain my excitement. After two and one-half years, I was returning to my favorite country away from home. It all fell into place nicely and neatly—too neatly. See? Something was afoot with the gods—the ones worshipped by countless generations of primitives on Dartmoor—but I was too caught up in the trip to recognize it. What fools these mortals be....

I also contacted two English friends I had first met in 1977 and continued to correspond with over the years. Back then, I was still in the Ph.D. program at the U of C, having passed those dreadful Oral Exams where I learned that "*all* history is in transition." My wife and I spent 1977 in England so I could flush out a thesis on Henry VII (died 1509) from the forest of documents planted in the British Library, Public Record Office, Guildhall, Westminster Abbey and local repositories. The first friend I hoped to revisit in 1992 was Anne Rose, whom I met when she was an assistant in the British Library's Manuscript Room— housed in the famed British Museum. The second was a world-renown authority on Tudor England, Sir Geoffrey R. Elton of Cambridge and Regius Professor of Early Modern History, who had kept up a lively correspondence with me for 15 years. Both gave me days and times we could meet in London and Cambridge respectively, and it looked like a fun trip was in the offing.

And yes, hope sprang eternal that I could make it back to Dartmoor, although it appeared a remote possibility given my schedule. I continually thought of the moors in between my last trip and the coming one, and the sheer joy of soaking in the eeriness of the area—I had joined the Dartmoor Preservation Association as a life member during the interim! But I doubted I could find the time to venture that far west on this trip, even if I knew a certain dart game might be in progress in the pub of old Sir Redvers, V.C. I was aware that the DPA was having an annual meeting the Saturday I would be in England in a town called Ivybridge in the moor, but I realized I would be lucky just to make it into the Cotswolds to the west of London at best, let alone into Devon. No, Chagford would have to wait and "The Hound from Hell" would have to howl at the moon without me awhile longer. Perhaps.

Chapter 6

Return

BEFORE I KNEW IT, I was on the plane with suitcase, camera and a new companion, a camcorder. I arrived early the next morning in London all bleary-eyed but too excited to consider sleep. Having booked a room at a students' lodge in the Bloomsbury area of London where Virginia Woolf did some literary howling of her own, I dropped my things off, wandered about the Old City on an unusually sunny day and met Anne Rose on the steps of the British Museum. We ate at a small Italian restaurant and caught up on family news. Since she is an ardent supporter of King Richard III, who in 1485 died at the hands of the fellow I had studied most of my adult life, we usually crossed swords before too long, especially over the murder of the two princes.

The detailed story of England's most infamous crime would require many paragraphs, but I'll just write three. King Edward IV died prematurely in early 1483, having overindulged in food, females and familial infighting. He left his realm to his two young sons, Edward and Richard, the elder one briefly appearing in history as King Edward V. (It is easy to get the impression that there were only five or six male names in all of 15th century England—like, if you yelled out "Richard!!" in the middle of London, a stampede of boys and men would have ensued.) The two princes were under the protection of the late king's brother, Richard—my point!—hence, their uncle.

Within a few months, the young princes were locked away in the Tower of London while their mother and sisters hid in sanctuary at

Westminster Abbey, afraid of the "evil uncle." Then Uncle Richard declared his nephews to be illegitimate and quickly grabbed the throne for himself as King Richard III. By July of the same year, it is surmised, the boys were no longer seen in public, or anywhere else for that matter. What actually transpired to make them go *poof* from the pages of history remains a mystery, although it is not difficult to conclude that you can only have one king at a time per country, and keeping a formerly legitimate one around didn't make much sense.[*]

Meanwhile, Henry Tudor, a Welsh exile on the Continent with an anemic claim to the monarchy, sowed popular discontent during Richard III's three winters on the throne. On 22 August 1485, the opposing forces met at Market Bosworth near Leicester, where Richard bit the dust and Henry became the first Tudor king, Henry VII. Henry and his supporters would later say that Richard offed the two princes. Richard apologists would later write that Henry VII found the kids locked in the Tower and bumped them off—even though Henry was married to their sister, Elizabeth of York. Or they would say that someone other than Richard did the foul deed during that woeful king's brief reign. I studied Henry VII for 20 years, and you can guess where I'm coming from on who sent the princes to the next level. Anne Rose, a former officer of the Richard III Society, knew where I was coming from as well.

As it turned out, détente was in the air on this sunny London day, for Anne and I focused the conversation on our lives, not those of long-dead kings. But the curious tourist should understand that England, with 2,000 years of recorded history, continues fighting its historical battles, and there are many. Americans periodically get caught up in "Who killed Kennedy?" three decades ago, or—if anyone under 60 remembers—what really were the circumstances of the Lindbergh kidnapping. The English still grumble about whether King John knocked

---

[*] For the record, bones were discovered under a staircase in the Tower of London in the 17th century. They might be the princes. They rest in a small coffin in Westminster Abbey.

off his elder brother's son and heir, Arthur, in the 12th century, or how true Alfred (d. 899) and the cakes story is before battling the Danes! "Old" in America is not old at all. It is in England.

The next day I was off to Cambridge in a rented car to meet Sir Geoffrey at his home. We had a wonderful visit and he brought me up-to-date on some history battles in progress between historians—those few animated academicians who act as surrogate knights for the original, long-dead historical participants. He spent some time relating a 17th century one centering on arguable efforts by my former U of C adviser, who was now at Harvard. Historians, like the English at large, pick up the gauntlet where their respective eras of history left off, and sometimes it gets professionally bloody. Having heard all the gory details, I then departed to drive around the countryside west of Cambridge for a few days, seeing if I could stretch it to Tintern Abbey just inside Wales, then maybe as far as Exeter at the entrance to Devon before heading back to London and home.

But then things started to happen after leaving Cambridge, perhaps the ancient Celtic gods up to their tricks again. My car was broken into while I was out exploring a Bronze Age something-or-other in Wiltshire. The goons kicked in the driver's door window but failed to make off with anything of import (or export, for that matter). I made a drafty drive to a petrol station and rang up the local rent-a-car office, which rang up other such clones before informing me that no one "in the vicinity" could fix it at this late hour, and that I should bring it to Bristol. No one had a replacement car, either. That meant cutting out a day of snooping in and around the Cotswolds, possibly two since I wanted to spend some time in Gloucester wandering inside the cathedral.*

So I rang up a terrific couple I stayed with in 1989 in their B&B in Tintern, near Bristol just inside Wales, and asked if I could spend the

---

* Two of England's more curious birds to perch near or on the pedestal royal are buried here and will catch up to us shortly: Robert Curthose (d. 1134), eldest son of William the Conqueror, and King Edward II (d. 1327). The East Window-72 feet by 38 feet-commemorating the English victory over the French at Crecy in 1346 and erected in 1352 by Lord Bradeston, is magnificent. So is the architecture from the various construction periods.

night. Myrna Mark, of the Holmleigh B&B, remembered me and said of course I could stay. She also suggested I call Monmouth when I arrived since it was near Tintern and had a fix-it station there. So I drove straight to Tintern, stopping only briefly at Chepstow on the Welsh side of the border to pay my respects to the splendid castle overlooking the river, built soon after the Conquest by William FitzOsbern, Earl of Hereford. Sorry—historians can't help themselves.

I pulled up at Myrna's place and was promptly greeted by her and husband, Gerry. They were warm as could be and let me use their phone. As it turned out, no one could replace the window, at Monmouth or anywhere remotely close. Worse, no one could fix it in Bristol, and they didn't have a car to replace mine. What to do? I sighed and took a stroll through one of the most beautiful valleys on the planet, the Wye. What were the gods up to?

The next morning I was up at 5:30 A.M. to catch the sunrise over the mountains that kept Tintern hidden. King Offa (died 796), the Saxon ruler of Mercia—one of seven Saxon kingdoms on the island at that time—built a dyke along the mountains to keep the Welsh out of England. In our century, it is the Welsh who would like to keep the English out! I ruminated on this change of perspective as I walked along the narrow path following the road through the valley opposite the river to Tintern Abbey. (I will eschew the temptation for yet another digression, sufficing it to say that the Abbey is an eerie, impressive ruin and I encourage people to see it but not touch it—I want it to be around awhile longer.)

When I returned to Holmleigh, Gerry was sitting up high on a terrace built into the mountain alongside the B&B, and he beckoned me up saying I could have breakfast here. I entered the front door and walked into the dining room where Myrna had a tray waiting for me, so I moved toward the back of the house through the kitchen and ascended a narrow, winding circular staircase to the terrace. I sat down at a table, tray in hand, and looked out at the river and the valley. If it were any more serene and bucolic it would have been an Impressionistic painting, probably Monet.

One last phone call determined my destination: a town not dreadfully far from Exeter, where they could exchange my car. So I said my farewells to Myrna and Gerry, entered an enormous traffic jam trying to cross the bridge into England and eventually switched cars. This detour put me in Exeter by mid-afternoon for a late lunch at Sir Francis Drake's watering hole across from the cathedral, The Ship Inn. Adventurous Francis helped harry the Spaniards in the late 16th century and contributed to the demise of their Armada in 1588, for which the people of Spain today are still miffed. I was not in the mood for visiting the cathedral—quite unusual for me—so I got into my second rental car for the week and headed out of Exeter....

And as night fell and I wandered closer to the northern rim of Dartmoor, I had a sinking feeling that something was being planned beyond my control. For as I saw the sun starting to set and I looked at my map for villages to explore for a B&B, the village of Chagford popped up as being only a few miles away. I couldn't believe it, yet there it was on the map, from a different direction than when I first encountered it in November, 1989.

My stomach was actually *butterflying* as I turned the car down a narrow lane and spotted my first white wooden sign for Chagford. Thirty months ago I had stumbled into the place. Nothing changes quickly in England, I knew. Hard as it is for an American to comprehend, I could still visit a fair number of historical places that Henry VII saw before his death in 1509. But was that really true for the *personal*, less monumental encounters we have in our own lives? My grammar school in Chicago no longer existed. Neither did my favorite childhood amusement park or movie theater or drugstore, to say nothing of the majority of childhood friendships. What of the places, sounds and people of Chagford I had "discovered" two and one-half years ago? Were they all still there? And what were the odds of running into any of those colorful characters on a night I just happened to show up, not in frosty November, but in warm May?

Odds, I was to learn, are strange beasties. Albert Einstein said that God does not roll the dice. Things happen because they are supposed to happen, given a set of circumstances. The thing was, other than a vivid memory and a yearning to get into the hearts and minds of Chagford's people, there *were* no circumstances. Just a broken car window and a detour.

Or maybe that was it.

Chapter 7

"Chageford tenebat Dodo"

I ENTERED THE VILLAGE OF CHAGFORD on a different road than during my previous drive 30 months earlier. Although evening, it was remarkably light and clear, and I rolled down the car windows to let in the smells of an enchanting, and very old, countryside. Coming around a sharp corner, I saw a sign for a B&B, missed the driveway, backed up and parked the car. It was a huge house and it looked deserted; several knocks on the door confirmed the suspicion. I climbed back into the car and carried on down a hill until the road leveled off and I started seeing more dwellings.

Up ahead I could discern where the village began in earnest, and just before it I spied a welcomed sign: Glendarah House.* A deft left turn of the wheel had me up near the front door of a large establishment that looked promising given the lights shining through the windows and several parked cars in front. After a quick meeting with the proprietor I was booked for the night—I figured I could only manage to stay one night since this was Thursday and I now had the opportunity to explore Dartmoor all day Friday. Because of my 'rush to the West' to fix my car, thus missing my intended exploration in and around the Cotswolds, the timing was such that I could spend Friday night in Ivybridge for the Dartmoor Preservation Association meeting on Saturday. Then it would be back to London and an airplane to Chicago.

* or "House in the Valley of the Oak" in Celtic. Clearly the gods were handling this little journey!

47

After unloading my things and reconnoitering for the rest room and shower (separate entities), I slowly descended the stairs, exited through the front door and stopped a moment to stare out at the sky. It was shifting colors, from bright blue to deeper hues, depending on which direction I faced, with only streaks of clouds suspended on a surprisingly windless evening. 'Chagford,' I thought, trying to confirm in my mind that I was really here. 'I am back in a moorland village I know nothing about save a handful of faces and a pub named after a late-Victorian general.'

I realized that much had changed in my life since my unintended visit here, and that the personal quest for the *simple life* was undoubtedly being pondered by uncounted millions of Americans, *Time* magazine's "Simple Six" notwithstanding. On the surface, it appeared that I had inadvertently discovered that simple life through the chance observations of lives being lived in Bullers Arms one chilly night in November. Obviously the romantic in me had once again overtaken the historian: I had become more intrigued with the *people of the pub* than the village they, and many of their ancestors, had occupied for a millennia and more. The question now would become, How simple has life in Chagford been through the ages, and has it changed at all?

In *White's Devon* (London, 1850), by William White, Chagford parish comprised 7,492 acres, most of which were under cultivation. Some 1,575 acres were common lands. The census in England is taken every 10 years on the "ones." In 1841, the population of the entire Chagford parish was said to be 1,836 people—possibly the largest in its history—although that number soon decreased to 1,740 because of "the Woollen Factory here being closed in 1848." (Wool was an important industry in the area, second only to tin and other metals.)

Chagford village itself had a population of 1,050. In F. A. Knight's *Devonshire* (Cambridge, 1914), the revised population for Chagford in 1911 was 1,548. This differed little from R. N. Worth's estimate of 1,530 in his *Tourists Guide to South Devon* (London, 1878) or the much later estimate of "about 1,500" from Charles Ward's *South Devon and South Cornwall* (1924). In 1961, the population was at a low of 1,240—about the same number of people that take the train to work each day from my small suburb to downtown Chicago! Chagford's population rose somewhat in 1971—to 1,250—and jumped to 1,400 in 1981, but it leveled off again, with 1,421 in 1991. Chagford parish has a total of 611 dwellings, including farms and cottages.

I learned all of this, and much more, after my return to Chicago, along with the strong impression that Chagford was a very old place. The name seems to have been derived from "gorse-ford"—*chag* or *shag* means gorse or broom—the stuff I saw growing all over the place when I first visited the village. (This, you may recall, is one of the numerous points I said I would get to "later!") Moreover, *shag* can refer to a tangled mass of shrubs or gorse, so it becomes clear that the village was named after a major factor in the local landscape. There have been many spellings for the village, and as the name implies, there was a bridge in the village fording the Teign River.[*]

The *Dartmoor National Park* book printed by Her Majesty's Stationery Office says that the lower ground in Chagford consists of "a network of narrow winding lanes, of Saxon and early medieval origin." In fact, following those lanes brings the curious traveler to many very old farmhouses at such places as Hole, Yeo, Rushford, Barton, Collihole, Whiddon Park and Yardworthy, the last one with medieval remains. Several of the farms are mentioned in *Domesday Book* (1086). Domesday Book? This will be quick:

After England, and its Saxon people, was invaded in 1066 by William the Conqueror (*aka* Duke of Normandy or William the Bastard, he liked both), William had this urge to ascertain exactly what

---

[*] Some sample spellings and the dates they appeared in writing:

Cagefort, Kagefort (1086)	Chaghford (1297)
Chageford[e] (1196)	Chakeford (1315)
Chageford, Kageford (1238)	Geaggeford (1363)
Chaghhford (1275)	Chegford (1675)

it was he had conquered. So he set about his Norman officials to take an accounting of the realm, down to the most minute details. Apparently the beancounters got carried away over the next 20 years. According to one conquered, and slightly annoyed, Saxon monk, William was a bit too curious. The monk wrote: "So narrowly did he cause the survey to be made that there was not one single hide nor rood of land, nor—it is shameful to tell but he thought it no shame to do—was there an ox, cow, or swine that was not set down in the writ."

And our high-tech government leaves out millions of people each decade when taking the census! They need a Norman in charge of the whole mess.

In Thomas Westcote's *A View of Devonshire* (Exeter, 1845), it was noted that the village was probably very old when records first mention a landholder of Chagford, Dodo the Saxon. A snoop into the *Devonshire Domesday and Geld Inquest*, which mirrors William's *Domesday Book*, rewards the reader with an entry beginning *Chageford tenebat Dodo tempore regis Eduuardi et geldabat pro i hida*...you expected English?

What that means is "Chagford was held by Dodo in the time of King Edward, and paid geld for one hide." Believe it or not, that *says* a lot. It says (take a deep breath) that a Saxon—one of those Germanic descendants whose ancestors first entered England in the 4th century A.D. or earlier, gave the Celts trouble, formed seven rival kingdoms, held the invading Danes at bay, united under Alfred the Great, became a subject of Edward the Confessor (the king mentioned with Dodo) until his death in 1066, and succumbed to the Norman invasion later that year through the demise of the last Saxon king, Harold Godwinson, on a battlefield near Hastings—owned the lands of Chagford for a payment of money. That wasn't too harrowing!*

---

* The Anglo-Saxon kingdoms alluded to earlier are interesting for their history as reflected in their names. To the east, East Anglia was, of course, where the Angles lived. It was divided into the North Folk and the South Folk, source names for present-day Norfolk and Suffolk. To the south was Essex of the "East Saxons"; then Kent, probably named after a local Celtic tribe; then Sussex, home of the "South Saxons"—guess who lived in Wessex! In central England was Mercia, bordering Wales—remember King Offa and his dyke? Mercia means "men of the border." To the north, beyond the Humber River, was...you got it: Northumberland.

One hide is not a huge amount of land. Yet according to *Domesday,* there was enough for six plows to work. Dodo also held the manor (*demesne*) along with four serfs, eight villeins, one plow and other things. Included in Dodo's deal were 18 acres of meadow, 60 acres of pasture and 15 acres of wood. And when it came to turning a profit, Dodo was no dodo. The entry ends *Olim xx solidos. Modo ualet xxx solidos*—"Formerly worth 20 shillings, it is now worth 30 shillings." That's a 50 percent increase on anybody's fingers, although "formerly" could mean decades and not just a comparison from last year's annual report.

From earliest times, Chagford was a center for the mining of tin. Along with Plympton, Tavistock, and Ashburton, these four Stannary (tin) Towns eventually came under royal jurisdiction in the early 14th century, and had a *stannary court* for regulating the tin industry. Such regulation, for the profit of the crown, included collecting dues and royalties on tin and determining the purity of the mined metal. A warden was in charge of this function—during the reign of Queen Elizabeth I (died 1603) it was none other than the chivalrous and temporarily trustworthy Sir Walter Raleigh (executed awhile later). It included responsibility for inspecting each block of tin by cutting off a corner, or *coin,* for analysis. Tin was thus measured by *coinage,* a word we use today but with a different meaning.

Knight's *Devonshire* observed that "a miner convicted of selling impure tin was punished by having some of the melted metal poured down his throat." Clearly tin was serious business and the English monarchs wanted to impress that fact in a memorable way. If this seems uncivilized for the English, understand that *civilized* has basically been an advertising slogan for a people that did some rather uncivilized things. Remember the two royal fellows buried in Gloucester cathedral mentioned earlier in a footnote? Well, Robert Curthose was imprisoned most of his adult life by his baby brother, King Henry I, and died in captivity. And King Edward II was starved, poisoned and eventually fitted with a hot poker up his posterior to underscore just how much of a royal pain in the ass he had become to his rivals. (Some, however, believe it to be a symbolic execution because of his well-known sexual orientation.) Civilized? But I digress....

Chagford was never a wealthy town, despite the nearby mining of tin. How do we know? By doing a little math.

According to documents, in the years 1383–84 during the reign of Richard II several collectors visited Devon to assess a tax on the inhabitants due the crown. Most of the cities and boroughs in the shire paid between one and 18 pounds, with ancient demesnes paying less. Besides these categories for taxation, Devon was divided into two "hundreds" (administrative units), each having numerous villages, hamlets and tithings paying from a high of 60 shillings (three pounds) to three pence. There were 240 pence, or 20 shillings, to a pound sterling, so we're talking from a high of 720 pence down to just three.

With me so far? Even if you dropped out, the answer is the same. Chagford was on the low end of the entire shire: *Chaghefor—12 pence.* This was out of a total collection of 476 pounds 17 shillings 6 pence for Devon. Put another way, Chagford contributed 12 pence out of a total of 114,450 pence, or .01048 percent of the kitty.

In other words—like plain English—by the end of the 14th century, Chagford still didn't amount to much. The king wasn't going to get rich off this village of future mean dart players, and from a purely revenue-generating perspective the village was rather insignificant to the country at large.

Although far from being even moderately prosperous, Chagford had its various festivals and activities for its villagers, some staying the same for centuries, others changing over time. White's *Devon* of 1850 states that by Victorian times, the village had "a market on Saturday, for meat, vegetables, &c.; and four annual cattle fairs, held on the last Thursdays in March, September, and October, and the first Thursday in May." Plays and festivals were also part of Chagford life. A 1988 article by Mary Morton in the *Chagford Times* noted, "from Medieval times onward, county people observed the Christmas festivals when the Mummers and the Lord of Misrule presented their bold and bawdy versions of the legend of St. George." Chagford men also acted out plays about Robin Hood.

Today, Chagford has a full calendar of cultural events that would amaze the dilettante and the doyen of the arts in America. Both traveling and indigenous artists stage plays and musicals, choruses, readings and other forms of entertainment from classical to folk to rock. Art fairs, antique shows, various association and society meetings, sports— it is a vibrant village life proffered the people of Chagford.

The church of St. Michael was a part of Chagford's temporal as well as religious life, with the church lands "vested from time immemorial for the use of the church." They comprised four acres, with a right of common land, "let for £14." The church incumbent received 99 acres of *glebe*, or lands belonging to the church that he could profit from to support himself while in office. The church also obtained the tolls of the markets and fairs, for a payment of about £10; "and a house, let to the overseers for 20 shillings, except the upper story, used as a school."

Although the current church is mainly of 15th century architecture, it was first built in the 13th century on perhaps a much older religious site. (The top of a square font discovered in 1865 dates to 1170.) The de Chagford family probably founded the church, which was dedicated by the bishop on 20 July 1261. An altar to St. Katherine—the patron saint of tinners—was placed in the church in 1555. Tinners were an important group for the viability of the village. On the church ceiling can be seen *tinner's rabbits*—three rabbits each with two ears yet only a total of three ears between them. (Some insist the symbol is for the Holy Trinity, and not for rabbits and tinners.)

Other religious groups in Chagford besides the Church of England were the Baptists (forming a church in 1829), the Wesleyans (1834), and the "Bible Christians" (1844). I also encountered a Roman Catholic church, which pops up in this story *later on*.

In 1790, John Weekes, presumably of the village, bequeathed £200 (the dividends on four percent stock) to Chagford for the schooling and apprenticing of poor children. Other philanthropists left varying amounts to distribute bread and money to the poor. The people of Chagford took care of their own, much as they did today. I was to see this first-hand during my 1992 visit. And I would also learn about a living descendant of John Weekes, whose family once owned Bullers Arms and gave it its name.

Chapter 8

Chagford Stories

GIVEN THE LOW POSITION of the village on the totem pole of tax collection, it would seem that Chagford could have remained a sleepy, *simple* village on the sidelines of English history forever. For the most part it did, and does today, although little glimmers of happenings do make it to the written record. R. N. Worth, mentioned earlier, wrote in 1886 that "For many a long year Chagford seems to have steadily thriven, and to have developed a sturdy independence of character that its comparative isolation on the borders of Dartmoor greatly helped to maintain." This included a villager's appreciation of warm summers and sometimes blustery moorish winters. In fact, according to several sources there appeared to be two well-known retorts by natives related to the seasons. In Worth's *Tourists Guide to South Devon* (London, 1878), he wrote "The story goes that if a Chagford man is asked where he lives, in summer he rejoins, with natural pride, 'Chaggyford, and what d'ye think, then?' But, in winter, his melancholy feelings find vent in the mournful reply, 'Chagford, good Lord!'"[*]

And no, neither of my visits to Chagford, in May or November, yielded these refrains. Obviously the indigenous population is either

---

[*] In Devon and Cornwall Notes & Queries for 1911 (William Crossing, editor), the rejoinders are stated as "Chaggevord, an' what d'e think o't?" and "Chaggevord, good Lord!" Either way, consistent spelling for the village name apparently was never a priority even for early-modern commentators on the subject. We already saw how medieval scribes spelled it.

unaware of what they are supposed to be saying to strangers or too befuddled by the whole thing to bring it up.

Although I surmised that an intensive study of local official records would divulge numerous transactions by Chagford villagers going about their business across the centuries, I simply had neither time nor money to take on such an exploration. Rather, I concentrated on wandering through secondary sources to gain an *overview* of the village. This approach yielded some interesting stories.

Market House, Chagford

Apparently the first major local disaster to be recorded occurred on 1 August 1616 in the reign of James I, although the date could be off. (See below) From information related by Westcote, Worth and a black-letter tract written close to the event, this is what happened:

The tin court was being held after dinner in the Market House (or court-house) in Chagford, but not all went well. "The chamber wherein it was kept stood upon pillars, and those decayed, and the assembly at that court greater than ordinary, the pillars and timber cleft in sunder and the walls fell in." The steward, a Mr. Eveleigh, (a "gentleman of good descent and a counsellor-at-law") along with nine other unfortunates, died. It continues to get ugly: "Many more had their arms and legs broken, being covered in the timber and stones: but that which seemeth most strange, a little child was taken up from among the slain not anything hurt; which is not to be slighted, though not to be made a wonder: for we know who saith that their angels do always behold the face of our Father which is in heaven." Worth viewed the catastrophe as "the chief event in the purely local history."

The parish burial register gives a different, more terse account of the event and puts it on a different date:

> Mem[orandum]. These five persons next in order following wer [sic] slayne by the fall of part of the market-house of Chagford upon tin courte daie sitting of the court, presently after dinner, on Friday, the sixth daie of March, 1617 [actually 1618]: John Cann, John Lillycrop, of Crediton; Gregorie Hele, of Colebrooke; William Adams, of Gidleigh; and Timothy Mole, of Ashburton.

Regardless, it was a sad day for the village.

Chagford did stick its toe into the pool of national affairs, if only briefly, during the Civil War between King Charles I and the Parliamentarians in the 1640s. And as it turned out, the event involved the Three Crowns Inn where I had spent the night in 1989, perhaps with a ghost.

Civil War? This will be painless: Let's just say that England and its increasing number of Puritan, anti-Catholic, merchant/business and anti-government groups of citizens were getting rather fed up with two awfully Catholic, increasingly absolute-ruling monarchs, James I and then Charles I. Worse, James was from Scotland—no love lost in England there. It came to a head, literally, in the 1640s, where Short and Long Parliaments and battle lines were drawn, mainly between Charles I and his royalist supporters on one side, and Oliver Cromwell and his Parliamentarian cohorts on the other, although loyalties blurred and crossed lines. Cromwell and company won, Charles lost his head in 1649 and old Ollie spent the next decade trying to find a legitimate form of government to replace the one he had successfully destroyed. As with most revolutions, a complete circle was made (that's what 'revolution' means), returning to where the revolt began in the first place. Cromwell died in 1658; by 1660, the dead king's son-in-exile, Charles II, was whisked back in as King Charles II. More happens, but it always does when you stop a story in 1660 and your speaking more than three centuries later.

In 1642, the Royalist supporters of King Charles I made an attack on the Parliamentary forces in the area of Chagford. One of the "four wheels of Charles' wain," or chief Royalist supporters, was Sidney Godolphin, poet, gentleman and second son of Sir William Godolphin, of Godolphin in Cornwall. Young Sidney joined the Royalists' advance through Cornwall to Devon, and he was soon confronted by Parliamentarians led by Sir Alexander Carew and Sir Richard Buller. (Buller? Any relation to Sir Redvers Buller of Bullers Arms? I don't really know.)

For Sidney Godolphin, like Charles I after him, it all came to a head—or rather a *knee*—at the Three Crowns Inn. The inn was originally built in the 13th century as the dower house attached to Whiddon Park. It had a thatched roof and ivy-ladened porch, with two stone benches recessed inside the porch, perhaps as waiting seats for expected carriages. That porch would now enter history.

What happened to "Little Sid," as he was called, is eloquently and defensively laid out in Murray's *Handbook for Travellers in Devon and Cornwall* (London: 1859):

> During the Rebellion the royalists made an attack on this village [Chagford], when, says Lord Clarendon [a Royalist supporter], 'they lost Sidney Godolphin, a young gentleman of incomparable parts. He received a mortal shot by a musket, a little above the knee, of which he died on the instant, leaving the misfortune of his death upon a place which could never otherwise have had a mention in the world.' Clarendon, it must be remembered, wrote before

handbooks were in request, for it is impossible to enumer-
ate all the romantic scenes round Chagford.

As if a handbook would have changed Lord Clarendon's starchy
mind about the village where his Little Sid checked out!

Indeed, the intrepid traveler John Leland, who trekked across Tudor
England from 1534 to 1543 and wrote of it before Clarendon's remark,
talked about walking across the Dartmoor to "Teign Hed," at the head
of the Teign River some 20 miles from its mouth, not surprisingly called
Teignmouth (pronounced Tin-mouth). Leland wrote on: "Jagforde
Bridge is half a Mile above the Towne, having a Market and 2. Faires,
[and] is a 4. or 5. Miles from the Hed." He, like numerous travelers since
his time, praised the village and its environs. Lord Clarendon obviously
was having a bad hair day—perhaps *wig* is the more operative word.

Three Crowns Inn, Chagford

And yet missing from this particular account of the attack on
Chagford is the actual place of
impact. Many sources say that
Godolphin took the bullet
while standing *in the porch of
the Three Crowns Inn*, that he
collapsed onto one of the stone
benches and that he indeed
died soon after, making the
skeptical reader wonder if the
bullet hit him *more* than just "a
little above the knee."
Moreover, Godolphin's ghost is
said to walk about the Three
Crowns, although I failed to
encounter him during my 1989
visit. Then again, I didn't know

there was supposed to be a ghost, making it less likely that I would have seen one. Believing is everything when it comes to apparitions, or so it would appear.

This story of the death of Godolphin is the most famous story Chagford has to offer the pages of history. Only minor, local events pop up after this time. The memorial to Mary Whiddon (died 1641) in St. Michael's church across from the Three Crown's Inn begins "Behold a matron yet a maid," cryptically alluding to Mary's untimely death—she was shot by a spurned lover as she left the church with her husband on her wedding day. Her ghost is said also to walk the halls of the Three Crowns, suggesting an interesting spectral tryst each night between Little Sid and Mary.

One curious note appeared in the *Devon Notes and Queries* for 1906–07, submitted by one W. H. Thornton, apparently a man of the cloth in North Bovey since 1868. The topic was "the Devonshire Matrimonial Market," and the minister offered the observation that *wife selling* was not an uncommon practice in that county, including the village of Chagford. He wrote of one instance shortly before he took up his church living:

"A man, whose name I can give, walked into Chagford, and there, by private agreement, sold his wife to another man for a quart of beer. When he returned home with the purchaser, the woman repudiated the trans- action"—Imagine!—"and, taking her two children with her, she went off at once to Exeter, and only came back to attend her husband's funeral, at which, unless I am mistaken, I officiated." Sounds like W. H. Thornton may have had a quart or two as well if he wasn't sure who he buried.

If the solid stones of medieval churches seem cold to unaccustomed travelers, they should read the words set upon those walls over the years. For while some may simply state the births or deaths of the important or the forgotten, sometimes a flicker of warmth exudes from the cool granite to remind us all that people through the ages in a small village continue to care about others. The memorial to Dorothea Ann Watts from the 1920s needs no introduction…and has no ending:

IN MEMORY OF DOROTHEA ANN
THE DEARLY LOVED WIFE OF HUGH WATTS
WHO DIED AT BETUL CP INDIA
ON 11TH JANUARY 1924

If in this Shadow land of life thou hast
Found one true heart to love thee, hold it fast;
Love it again, give all to keep it thine,
For love like nothing in the world can last.

Chapter 9

Chagford Lords

DODO THE SAXON HAS BEEN MENTIONED as an early holder of the lands and manor of Chagford. Several other families were to become connected with the village. After Dodo and the Norman Conquest of 1066, the next landowner to be recorded was Hugo, who took his surname from the village: Hugo de Chagford. In about 1150, Hugo and his wife, Alice, were granted a lease of lands near Chagford Bridge. Tin was already being mined. In fact, in 1185, four baddies—Eilward, a smith in Chagford, Richard of Querrendon and his brother, Ailric, and Robert de la Cnolle—were fined for false smelting. The lands then successively descended to Henry de Chagford, Hugh de Chagford and then Thomas de Chagford. Upon Thomas's death in 1299, Simon de Wibbury (or Wilbury) and his family acquired the manor and rights to church appointments for about £66. Then, during the reign of Henry III in the 13th century, the Hiwise (or Huish) family received the lands of Chagford.

Parenthetical spellings driving you crazy yet? Problem is, until the King James Bible of the early 17th century, spelling wasn't standardized, even by people writing their own names, if they could write at all. That's why Chagford has had so many spellings, and even in early-modern times they couldn't agree on it! I will therefore provide the other derivatives for the interested sojourner.

The Coplestons held the title but it reverted to Sir John Whiddon (Whyddon) and his family, who held it for centuries. The above-mentioned Mary Whiddon—murdered on her wedding day—was a descendant. So was Sir John Whiddon, Justice of Queen's Bench, who according to his tomb memorial died on 28 January 1575 and was also buried in Chagford church. If John's inscription was in fact written when he died and not updated later, then he left this world in 1576, not 1575. Why? The New Year in England began on March 25, not January 1—and stayed that way until the mid-18th century!— making John's death on 28 January an event for 1576, not 1575. It is a little trick English historians have to know if they want to keep battles, coronations and zillions of documents in the correct years.

The Whiddons also owned the Three Crowns Inn. It was built, or possibly rebuilt, by Judge Whiddon, and we have seen that Mary Whiddon may yet roam its dark hallways. Whiddons were everywhere, with their main seat of power at nearby Whyddon Park, consisting of a very old mansion and 300 acres.

And if you will recall that little story about Tom Cobley and his overserved friends riding an ill-fated white mare to Widecombe Fair, one of the companions was "Daniel *Whiddon.*" I'll bet a bouquet of gorse that old Daniel was a real person, maybe the black sheep of the Whiddon family.

Another prominent family holding lands in and around Chagford was the Prouz (Prowse, Preaux, Le Paux) family. They held the manor, lands and Norman castle of nearby Gidleigh from the time of the Conqueror, whom they accompanied on his business venture in 1066. The family held onto the lands down to the reign of Edward II, he of hot poker fame. Many Prouz family members were involved in the events of the country. For example, three of the five sons of Osbert de Prouz accompanied Richard the Lion Heart on the Crusade to free the Holy Land in the 1190s. In following the exploits of Osbert's boys, a curious particle on the pages of history caught my eye related to the somber-looking Sir Redvers Buller, he of the pub in Chagford. I had already run into the name Buller when digging through secondary sources, the earliest during the Civil War. But the name *Redvers*—a name I had never encountered prior to seeing the General's portrait inside his namesake pub—I felt uncommon enough never to run across anywhere else.

Prouz coat of arms, St. Michael's church, Chagford

Not quite. The fifth son of Osbert, a lad called Peter, married a woman named Mary in the year 1200. She happened to be the eldest daughter and co-heir of William de *Redvers* de Vernon, earl of Devon and lord of the Isle of Wight. (Some accounts referred to him as William *Rivers*, another version of Redvers.) Furthermore, on the Prouz family shield of arms found in Chagford church with 22 heraldic arms, showing the various marriages made during the centuries, one of them is Redvers. Obviously there was more going on in and around Chagford with these past patricians than I would ever discover any time soon.

The *Devon and Cornwall Notes and Queries* volume for 1916–17 walks through the marriages made with the Prouz family, and not without controversy. Arguments abound about correct heraldry, exact relations and the like—boring stuff to us moderns but important to those medieval families at a time when marriage and land was the bond that mattered. The Prouz family seems to have petered out some four and a half centuries after Peter married Mary. A memorial in Chagford's parish church for *John Prouz, esquire*, who died 19 May 1664, noted *in Illo Ultima Prouzou Proles (De Stirpe Virili) Arvit Extincto*—"With him the race of Prouz (in the male line) became extinct."

As George Harrison called his post-Beatles album—through a borrowing from the Bible—*All Things Must Pass.* So it was with the Family Prouz and other lords connected with the parish of Chagford.

Chapter 10

Arrival

OF COURSE I WASN'T AWARE of Chagford's intriguing and relatively quiet past when I stepped out into the small car park of Glendarah House one day in May, 1992, and began pondering my precarious position on the planet. All this was learned a few months later. My only thoughts then were about my own present, and the present of millions upon millions of my generation, all striving to find the *simple life* and discovering that the pursuit of money wasn't necessarily going to get us there. Here— here in Chagford was a life of quiet and contentment. From what I read later on about the place, the only stress and violation of a peaceful existence in a thousand years had been a collapsed Market House, a wife for sale, a murdered wife-to-be and the death of a foolish poet from a bullet wound "a little above the knee." Now, on this tranquil evening in May, the fantasy of sheer peace and simplicity about a village in wild Dartmoor bathed my mind as I started my car and turned left out of the car park to enter Chagford.

It was a rude entrance. Before the full meaning of a sign stating TRAFFIC CALMING AHEAD sunk in, I was running over seven pairs of speed bumps. By the time I hit the seventh I had come to a complete stop. 'Well, I may not be calm, but I seem to be moving a lot slower now,' I thought. I looked in the rearview mirror and still *couldn't* believe it. If the Hell's Angels ever decide to descend upon Chagford—perish the thought—they had better enter from a different direction. Otherwise, the neighbors can instantly open a Harley-Davidson Used Parts Store, because parts will be flying everywhere.

I drove up the hill toward the Market House and circled the square once before finding a parking place. The air was cool and fresh as I took a deep breath after locking the car. It was 6:45 PM, and shops were closed on this Thursday night in mid-May. For long moments, no cars could be heard—those little lawnmower jobs. Only a few people walked in different directions, voices muffled. I walked past a woman carrying a shopping bag; she smiled and scurried away. I reached the High Street upon which stood the Three Crowns Inn to my left—Judge Whiddon's place, but I didn't know that yet. By squinting at the entrance to the inn, I might have seen the stone porch bench where Little Sid sat for his last sit. To my right I noticed the large outfitting store, where Dartmoor explorers can suit up or find anything necessary to make a pleasant day of hiking on this ancient moor: Chagford has 18 marked footpaths and five bridle paths. I would buy something personal in the outfitting store near the end of this trip, but of course that comes up a little L-A-T-E-R.

I turned away from the Three Crowns Inn and looked down Mill Street, a continuation of High Street past the Square, and to my right. There stood Bullers Arms, same as when I had left it in 1989, or so I thought. I slowly walked towards it, almost with tentative steps, as if something foreboding was lurking inside the pub. And my mind started racing as I reached the front door: 'Would anyone from 30 months ago be here that I would recognize? Could I be so lucky as to walk into a *Dart Game In Progress*, with all my cast of characters who had provided me with a most memorable evening? Would the triumvirate of Messrs. Crafty Cool, Pipes & Pits and Sloppy be already in triangular formation, setting up the topics for the night's discussion? What about red-cheeked Chirpy, or the cloned "Hugh Griffith"—would they be slurping away and enjoying the evening's festivities as if it were their very first cele-bration in Bullers Arms?

'And how about Captain? Would she be there? Did she even still *live* in Chagford, or did she move away? Would I be entering not the familiar pub I left *on hold* in my mind two and one-half years ago, but a totally different pub, with different faces, a different atmosphere and different activities? Was this still the pub of my mind, the embodiment of the simple life?'

It was strange, but I slowly, warily took a deep breath and carefully opened the door. Then I pushed through the second door and walked into Bullers Arms.

Bullers Arms, 7 Mill Street, Chagford

There were changes...and in a country that wasn't supposed to take readily to change. I noticed the dart board was still to the far left, the one the intrepid village dart players used for practice prior to tournaments. The bar was still ahead and to the left, with just two people sitting on barstools. But direct on, where there had been a wall and the tournament dart board, there now was an open space—a kind of serving area where food could be ordered and retrieved from the kitchen in the back. (Indeed, a sign noted the words *Food Servery*.) I could still see the hallway leading to the loos, and I discovered that there were several tables for dining on a lower level behind the new open space. It may have been there before and I just hadn't taken notice.

Modernization had come to Bullers Arms, it appeared. Then I looked up above the serving area high on the wall. My eyes beheld a large chalkboard of sorts with numerous entries concerning entrees and other tidbits that looked positively, well, enticing...in an English pub...actually a Devon pub.

Examples:

Pork in cream and wine casserole with potatoes (chips, boiled or jacket), stirfry veg's and peas: £3.75

Chicken kiev, chips and peas: £3.75

Homecooked vegetarian, either Mushroom stroganoff or Tagliatelle Verde in a cream cheese sauce with stirfry vegetables: £3.75.

I blinked several times. I knew things had become better in the culinary department, but I wondered if the French hadn't tried another invasion on the southern coasts during my absence, landed, changed their minds and inadvertently left their cook (excuse me—*chef!*), who was now holed up in Chagford eking out an existence by preparing repast at Bullers Arms! Stranger things have happened—remember those French tombstones in Moretonhampstead from the time of the Little Corporal? Still and all, the verdict was in: Dining had arrived in Dartmoor.

I walked over to the bar and saw two faces, but they weren't those of Mr. and Mrs. Properly Attired. One belonged to a lively, roundish woman chuckling about and serving pints; the other to a bespeckled, friendly fellow chatting away and serving brew as well. He asked me what I wanted and my mouth went into English Automatic Pilot: "I'll have a half-pint of cider. Medium if you have it." He did, I received it and he asked if I was from America.

Déjà vu all over again.

We went through the drill and then I took the cider to a table near the door, my back to the entrance, staring straight ahead at the menu and the newly-formed Food Servery. My eyes now located two very busy female forms, moving about with such alacrity that I couldn't hold an image of what they might look like. Suddenly time stopped—not a big surprise for an ancient village—as both ladies seemed to slow down and stare at me across the tables. One was a pretty young blonde, the other a pretty young brunette.

Beware, you say. Here we have a 42-year-old hubby *sans* wife and kids staring across the empty—and not very distant—space between table and Food Servery at two 19-or 20-year old ladies in the middle of a pub in the middle of a lonely moor. My thoughts, however, were not only pure, they were extremely basic: I was starving!

I tried to catch their attention without the Ugly-American-Waving-His-Arm atrocity I had often seen acted out in restaurants in foreign lands by United States Citizens—an action that should be legal cause for banning them from travel beyond the Illinois Central Gulf rail line. Fortunately, the reason for their sudden slowdown in motion stemmed from their innate wonderment at a Stranger-In-*Their*-Pub, and not from any covert hostility toward non-Chagford folk. I fully understood; I just hoped that curiosity would eventually lead to a meal.

I started to rise, figuring I had to trek over to the service area to place an order, when Young Blonde magically appeared out in front of the counter and glided over to my table. With a big smile she said "Do you know what you'd like to have?" To this weak and hungry sojourner, Young Blonde's question was a call for salvation. "I'd like to try the mushroom stroganoff. Is it good?" Ugh. *Is it good?* No, she was going to tell me that several hundred German tourists died from it last week, but they kept it on the menu because someone pinched the eraser and they couldn't extricate it from the chalkboard. Sometimes I wonder how we manage to program our dialogue to the point where it is void of meaningful discourse.

Happily, Young Blonde was forgiving. "Yes it is. It's really good." We struck up a contract—if she delivered it, I would eat it and pay for it. She then glided back behind the Food Servery and disappeared into the bowels of the pub, as it were. Young Brunette shot me a nice smile and also disappeared. Then Young Blonde reappeared, smiled at me— I guess I could no longer be viewed as a threat of any sort, seeing that I was a paying customer—and received a phone call, which she took, one of a series during the course of the evening. I smiled back—it couldn't hurt.

And then the boom was lowered, the ceiling caved in and all my fantasizing of 30-odd months seemed to blow up in smoke. The proprietor came over—I now knew his name was Keith—to ask if I would like another cider. I declined but then inquired "Is there a dart game here tonight?" The reply: "No. But there's a foot-…uh, soccer game. Chagford's playing Dartington in their village. Everyone'll be there."

Everyone. All those wonderful faces of 1989—at least those that survived the "Good Lord!" winters of Chagford—were far and away from Bullers Arms on the night I happened to parachute in. It was a hard blow. I looked at my watch—it was after 7:00 P.M.—and it appeared that the pub would not get any more crowded beyond the sparse crowd already occupying it. I stared at General B on the wall. No consolation was coming from the old boy, as if to let me know that life works out that way, and that if I wanted to further explore the simple way of life on the mystical moor, I'd have to come back and try again. 'Not likely,' I thought, sipping my cider and watching Young Blonde materialize behind the Food Servery, plate and cutlery in hand.

Wealthy individuals can hop across the ocean at will or on a whim, and more likely than not they wouldn't come to Dartmoor anyway. I was on the other side of rich, just past the street marked HANGIN' IN THERE, with debt to prove it. Both England and my fantasy would have to remain one of those intangibles, alongside the Holy Grail and the Retirement of the National Debt. No, I wasn't going to learn more about what *Time* magazine was so sure existed. I thought I had it in my grasp the first time round; the second time it slipped through my hands.

It didn't help when I realized that I had bought a pair of boots for this trip, and that they were starting to look worn—magazine cover stuff.

I smiled weakly at Young Blonde as she placed my food on the table. The gods, perhaps, were having yet another little joke on me. It went something like "Let's mess up his England trip with a little break-in of the broken car window variety and make him end up in Chagford. We'll empty the village, then have him leave none the better for it. Great idea!"

The gods had a lot to answer for, especially if my insurance didn't cover the cost of the auto repairs.

Chapter 11

Reunion

CURIOSER AND CURIOSER, ALICE SAID during her journey through the Looking Glass. She had no idea how her story would end. I didn't either, but I had this itchy feeling that, perhaps, I ought to start recording some thoughts in case the gods actually screwed up their wicked scheme and accidentally let a beam of hope slip through a crack in the heavenly ceiling.

So I took out a small note pad reserved for taking notes at my London business meeting and started to jot some things down. Here's how it started to come out.

Young Blonde just delivered the mushroom stroganoff with great flair and a smile. Don't know why I'm writing this, but now that I've learned about the uneventful evening to come, maybe some jottings will keep my mind off the disappointment of not being able to relive 1989 in Bullers Arms.

Then again, I invented that night, not the people of Chagford. If they refuse to cooperate and show up for my further enjoyment and 'exploration' it's not their fault. Still, I want very badly to believe that there is something special here. That people can find a common ground to enjoy each other, support each other. That the Slippery Sidewalk of Life doesn't run through Chagford.

Who knows.

I just tried the stirfried vegetables and the stroganoff. Very good. Better than the hot food I had in 1989, when the menu was limited. I noticed a strawberry cheesecake with clotted cream on the menu. Oh God, Devon clotted cream! I should have brought a portable angioplast gizmo—instant heartclog! It's sort of like 'dairy mortar': you could lay bricks with it.

It's about 7:30 or so and....

Well I'll be. Bullers Arms was just invaded by a flock of females, nattily attired and heading past the Food Servery along the Loo Run to the lower dining room. I've never seen so many short skirts. (Don't they know Hendrix and Morrison and Joplin are long gone?) And the cigarettes are puffing away with Marlene Dietrich adroitness, like so many exhaust pipes waiting for the green light to start the drag race—the one with wheels, that is.

I can only see a few faces since they have their backs to me as they descend. Most are of the youngish sort, 20's or so. It must be some kind of party. Young Blonde and Young Brunette are now hyperventilating to keep up with the drink demand, as is Keith who welcomes them, jokes with them and keeps the female flow streaming into the lower room....

Young Blonde did it again—she somehow materialized right near me while I watch the ladies file into the subterranean dining area. Our conversation:

"Would you like some dessert?"

"Yes. How about the strawberry cheesecake with clotted cream." (*If you ask her 'Is it good?' I will give you a cerebral hemorrhage!*) Uh, and a cup of coffee."

"The cheesecake's very good."

"I'm sure. Say, is there some kind of party going on? And why only women?"

"Oh, it's a wedding party. One of them is getting married this Saturday. It's for her."

"I see."

Young Blonde smiles and walks away. "I see." And you wonder why speakers' bureaus aren't ringing your phone off the hook to book you for speaking engagements! Maybe I should finish the cider before the coffee arrives. Might numb my tongue as well as it's numbed my brain....

I just chugged it. Gosh this is good stuff. Wonder how they can function after drinking a few of these. Right now I wouldn't trust myself with the remote control for the VCR!

Yet again. Young Blonde beams over to me with precision that would shock Scottie and Captain Kirk. (Maybe not Spock. Too logical.) The luscious cheesecake with its deadly cover of clotted cream stares up at me as if to say "Yeah, but it's worth shortening your life a little. Proceed." So I do....

My God, this just isn't happening! But I'm still moving the pen and the cider hasn't put me away, so it must be real. I am sipping the hot coffee—leaning over to hold it up close to my mouth—and as my eyes look up I see...the Captain!

The Captain. It's her...in a suit...asking for a drink from Keith. She ascended from the dining room and rounded the corner where in 1989 she almost killed me with a stealth backhand . Now she walks over to the bar.

And from behind me the Triumvirate of Rome has just walked in and settled into the right side of the bar next to where Captain is waiting for her drink: Crafty Cool, Pipe & Pits, and Sloppy. Bloody unbelievable!

And talk about the gods having a little fun! The Three Men in a Pub are basically wearing the same outfits from yesteryear! CC is in sweater, shirt, blue jeans and athletic shoes, with that cigarette box still grafted onto his back left pocket. P&P has his slacks, vest and short-sleeve white shirt with very shiny black dress shoes...and the ubiquitous pipe skewered unlit into his mouth. Sloppy maintains his white wooden Dutch shoes and wears a sweater-shirt and gray sweat pants. Clothing designers wouldn't get much business in Chagford.

I put the coffee down, and I am now waiting for a little Twilight Zone music, maybe with Rod Serling sitting at the bar staring at me with that wicked grin responsible for unsettling much of my childhood.

And don't you know—Young Brunette walks by and Crafty Cool all but hitches a ride on her fanny! Old habits never die, etc., etc.

I'm looking down at the note pad, almost afraid to look up. But I do...and I see Captain graciously accepting her drink and retracing her

steps to the wedding party, her thick straight hair bobbing with each move-
ment. She doesn't look my way, but that's hardly important. It is doubtful
that she would remember her two attempts at murder and mayhem on an
innocent American. (Is that an oxymoron: Innocent American?*) Indeed,*
she would not remember them happening, because they happened to me*!*

I put my pen down for a moment to take in the scene, which I still couldn't believe was forming before my eyes. Mr. P&P was now chomping on the stem of his pipe—probably the same one he masticated all over in '89. He was half-heartedly listening to Mr. Sloppy, hair as tousled as ever, tell an animated story that sounded suspiciously like a defamation of character assault on a member of parliament. Mr. CC moved in and out of the conversation, watching the curves of passing females and occasionally joking with the jovial lady behind the bar, who I overheard was called Gwen.

Sloppy remained undeterred by his inattentive audience. His white wooden Dutch shoes often clicked together when he made a point, and I now wondered if he might accidentally send himself to Kansas should he click them three times in a row á la Dorothy of *Wizard of Oz* fame. It could prove to be a busy night: Young Blonde materializing at will, Sloppy dematerializing in search of Toto and companions.

Pipe & Pits now folded his arms in cross-pit fashion, and I marveled that after 30 months I was witnessing behavioral patterns that hadn't varied a millimeter. I supposed I shouldn't have been surprised—people continue to do what they are comfortable doing. Only, I was just here for a few hours two and one-half years ago, and those patterns stuck like magnetic glue to the hard-drive of my mind. The images were now being repeated with uncanny accuracy, down to CC's post-posterior proclivities.

I reached for the pen again, although my true inclination was to stand up and look for Captain. Yet part of my mind dismissed that desire: 'She doesn't know you from an empty pint glass lingering about a pub bar. Forget it. Just write.'

I just took a last bite of the artery-blocking clotted cream and gave myself an inward smile. All of this is just amazing.

The Servery, Bullers Arms, Chagford

I need to stand up and stretch my legs. I'm also at a loss for what to do next! After all, I came here with a wish in mind: I wish I could see and watch these people again—possibly even talk to one or two—to learn if the simple life my generation yearns for really, truly exists, here, in Chagford. I want to know if all the diverse faces and appearances and conversations and concerns occupying Bullers Arms have a common foundation, one of contentment, of being at peace, of not needing to climb the next mountain (corporate or geographical) or to outperform the financial results of one's parents. I want to learn if they ever feel alone, or if they know they can always rely on each other—one out of four Americans lives alone, a scary reality. I want to discover if they are haunted by a past, much as the early Boomers are haunted by Vietnam, assassinations, civil rights and other raging issues from their formative years that just won't go away. How could such hauntings be even possible in the ancient village of Chagford? How could they share a collective guilt?

Well, buddy, through a strange series of circumstances, you are here and so are they. That's easy for me to say! Although only mildly shy, I just can't see myself trudging up to someone and saying 'So, about your life—let's talk.' Lord! And how could I ever approach Captain? Her life and the lives of these people are locked in stone—the granite, eternal stone of Dartmoor. The last thing she needs is for some comfort-seeking ex-Colonist with a funny accent probing into her life in Margaret Mead-like fashion to 'learn from the natives.' No, I'm truly stuck. I will watch the evening unfold and enjoy a rerun of my incredible first visit to Bullers Arms...but that's about it. I failed.

Would that I could meet Captain Courageous, Dart Queen of Dartmoor, unarmed....

I have just had a conversation, which I will record while sipping my second cider and sitting at my table. (Warning: A second cider could mean loss of many functions to this writer! Don't try this at home.) I should note that the pub is filling up—there are at least 20 people in the pub proper while the wedding party rumbles on in the demi-basement.

I had walked over to the bar and caught the eye of Gwen, mentioned earlier as a round, smiley lady who serves patrons along with Keith the proprietor. (There was no trace of Mr. and Mrs. Properly Attired from 1989. Nor had I seen Chirpy, "Hugh Griffith" or Short Blonde.) Gwen has a space between her teeth that would match up well against the late Terry Thomas, and her grins are positively endearing.

The conversation:

"Yes?"

"I'd like another half-pint of cider. Right—one of those in the bottle."

"You're from America."

"Yes. Chicago."

"The gentleman here is from Canada."

Gwen gave me my cider, accepted payment and pushed off to the next dehydrated arrival. The 'Canadian' was a normal-looking fellow, and like a hand-off in a relay race, Gwen passed the conversation to him.

"Chicago you said?"

"Yes."

"How are the Black Hawks doing?"

Chicago, we have a problem. Talk about skating on thin ice! It is dangerous and often unlawful for an American to talk about ice hockey with a Canadian. Before answering, I stood on my tiptoes to try to see past all the talking heads, beyond the Young Blonde-Young Brunette alcove, to catch a glimpse of Captain and company. No luck. Guess I had to walk through the mine field, or rather skate through it.

"Um, I don't really follow them. I know they swept Detroit in four during an early round of the Stanley Cup playoffs, but I'm following the Chicago Bulls, uh, basketball, to see if they can repeat their championship from last year."

I'm worried about the Bullies. It's been a long basketball season—82 games worth—and when I left them almost a week ago they were exhausted, bewildered and beaten up by the hands, elbows and glares of the New York Knicks in the playoffs. The Bulls were tied 2–2 in the series and I was prepared for the worst once I eventually had to board the airplane for home.

"I don't know much about basketball. Do you think the Black Hawks will go all the way? They really blew it last year."

Yeah, they did, and this guy just won't let go. But putting the Bulls aside for a moment, 'blowing it' is a Chicago tradition and art form, led by the hapless, hopeless Chicago Cubs. It works like this: Raise the hopes of Chicago fans by winning a few games, then dash those hopes upon the rocks through sudden and inexplicable failure before the end of the season.

"I hope so. The Black Hawks were embarrassed by last year's disaster. I'm sure they'll want to avoid it this time."*

I bade the Canadian a polite adieu and only later on learned that he was part of the wedding party, because the groom was a Canadian. Fortunately, he didn't raise questions about what I thought of the

---

* As it turned out, the Black Hawks did make the finals...and were blown away 4–0 in massive, Chicago-style humiliation. The Bulls, on the other hand, obviously took collective amnesia lessons when confronted with the word CHICAGO emblazoned on their jerseys. They won their second NBA championship in a row, with superstar Michael Jordan sweeping the honors. I watched it on TV, and I still can't understand how everyone and Michael can go up for a ball, then everyone but Michael come down on the floor, then—days later after making the basket—Michael slowly alights to earth while several players have already retired for alternative employment. That and the Big Bang have always confused me.

Toronto Maple Leafs or other North-of-the-Border entities. Ignorance is bliss at times; it can be deadly if you answer incorrectly.

I looked at my watch and couldn't believe the time: 9:00 PM. 'How did *that* happen?' I thought. I assumed my conversation with the Canadian hadn't taken that long, and that most of my time at the table was spent sipping cider and *listening in* on snippets of conversations. I hadn't realize how quickly time passes between sips and snippets. My rough guesstimate of attendees in the pub now came to about 50, including some 18 women in the lower dining area. It could have been more, since there was movement to and fro from bar to loo and back again.

As if someone wanted to help me complete the count—the gods feeling remorse for their mistreatment of me?—I suddenly spied Mr. and Mrs. Properly Attired, former proprietors of Bullers Arms, who were now in full view talking with the Triumvirate. Mr. P.A. was—surprise!—impeccably dressed, with a handkerchief around his neck and his graying beard neatly groomed. Mrs. P.A. had four-inch black high heels with white squiggles on them. Her short graying hair bobbed about when she laughed, painstakingly loud I might add. She perniciously held the attention of CC, P&P and Sloppy, taking up lots of air time with periodic lapses for her husband to chime in. They were all having a splendid time, it appeared.

And then, almost out of nowhere, my eyes ran into Chirpy and "Hugh Griffith." Chirp didn't have his heraldic sportscoat on, but his cheeks were as red as ever. He was chatting with one of the pubdwellers to one side of the crowded bar. Near the other side, I first caught the eyebrows and then face of Hugh. He was missing his cap but the ruddy face was undeniably Hugh. (Isn't that a song or something?) To complete the return of 1989 for me, Miss Short Blonde strolled in and walked over to the Properly Attireds. Her hair was still thick and shoulder-length, and she continued her tradition (at least in my mind) of wearing black. But Miss SB was hardly in mourning; she jumped right into the conversation, with even Mrs. P.A.'s attention now redirected to the new arrival.

I am feeling completely fulfilled at the moment, I wrote. *My worst fear—that the Dartington soccer game would prevent a reunion of my 1989 "mental acquaintances"—is now dissipated into emotions of happiness and contentment. Here are the participants in this easy-on-the-nerves life that few in America will ever realize. Oh sure, they work all day—the farmers probably have very few days off. But it's healthy work, (remember the 'healthy tired' in the* Time *article?). Healthy work and acceptable work—life on the corporate fast track was neither for those in the race. Work that leads to the comfort and honest camaraderie of friends, if not to material things that rarely bring long-lasting comfort anyway.*

I feel all this as I watch them: Mr. & Mrs. P.A. now jollying it up with P&P, CC and Sloppy; Miss Short Blonde, returning from a brief hiatus from the pub with a slightly taller version of herself; different ages and sexes playing darts, with scorekeepers tallying results at a speed rivaling a Cray computer and using only occasional swigs of beer as a power source. This is their home. This is their life. The warm smells, the old, crowded walls hiding old stones and beams, the mixture of young and old, of Young Blonde and Short Blonde. It's that simple.

Chapter 12

Chagford Pubs and People

KEITH, THE SUCCESSOR TO Mr. and Mrs. P.A. at Bullers Arms, came over to my table and asked how I was doing. I told him quite well and he explained that the soccer game ended awhile ago and everyone was coming here afterwards to celebrate. They won. 'Nice goin', 'Mark,' I thought. 'You didn't think to ask about that. Nothing like needlessly worrying yourself over the prospects of sitting in an empty pub—a very special pub to you—just because no dart tournament was scheduled. See? Americans are too quick to take on disappointment and accept the status quo, rather than ask a few pertinent questions. That's why some of our corporations are going down the tubes.'

I asked him about the pub and we had a mini-conversation amid the loud noises of numerous oral outputtings.

"How old is the pub, Keith?"

"Oh, that's hard to say. Parts of the pub are over 400 years old, mainly the stone parts. Chagford's had one or more fires, and anything originally built of wood no longer remains."

"How about the name Bullers Arms?"

"I believe that was changed in 1902. Before that, it was called Bakers' Arms. If you look high up on the outside front of the pub, you'll see the initials JB in the wall. I think it stands for John Baker. But I'm not sure."

Gwen gave Keith a glance that suggested aid was required to fill glasses, and he politely excused himself and headed back to the bar. I looked around at the walls and ceiling, trying to discern a 400-year-old stone among the various structural parts of the pub.

It wouldn't be until summer, after my return from Chagford to Chicago, that I would come across a section in White's *Devon* (1850) that gave an actual census of the principal dwellers and business folk in Chagford before the pub had acquired its present name. If we can assume that the list was current for the 1840s, we have a glimpse at the names and professions of the villagers of Chagford when Queen Victoria was in her 20s, revolution was a fad in Europe and Britannia ruled the waves, or at least certain sea lanes.

To begin, Keith hit the nail on the head. Six "Inns and Taverns" were listed for Chagford in the 1840s, including Bakers' Arms, along with the proprietors and their vocations. There was no JB at Bakers' Arms at this time, but the Three Crowns Inn coincidentally had a "John Brock."

Bakers' Arms, Rd. Holmes, *wheelgt*
Globe Inn, Henry Gregory, *cooper*
King's Arms, John Hooper, *butcher*
Royal Oak, George Harvey, *butcher*
Ring O' Bells, Richard Stanbury
Three Crowns, John Brock

Several other vocations and their practitioners were listed, which should be quickly skimmed rather than studied—this is *not* a test:

Bakers
My. Ann Heard
Ann Stone

Carpenters
John Aggett
Thomas Ball
W. Brimblecombe
James Collins
John Luscombe
Wm. Underhill

Blacksmiths
Samuel Hill
George Murch
Wm. Stoneman
Wm. Stoneman jun
John Stott

Grocers & Dprs.
Joseph Gale
Wm. Gibbons*
My Ann Heard
Wm. Morrish
Thomas Pearse
James Pike
Elizabeth Pratt

Boot & Shoe Mks.
James Aggett
George Clampitt
George L. Gill
John Harvey
Robert Holman
Edward Lyddon
George Lyddon
William Scott

Saddlers
John Braily
J Thorn

Elizabeth Pratt also had a post office in her store, and letters addressed to the town folk needed to include the phrase *via Moreton Hampstead*. And it is interesting to see how people worked: William Stoneman training his son as a blacksmith; the proprietors of four of the pubs having other employment, two of them butchers; family members branching out (George Harvey, butcher, ran the Royal Oak, and John Harvey, boot-and-shoemaker, was probably a relative). These were the people that supplied the town with basic needs, a situation that hadn't changed 150 years later.

There was a separate listing for the important citizens and the corn millers and farmers, along with their professions or their farms. While not trying to simply dump a series of old lists on you, I think it interesting to let the names, professions and places from early-Victorian times "paint a picture" of the inhabitants of a village that was very old even then. First, the people of importance, exactly as they were listed.

Edward Seymour Bayley, Esq., *Whiddon Park*
Richard Leach Berry, gentleman
John Coniam, Esq., *Way Barton*
Mrs. Susan and Miss Eliz. Coniam
John Collard, ironmonger & brazier
Mr. Wm. Courtier, *Westcote Cottage*
Rev. Wm. Hames, M.A., rector of Chagford and of *Ham*, Kent
Samuel Hunt, surgeon
Thomas Miles, watch and clock maker
George Murch, wheelwright, ironmonger, and glass, &c. dealer
John Pardon, sexton
Thomas Penrose, mine agent, *Whitebury Cottage*
Richard Thorn, registrar & par. clerk

Following this small group of professionals and VIPs—for my money, being "Richard Leach Berry, gentleman" sounds like a nice profession, although Mr. Edward Seymour Bayley, Esq. lived on the *prime*

* & woolcomber

real estate—was a listing of the bread-and-butter of Chagford, so to speak: the farmers. Four were listed as "Corn Millers, &c."—Edward Aggett, *Holy street*; James Collins, *Batworthy*, Joseph Nicholls, *Sandy Park* and Peter Torr, *Rushford*. The farmers with asterisks (*) after their names were the actual owners, and not all farm names were listed. The list gives us a little more information about the lives in Chagford as they probably would have been lived for centuries: lots of farmers.

William Austin, *Drewston*
John Bennett, *Teigncombe*
*George Brock, *Drewston*
*John Brock||Wm. Collins
Gabriel Clampitt, *Middlecote*
Nicholas Clampitt, *Holy street*
*John Dicker, *Drewston*
James Dodd||John Ellis
*John Ellis, *Westcote*
*Wm. Ellis, *Great Wicke*
*Wm. Ellis, *Stinial*
James Endacott, *North hill*
John Ford, *South hill*
George Harvey, *Cleeves*
*Humphrey Harvey, *Corrindon*
*Humphrey Harvey, *Yardworthy*
John Harvey||Richard Harvey
*Robert Harvey, *Forder*
Wm. Harvey, *Easton*
Wm. Hast, *Nattadon*
Richard Hellyer, *Calla hole*

William Hellyer, *Masher-hole*
Alexander Holmes, *Easton*
George Holmes||Richard Holmes
*Henry Hooper, *Yelham*
Lydia Hooper, *Great Weeke*
John Hooper (survyr.), *Withecombe*
Wm. Hooper, *Rushford*
William Morris, *Little Weeke*
George Mortimore, *Frenchbeer*
Thos. & Wm. Northcote, *Teigncombe*
*Wm. Nosworthy, *Broadhouse*
John Nosworthy, *Willan head*
*John Perryman, *Yeo*
*George and John Rowe, *Easton*
James Rowe, *Calla hole*
Henry Scott||John Scott
John Stanbury, *Frenchbeer*
Richard Stanbury||John Stanbury
Wm. Strong & Geo. Wills, *Waddicote*
Peter Torr||Richard Thorn
George Webber, *Whyddon Park*

Although I have read thousands of documents over the last two decades and written some scholarly things and given lectures and papers based on many of them, I do not pretend to understand fully what is meant in any document at any given time period, whether from 1140 or 1840. Nevertheless, even to the layman (and woman) it is fun to look at the above listings and conjure up what was taking place in the Chagford of the 1840s. For example, we see that Richard Holmes, who ran the Bakers' Arms, was apparently the son of Alexander Holmes, who worked on the farm at Easton. He may have worked there during the day, along with his brother, George.[*]

Then there were the few family "dynasties" in Chagford: the Ellis's, owning three farms; the Harveys, owning or working on several properties (one of the Harveys—George—ran the Royal Oak and was a butcher; John Harvey, perhaps a son of Humphrey, was a boot-and-shoemaker); the Hoopers (George, probably a relative, worked the King's Arms); the Stanburys (Richard ran the Ring O' Bells—you can still stay there today). It would be easy to make up stories about them, just as it was easy for me to create names and behaviors of the present villagers in Chagford.

And how could I leave out Tom Pearse, listed under Grocers and Drapers? Was he a descendant of the 'Tom Pearce' who loaned Tom Cobley his white mare to go to Widecombe Fair?

The point to all this, for me, was that Chagford had a long history of *history*, and little had changed in the way the villagers supported themselves, yesterday, today and probably tomorrow. Nor had there been much of a change in a seemingly simple life. Many of the farms— some listed in the *Domesday* Book of 1086—continue unto today, as do the pubs, the shops and the sprouting of family members into the next generation. It would be hard to say that about small-town America. When Chagford people were tilling the soil as a young Victoria sat on the throne, 90 percent of the U. S. was agrarian, with "Chagfords" everywhere and the BIG CITY only a rumor and a dream. Today, the numbers are reversed, with the megacities housing much of the

---

[*] I could not know that I would later run into the great-granddaughter of Richard Holmes: Edna Maggs, who works in the Post Office. She told me Richard was a wheelwright and employed three men who worked in the back of the pub. He married Mary Murch, she of a blacksmith's family, thus merging two compatible trades. Richard died on 30 June 1853, age 46. Eight years later, Mary married George Bond, 46, who was listed as an innkeeper. He probably took over Bakers' Arms. I was amazed how easily I could touch Chagford's past through its current inhabitants. But read on for more...

population and megafarms owned by large consortiums providing most of the food for a nation. Yes, things changed where I lived. They didn't change much in Chagford, from the worn boots to the trusty bicycle…just like on the cover of *Time* magazine.

Chapter 13

Meeting the Captain

9:25 PM. THAT'S WHAT IT SAYS on my watch as I continue to watch the villagers in Bullers Arms enjoy their evening. I don't want it to end, but I know it will. Hmm, perhaps the end has just begun. Mr. Crafty Cool is drifting toward the door, having exhausted every last drop of coolness for the evening. He spies a dart game in progress between two male patrons and leans against the side of the door to watch it. Now I see him speaking with an older gentleman. Oops. A little comic relief from an unlikely person. Mr. CC has just fallen into the inner door, the victim of an eager villager briskly opening it to enter the establishment. Deftly—and with great cool, no less—CC recovers in Olympic gymnastics adeptness—even plants both feet on the landing—only to look about him quickly to make sure that no mortal witnessed the faux pas *of his life. He's in luck. I'm the only observer, and I'll never tell. (Well, actually, I guess that's what I'm doing right now!) Exit Crafty Cool.*

It was now 9:30 in the evening and the noise level was not unlike a crowded night at the old Chicago Stadium, where Bulls and Black Hawks fans alternate nightly at attaining vocal decibel levels that could reach intelligent life light years away far better than any of the stuff we're presently beaming out. I rested my pen a moment and sipped some more cider, taking in the din of voices as if it were waves of warmth and well-being flowing over not only me but the current inhabitants of Bullers Arms. It was so crowded I couldn't even see old Redvers on the wall, although he would have enjoyed the company and especially the spirits—I was to find out later that the general was especially fond of drink.

I completely lost visual contact with the wedding party far off and below my current level of viewing. However, periodically one or two ladies emerged from the lower level, approached the bar as Rumpole would at Pommeroy's for his plonk and ordered a drink for themselves and perhaps a companion female imbiber. Service was swift. So were the occasional dashes to the loo at the back of the pub. The Myth of the MAGI (Males Alone Get Indisposed), whereby *only* men are magnetically pulled to the rest room after a few beers, can now be confidently dismissed. Females are just as proficient at making quick exits and equally relieved entrances without skipping a beat.

9:32 PM. Mr. and Mrs. P.A. are now left with Short Blonde and the slightly Taller Blonde, and Mrs. is taking the lead with Mr. filling in the odd gap. Short Blonde again seems all listened out. No one in the original group except Mr. Crafty Cool, Mr. Pipe & Pits and Mr. Sloppy have sat on a bar stool or at a table. This may be strategic: it can be no coincidence that the "Three Sitters" are no longer with us—I now realize that, unbeknownst to me, P&P and Sloppy flew the coop. The "Four Standers" are still here and holding their own, as it were. Perhaps the legs cramp up from oversitting.

9:40 PM. Keith the proprietor is coming over to chat. Time to stop writing.

Keith's inquiries about my previous visit to Chagford led me into the whole story of November, 1989, including my near brushes with death at the hands of Captain. And lo and behold, Captain was now revealed to me by Keith, much as Lois Lane found out that Clark Kent was the Superguy, and Americans discovered Richard Nixon was taping his gutter-inspired conversations in the Oval Office of the White House.

"Oh, you mean Julie."

"Judy?" I couldn't get the exact pronunciation because of all the noise.

"Julie. She plays darts and drives the taxi. Very nice."

"I saw her come in for the wedding party."

"Yes. She's downstairs."

Keith was about to leave when he suddenly threw me a curve that might have made Nolan Ryan smile. Not only was it unexpected, it started me on a path of research that was to slowly chip away at the vision of innocence I had created for Chagford—a village I thought had successfully retreated from that "real world" 77 million of us were trying to escape.

"I meant to tell you about General Bullers. You asked about the origins of the pub before. Well, Bullers fought in the Boer War, and was a real hero. Ladysmith and all that. It was Buller who started concentration camps, you know."

"!!#$%&*|!??" That's about all I could hiss out, give or take a %&*|!, because Keith was already making a hasty exit from my table to the back of the pub where more thirsty mouths required quenching. And as if Charleton Heston had now entered the pub on cue to part the sea (to me, Charleton did it, not Moses), a sudden parting of the mob of people to the right of me opened up a two-foot wide, head-on clear path to the portrait of General Sir Redvers Buller, V.C., looking out at the world, innocently, quietly.

Ladysmith? Concentration camps? What does Keith mean? I wrote. *I had once read something about the British being the originators of that ghastly inhumane edifice, and that Hitler may have taken notes. But how come I never heard of Buller, if it was his baby? And wasn't the Boer War a national disgrace for the British? How could Buller walk away from it with a Victoria Cross and a pub named after him?*

Here comes Keith again, in a big hurry. I've been staring at Buller for several minutes now, and I can't just leave him up there on the wall without a few answers.

I hailed Keith, hoping to fire off some quick questions about his last statement before he retreated behind the bar. ('And what was Ladysmith?') As it turned out, he complicated my life even further, and indeed set the stage for the writing of this story.

"Uh, Keith, what did you mean by—"

"Sorry, got to run. Oh, I told Julie your funny story. About her almost running you over and all that. She said she'll be up in a few minutes to join you."

In perfect *deux ex machina* fashion, Keith disappeared faster than Young Blonde could have accomplished on the U.S.S. Enterprise (the spaceship, not the aircraft carrier). I was left with two sets of butterflies going at each other in my stomach. I wanted to know more about Buller, true. And now—ugh!—Keith had done what I was unable to do. He let Captain know I was alive and had survived her assault & battery blitz. And she was willing to talk to me about it!

A 42-year-old American in Bullers Arms was suddenly terrified.

9:44 PM. Several of the women-at-the party leave, saying their good-byes to Keith. He is furiously working the brew levers while looking up to smile and bid farewell. I swear, I've never seen so many polka dot dresses. The old Lawrence Welk show, maybe?

9:48 PM. Can't believe I'm keeping track of the minutes, but it's either that or go out and wallpaper the market square. Amazing, but I am truly nervous. I wonder what my mouth is going to say to Captain—to "Julie?" I just looked around me. The pub seems to be moving into lull mode, although it's still noisy. I continue to sip my second half-pint of cider—always the cheap drunk. At least I can move this pen without sliding off the table, but it's getting harder to concentrate. I'm also afraid to enter the "Dash to the Loo" competition—although my bladder is very unhappy— lest Julie and I cross paths. After all, I'm unarmed, and if she's the meticu-lous type she may want to finish the job right!

9:50 PM. Keith just helped dissipate some of the butterflies, but also hatched a few others. He came over to chat a bit more about General Buller and told me that the house next door is called Ladysmith House, after the campaign. (What campaign? Ladysmith again?) I quickly asked about Buller's Victoria Cross, and Keith said he received it during the Zulu Wars much earlier. Oh.

"Buller decided to stop the Boer farmers from supplying the Dutch soldiers with food by concentrating them in one area. That's where we got concentration camps."

Keith then changed the subject and told me about an 88-year-old woman who still comes to the pub for a pint. Her father and grandfather built many of the houses in Chagford, and apparently the family had ties to the pub.

I wanted to ask more about Buller and the camps, but two things happened simultaneously: Keith quickly departed, summoned by Gwen. And Julie emerged from the depths of the party.

I think it was Martha and the Vandellas, or the Supremes—maybe both—who sang *Nowhere to run, nowhere to hide.* Too true. I came to view Keith as a buffer, someone who might hang nearby should I run into anything unsettling in the pub, like having a conversation with someone. Naturally, this was absurd, as was my behavior. After all, I survived the Canadian and his shots on goal. I was going to meet Captain. No big deal.

Sure. Neither was the little ice cube the Titanic bumped into. After 30 months of wondering, fantasizing, daydreaming, I was going to meet someone who represented the cover of *Time* magazine in my mind, much as she would have for countless others. Worse, it wasn't her fault. She didn't ask for the role I created for her. Julie was being Julie and I was being Isaac Asimov, creating worlds and futures in my mind, but nowhere else.

I looked at Julie. She was waylaid on her way into the main room by several people, and thus fell into conversation as easy as a 10-year-old hops onto a waterslide, all smiles. Meanwhile, the dart game continued, with new players and that lightning-quick tally ability that young and old seem to possess.

My watch said 9:56. I looked down at pen and pad. They both looked up at me, as if to say 'You're on your own, Shakespeare. No good scribbling around with us to look busy and calm. Just keep knocking those knees together and hope for the best. Besides, she doesn't *look* like a killer.'

9:57 to 10:39 PM: Julie. I am writing this in my room at Glendarah House. It's just after 11:00 and I want to be sure to record everything as it happened, including the conversations still in my mind.

Of course the inevitable occurred, given the chain of events and words imparted all evening. Celtic gods at work, right? Julie came over to my table, sat down, shook my hand and said "I understand I almost ran you over two years ago." It was an auspicious beginning.

Chapter 14

Julie

JULIE JEFFERIES GAVE ME A BIG SMILE and looked at me through her cat eyes, which were alive and piercing. It was a smile full of life, and it sent out vibrations that let me know how easy it was for her to gain attention. During that brief pause before answering her about my near demise at her hands, I zipped through the rolodex in my mind that listed the last 30 months of events, problems, dreams and wishes…and the thought of coming back to Bullers Arms one more time to see if I had simply made up a simple life or if, in fact, it really existed.

And here I was, sitting in the pub next to the leader of the pack. Just incredible. I was nervous, overwhelmed—grab a thesaurus and make a list.

Here's how it began:

"Yes, but as you can see, I lived to tell the tale. Barely."

"Are you here on holiday?"

"Mostly. I had some business to attend to in London. I'm staying at Glendarah House tonight. Nice B&B."

"Do you always take notes on holiday?"

Oops. The note pad laid bare for all to see, and I forgot about it. I explained that I remembered several of the people in Bullers Arms from late in 1989, and that I thought I would write down some thoughts about the evening as it unfolded. I also confessed to being a writer, whenever feasible.

"Well, tell me some of those people. I assume you remember me because of your near-brush with death."

Cute.

"Kind of hard to forget." *If she only knew.* "Well, for example, there was a red-cheeked gentleman here—I began thinking of him as Mr. Rosy Cheeks—who wore some kind of sportscoat with an insignia or badge on it last time."

Julie looked around, silently nudged me to look near a corner of the bar.

"That's Chirpy."

"Chirpy?"

"His real name is Leonard. Leonard Mortimore. There are lots of Mortimores around here. Gwen, over there. She married a Mortimore. Chirp's a sheep farmer."

[A quick look at the Chagford folk of the 1840s does, in fact, show a "George Mortimore" at Frenchbeer. I didn't know at the time if that was Chirpy's farm or family. I would find out much later that it was Gwen's husband, Arthur Mortimore, who was the grandson of George. There were three branches of Mortimores in and around Chagford. Arthur and Chirpy came from different branches.

"Why do you call him Chirpy?"

We both looked over at him again, talking away and drinking a pint.

"That's because Chirpy likes to talk a lot. Chirp's quite a character. Very Devonian and not keen on changes in Chagford."

"Changes?"

"Some people in the village trying to change the way things are. He's farmed all his life, apart from his national service in the army. He once told me he would have liked to have made the army his career. Unfortunately, he had to come back to look after his sick mother."

We then talked about some of the other "characters" in my Chagford cast. She couldn't put a finger on Crafty Cool, Sloppy or Pipe & Pits, but she had a notion about Short Blonde, who had left the pub before Julie's arrival at my table.

"I'm not sure, but that might be Mrs. May. She owns the Claremont Guest House below the Bullers."

She didn't know who Tall Blonde might be. "Hugh Griffith" sounded familiar, but she needed to see him. At the moment, Hugh could not be located.

"What about the new proprietors? And the old ones?" *I was thinking of Gwen and Keith, and of course the Properly Attireds.*

"Edwin and Audrey formerly owned the pub." *Edwin and Audrey? If I ever meet them, I will encourage them to change their names to Richard and Elizabeth. To be properly attired means having properly-attired names as well.*

Julie continued. "I believe Edwin owns a plastics factory up north, but they are retired and live in Throwleigh." *I glanced over at them, chatting away. They didn't seem old enough to be retired, let alone* properly *retired. Then again, I'm not old enough to retire but I'm more than willing.*

"How about Keith and Gwen?"

"Keith Wright. I don't know anything about him. I believe he owns the pub with Bob, his brother-in-law. Gwen works for them. She's worked in Chagford pubs a long time."

Amazing. So much to learn, so little time. "Keith told me about an 88-year-old lady whose family built many of the houses in Chagford."

Long pause, in thought. "The person who springs to mind is called Nesta Weeks.* Her father was called Stone and he owned the local builders, which were also the undertakers. Her nephew married the daughter of the then owners of Bullers' wife's sister. Does that make sense?"

"Oh, perfectly."

I was having such a good time in this impossible setting that she could have been speaking Icelandic and I would have grinned in gratitude. How many times have people spied other people across a room, or seen someone

---

* Any relation to John Weekes, mentioned earlier, who in 1790 left the village a grant to help poor children? There must be many connections from past to present in Chagford. As it turned out, Nesta's grandparents, the Lyddons, owned the pub at the turn of the century, and in 1902 changed its name to Bullers Arms in honor of Sir Redvers. Mrs. Lyddon hated the thought of living in a pub, so she made Mr. Lyddon wall off a separate dwelling attached to Bullers Arms. They called it Ladysmith House. We'll get to Ladysmith—promise.

up on a movie screen, or at a gathering, wondering what it would be like to meet that person…realizing, of course, that it would never happen and that both the face and the expectation of 'what-might-have-been' would dim and fade over time? Here I was, meeting a memory and listening to her tell me about her village, or rather certain people in 'my village,' the one I created in my mind from real, live characters. And all the while the pub oozed warmth and chatter and safe haven. That port we all look for.

Then I turned to the matter I wanted to explore most over the last two and one-half years, only I didn't know if it were possible, or how it would be received.

"Uh, Julie. Would you mind telling me a little about yourself?"

Again that intrusive smile that was so easily absorbed by whatever targets she selected. Again, a thoughtful pause to reflect.

"Well, I'm one of eight children. I'm half Irish. My father came over to England in 1937 to work on a reservoir near Chagford. He met my Mom here and married her. I've lived here my whole life, and have never wanted to leave."

"Have you traveled much?"

The smile. The head bobbing with her hair bouncing about. "I've been to Austria, Portugal, Spain. But I've always wanted to come home. I'm not interested in travel."

I was going to ask her more about her life, about her view of the world, of Chagford and its people…about the joys and sorrows of a 'simple life' that she enjoyed living so much. About to—but then Chirpy arrived.

"Chirp. This is Mark. From America. I almost killed him two years ago playing darts…and in my taxi." *She was laughing away.*

Chirpy, glass in hand, pulled up a chair and joined us. He shook my hand and gave me a warm smile that made those beet-red cheeks swell up like, well, beets.

"She's pretty good with darts, you know. Wins lots of tournaments."

And Chirpy then did what I should have done and wanted to kick myself sideways once he did it.

"Let me get you a drink," *he said to Julie.* "How about you?"

"No thanks. I'm fine." *Chirpy took off.*

I have always prided myself on being of the gentlemanly ilk, raised by polite parents who imparted the virtues of walking on the street-side when accompanying a female and never failing to open the door and pull out the chair, preferably before she was seated. Yet when Julie sat down, all past training and reflex seemed to fly out the window, along with everything else except the thought that I was face-to-face with a face I've been wanting to face for a very long time.

"Do you like the pub?" *she asked, before I could resume learning more about her life.*

"Yes, very much. You know it's interesting. I assume that you all have your favorite pubs. Otherwise, I never would have, uh, run into you and Chirpy and the others again. I mean, there are other pubs in Chagford."

"That's right. A lot has to do with the owners and their attitudes and personalities." *She leaned forward over the table so I could hear her better, the pub now oddly becoming more crowded at what I thought was a late hour. In fact, we were slowly finding ourselves surrounded by people standing and downing pints, with lots of smoke and various aromas filling the air. But rather than being stifling, it was actually comforting, if that's the right word for second-hand smoke. I sort of coughed with delight (!).*

"Groups of people will change pubs because of an owner," *she continued.* "I remember one pub didn't treat young people very nicely, so they left for another. Then the owners changed, and some of them came back. Some owners hold a grudge and won't serve certain people. But"—*and she wanted to make certain that I understood her next words*—"There's no viciousness in Chagford."

Julie now hit the one brick that could make the entire Simple Life structure collapse for me, one that I didn't want to think about during my cerebral construction of Chagford after 1989. But I didn't run from it. I asked.

"You know, I wondered about how people in a very old, small village get along with each other," *I began, finding myself leaning over to be heard. Seems there were now lots of young people pushing into the pub and ordering drinks.* "What happens when there's a falling out among neighbors or friends? Doesn't everybody find out about it? And if you don't patch it up, doesn't it make life rather awkward, day to day?"

Chirpy arrived with a clear drink in one hand, a lemon floating in it, and his pint in the other hand. He sat down and handed the clear one to Julie, who accepted it and kept talking. Apparently he knew what she drank.

"Ta. *(That means 'thank you.')* You're right, Mark. It's a small village and everyone knows everything about everybody. That's why we can't afford to be mad at each other for very long. Right, Chirp?"

"Right," *Chirp said into a slurp of beer.*

As if the slurp were a clandestine signal, a large group of young men began whooping it up. Julie started laughing and Chirpy grinned and initiated a conversation with one of them.

"I take it this hasn't anything to do with your victory in the Falklands," *I yelled, trying to be heard.*

"It's our football team. Your soccer. They beat Dartington and now they've come to Bullers to celebrate."

We both looked up and watched as the players let out war chants, raised pints and generally caused havoc. I noticed older Chagford folk sitting at tables drinking beer and smoking. But rather than being irked at the noise, they seemed rather excited and amused. Even proud.

Two of the young men came over to the table and looked at Julie. The first was good-looking—you see guys like him in commercials on television for after shave or men's designer jeans. Hollywood features. His hair was perfectly groomed and he had an air of confidence that was positively unsettling. Though not tall, at least from where I was sitting, he was well-built, with two arm-length tattoos and an earring for decoration. The fellow standing next to him was pleasant-looking but didn't quite stand out the way his cohort did.

Julie looked up at the tattooed gent, smiled and introduced me.

"Mark, this is my brother, Nick. He plays football for Chagford's first team. They won the Division I League."

With nary a smile but enough recognition to let me know he took in the introduction, Nick nodded. I got the distinct impression that offering a handshake wouldn't go over well, so I nodded back.

"And this is Nick's future brother-in-law from Canada. He's marrying Nick's wife's sister."

Those last two lines weren't quite the lines Julie delivered. She did in fact mention his name. I just couldn't hear it. No big deal, since he smiled and we offered our hands at the same time. I now realized that my earlier conversation about hockey was with a Canadian attending the wedding in Nick's family.

Nick, the brother, huh? Interesting. And who's he mad at? As I found out later on, perhaps the world, and for good reason. But clearly not at Julie.

And then I saw an opening to get back to Julie's origins. Nick and brother-in-law wandered off to regale with Nick's compatriots, and Chirpy was turned away talking with two pubdwellers. I looked over at Julie, who was somehow serenely sipping her drink amid the chaos of the universe that was now Bullers Arms.

"Julie, you said your Dad was from Ireland. Was there a problem fitting in with the people in Chagford? And I would guess that he was a Catholic coming over to a largely non-Catholic country."

She put her glass down and moved closer again. I could see that she was going along with me out of a sense that it was important to me, and not because she enjoyed talking about herself. I knew I probably shouldn't have been so overtly interested in the life of a stranger...and yet, I had this opportunity—maybe the only opportunity—to learn about the one person who, in my mind, represented a life I had longed for my whole adult life. If I could confirm in my mind that I hadn't 'invented' Chagford, but rather Chagford was indeed the way I wanted it to be, then there was hope for the Boomer millions back home. And that confirmation would have to begin

with the embodiment of a simple life, namely the people of Chagford. Julie
was their symbol to me.

"The people were very nice to him when he arrived." *She was more*
serious now. I had opened a dusty file in her memory. "It was just before
the war, and everybody was pulling together. Then he met my Mom
nearby and they married."

She sipped her drink and opened perhaps a more hidden file. "My Dad
was raised a Roman Catholic. You know the church down the road, near
where you're staying at Glendarah?"

"Yes." *I had seen the sign for 'RC Church' and recalled viewing the*
building up a lane.

"One day my Dad was sick and the priest didn't come to visit him at
home. So he tossed off the Catholic church."

Part of me didn't want to ask this, but it seemed the logical thing seeing
she had gone beyond my initial query. "Where is your Dad now?"

Julie fingered the stem of her glass and looked down at the lemon, float-
ing off to one side. Then she looked up, gave me a warm smile and spoke.

"He died in an accident, a long time ago. When I was 13."

We caught each other's eyes and smiled. Mine was weak, sorry that I
had asked the question. Hers was almost sympathetic, as if sensing how I
felt at that moment.

Our conversation quickly moved to the general area of the Troubles in
Ireland between Catholics and Protestants. I chipped in my two historical
pence about a long history of Anglo-Irish adversity, dating back to the 12th
century and Henry II. Julie had strong opinions about the politics of the
problem, then hesitated before confiding in this stranger who took notes in
her pub.

"It's a terrible thing to say, but if my Dad had lived I could see him
supporting the IRA."

Another hesitation, then a quick shifting of gears. "So what will you do
with your notes? Are you planning to write something?"

It was no lie that, after I began jotting things down and the people from 1989 started reappearing in 1992, I had considered writing a piece at some point about Chagford. Problem was, I didn't know anything about the village, the people, or the General on the Wall—at least, not at this time. The notes were therefore things I didn't want to forget in case I had use for them later.

Chirpy somehow reappeared in our faces, leaning over to talk to both of us.

"You'll be staying for the dart tournament tomorrow, Mark?"

Say what? I looked at Julie with askance and she radiated her smile back.

"The tournament at the Jubilee Hall tomorrow night," *she said.* "All the pub teams in Chagford compete for prizes."

Chirpy chirped in. "Yeah, and Julie and Nick are in several competitions. You'll be there, won't you?"

Julie looked at me as if she wasn't quite sure what my answer would be. Thing was, I didn't know either.

"Well I'll tell you, Chirp. The last time I watched a dart tournament in Chagford it nearly cost me my life."

Julie suddenly flew into a fit of laughter and shattered the stem of her glass on the tabletop, leaving a small glass bowl that was the top-half of the glass still in her hand. I grabbed the cup while Chirpy did the only gallant thing a Devonian could do: He jumped up, ran over to the bar and ordered her another.

"You *are* a dangerous sort, aren't you?" *I offered, wiping the table where some of the fluid had spilled. She picked up the stem pieces and put them in the ashtray, tears in her eyes and laughing.* "Still trying to show me how lethal you are, right?" *I continued.* "Never saw someone crush a glass before. At least not up close and personal."

I know. I shouldn't have gone after someone as vulnerable as a lady laughing uncontrollably. Best part was, she wasn't embarrassed at all. Just tickled.

Chirpy returned with a backup for her, which she politely exchanged for the stemless cup. He took it away and returned while Julie caught her breath. I figured enough was enough so I picked up where we left off.

"I would love to go, but I've got to start heading back to London. I was hoping to try to attend a meeting of the Dartmoor Preservation Association in Ivybridge on Saturday. Spend the night there tomorrow."

"Ivybridge's not far from here," *Chirpy said, all serious. Hey, we were talking darts.* "You could spend tomorrow night here, leave first thing Saturday, then make your meeting and get to London."

Then suddenly Chirpy stood up, ready to leave. It was getting late and, I remembered, Chirpy was a farmer. "Hope to see you tomorrow, Mark. Nice meeting you." *We shook hands.*

"Good-night, Chirpy," *Julie said, flashing a smile to him that obviously warmed his heart. He smiled back and left.*

"Dang! I forgot to ask him about that insignia he had on his sports-coat. Maybe it wasn't him I remember. I've seen lots of red cheeks around here."

Julie and I started to rise as we saw people pouring out of Bullers Arms, the festivities over and a work day looming beyond the bright moon outside.

"I can find out for you."

"That would be great. And I'd like to send you my notes once I've written them up, to see if I've got everything right. I'm just sorry I don't have more time to learn about the people here."

"I'll look forward to reading them."

Again the eye contact. Again her smile. And my mind placed her in the setting of Bullers Arms, with people moving about, laughing, saying good-byes, readying for the way home and a contented sleep before another day in ancient Chagford.

Just then a few of Julie's friends came over to talk with her as the pub continued to empty out. I suddenly felt redundant and very much an out-sider. I mean, let's face it—I burrowed into this village and the next thing you know I'm interviewing a villager and asking way too many questions. Keith probably thought I was from Inland Revenue. And Nick—well, I didn't think he'd be waiting outside to encourage me to stay.

Julie momentarily turned away from her friends and looked me in the eye. It was a brief moment of recognition, from her to me, as if her eyes were saying 'Yes, we did meet and talk and I didn't mind that you snooped about my life.' She extended her hand and I took it.

"Nice meeting you, Mark. I enjoyed talking to you."

And then she moved close and kissed my cheek and turned and went back to her friends.

I looked back only once as the inner door closed to the pub. She was still talking away, and beyond her I had quick glimpses of Young Blonde. (I couldn't locate Young Brunette, but there were lots of brunettes in the pub.)

I entered the street of Chagford, looked up at the moon and took a deep breath. Now *what?*

Chapter 15

"A Thorough Soldier"

AS I STOOD OUTSIDE THE PUB and stared at people slowly filing out into the cool, clear night on Dartmoor, it occurred to me that I knew far less about Bullers Arms and the people frequenting it than I might have supposed after the events of the evening. My conversation with Julie Jefferies—the Captain, whom I actually met!—in some ways was frustrating for what I *didn't* learn about this home-grown, interesting individual. The pieces I did manage to hang onto—one of eight children, father died when she was 13 having fallen out with the church (not related events), an almost dangerous-looking younger brother—let me know that there were hundreds of other pieces about her life, her joys, her concerns. I had no clue as to what I was missing or how to put it all together. My fear was that I would never have the chance to find all those pieces, and simply *keep* Julie in my mind as the lively Captain with a not-so-perfect past that managed to live—and to help her village maintain—the simple life. As it turned out, I got my chance to find some of those pieces…for better and worse.

Better and worse? Yes, for at that moment, standing outside the pub on a moonlit night, it occurred to me that something was wrong. It was more than just missing pieces. There was some tragedy here, something very hidden about her past that extended into her present and future. Why did I think that? The readily-available smile? The pointed hesitations before speaking? What might the matter be? Maybe it had to do with her brother, or other members of her family. Maybe even her crystal-clear drink with the lemon slice floating about. As it turned out, it had to do with all of the above.

The situation was even bleaker for Bullers Arms. Between Keith and later snooping about the village of Chagford, I would learn precious little about the pub prior to its current name, let alone who Redvers Buller was. Other than Keith's mention of him as a hero in the Zulu wars and a participant in the later Boer War, the surface was less than scratched on this representative of Victorian England who had a pub named for him after the turn of the last century. My confusion over how he could have earned his glory from an unpopular war was partially resolved when Keith said Buller won his Victoria Cross in the *Zulu Wars*, not in the Boer War.

The suggestion that he somehow cranked out the first concentration camps didn't make me feel any better about the man.

And yet I felt it was somehow important to get behind that portrait of the general in Bullers Arms to understand Chagford and its people. Standing outside the pub that evening, smelling the pungent, somehow satisfying aroma of burning fireplaces and feeling the cool air on my face, it gnawed at me that there were stories to be told and learned that could either confirm I had discovered a simple life with a proud but simple history, or I had stumbled upon the same kinds of ghosts that haunt a generation of Americans thousands of miles from Dartmoor. But to find those stories I had to dig not only into the life of a general, but into a war that, in many respects, was the 'Vietnam' of a declining British Empire. If there were parallels for Julie and me, rather than differences—if we both had ghosts to contend with, making our lives less than simple—I had to know. So my quest would have to take me into the pasts of a Captain…and a General.

I realized there was a risk. Such a journey could destroy my vision of the simple life I had stumbled upon in Dartmoor. Truth does that.

My vision became more focused as I walked a few steps away from the pub toward the center of town, then turned and looked back.

Although late—it was approaching 11:00 PM—I could still discern the pink hue of the smooth wall of the pub's façade, with white borders surrounding the large windows on either side of the white door. To the left of the door was a white sign, the top of which had a caricature of the general. Beneath his bust and the drawings of four British flags was simple writing telling of what the place was about:

RESTAURANT
BAR MEALS
SNACKS
COFFEE

But it wasn't that simple. Bullers Arms began with a man and ended with a war and the loss of honor. The loss of innocence, like Vietnam. What follows is, to most historians, a brief description of that man, with only casual digressions to underscore a thought. Rather than give it an Appendix (not in the medical sense), it seems to fit just about here.

Argent a cross quarter pierced sable, between 4 eagles displayed of the second. That is how the armorial bearings for Buller are listed in a discussion of the family arms displayed in St. Thomas Church in Exeter. The quest for Buller begins with the Dissolution of the Monasteries, that financially-timed activity of the 1530s when Henry VIII's principal minister, Thomas Cromwell, took advantage of his king's permanent separation from Rome by orchestrating the mass stripping of wealth from the monasteries in England and the sale of their lands to secular investors. Lord Russell, one of the many beneficiaries of the Dissolution, held the manor of nearby Cowick and the properties of St. Thomas Church in Exeter.[*] According to *Devon and Cornwall Notes & Queries, Exeter Churches*, Beatrix F. Cresswell, ed. (Exeter, 1908),

---

[*] The Russells—earls and dukes of Bedford—are an old family with a history of service to the crown. One recent descendant was the philosopher, Bertrand Russell. His son, whom I befriended while in England in 1977, is Conrad Russell, a well-known Stuart historian who moved from Bedford College (family reminder!) to Yale, and now sits in the House of Lords.

In 1639, the then Earl of Bedford sold this part of his property to Mr. William Gould, whose great-grandson, Mr.
William Gould, of Downes, Crediton, left two daughters
co-heiresses, of whom the elder married Mr. James Buller
of Morval, Cornwall. In this way the property was inherited
by the present Lord of the Manor, General Sir Redvers
Buller, V.C.

The general had taken some interest in the church. When the treble
bell cracked on New Year's Day, 1900, it was recast and rung on Easter
Sunday, 7 April 1901. An inscription on the bell included the words
"When I begin ye all strike in. Recast 1901, 1st year of King Edward VIIth.
General Sir Redvers Buller V.C. patron." The *Notes & Queries* for 1908
also mention other gifts by Buller and his family to churches in Devon: in
1899, the district church of Emmanuel was erected on a site given by
Buller; at the church in Erwick, the general's father laid the cornerstone
in 1841, and Sir Redver's wife, Lady Audrey, and her daughter designed
an altar frontal of primrose and daffodil flowers "with extreme suitabil-
ity, as anyone who has paid a spring visit to the hamlet would testify."

What *N&Q* for 1908 failed to mention, no doubt because it was
already in print, was that on 2 June 1908, General Sir Redvers Buller,
V.C., passed away at age 68. According to the *Dictionary of National
Biography (DNB)*, Second Supplement (1912),

> His health was beginning to fail, and he died at his home
> near Crediton....He was buried at Crediton with military
> honours, the escort consisting of a battalion of rifles and a
> battalion of the Devonshire regiment, which alike laid
> claim to him. The depôt of the rifles is at Winchester, and
> in the north transept of Winchester cathedral a memorial
> of him, a recumbent figure in bronze on a tomb...was
> unveiled by Lord Grenfell on 28 Oct. 1911. There is also a
> memorial in Crediton church.

The *Country Companion* guide to Devon (1984) notes that Crediton "is the famous birthplace of St. Boniface in A.D. 680." Little else of importance is mentioned about the town, except that in the Holy Cross Church "there is a fantastic memorial to Sir Redvers Buller who relieved Ladysmith in the South African War." As the crow flies, should it be so inclined to take the journey, it is 11.8 miles (19.7 km) from the Holy Cross Church in Crediton to the church of St. Michael's in Chagford. Another 200 yards or so and you are at Bullers Arms.

Buller Memorial, Winchester Cathedral (inset of head)

I would learn this later that summer, and not on the night I stood outside the pub after saying good-bye to Julie Jefferies, Captain. But starting at the end of a life rather than at the beginning only confused things. Redvers Buller, from this perspective, was to the manner and manor born, a patron throughout Devon, an inspiration to his troops, a war hero worthy of a local memorial (Crediton) and a national one (Winchester). But to begin at the beginning provided a very different view, both of his own personal life and of the events of his generation that, in many respects, were far beyond his control. His life would provide clues for my quest— clues as to whether I had found a simple life void of the guilt and responsibility of the past, if that were possible. Could Chagford's inhabitants be unattached, unlike my generation? The general whose name was on a village pub suggested the answers.

Redvers Henry Buller was born on 7 December 1839 in Downes, Crediton, the second son of James Wentworth Buller and Charlotte Juliana Jane, third daughter of Lord Henry Thomas Howard-Molyneux-Howard, a younger brother of Bernard Edward, twelfth

Duke of Norfolk. (The Howards, of which there were legions, were the earls of Surrey and dukes of Norfolk all the way back before the 16th century.) James Buller, often referred to in writings as J.W., graduated B.A. from Oriel College, Oxford in 1819, the year Victoria Alexandrina—the future Queen Victoria—was born. He received his B.C.L. (Bachelor of Civil Law) in 1824 and D.C.L. in 1829 from All Souls' College. He later became an M.P. for Exeter and for North Devon. The Bullers had been settled in the west of England for over 300 years. This recent addition to the line, Redvers Henry, did not have his parents around as long as many of his peers. On 15 December 1855, just after his sixteenth birthday, Redvers' mother died in a most unsettling way. (See below) Less than 10 years later his father passed away.

Young Redvers presumably planned to begin his education at public school (read "posh private school") much as his other upper class peers intended to, only his coming out had an interesting twist. According to Ruari Chisholm in his book, *Ladysmith* (1979), "Redvers Buller's first distinction in life was to have been admitted to Eton, having been asked to leave Harrow"—read *expelled*—"thus establishing himself as one of the few Englishmen to have been educated at both schools." It was while traveling to his family estates in Devon during Christmas holiday that his mother died. After embarking from the train at the Exeter station, Redvers saw his mother collapse on the platform just as she came to meet him. Long-known to suffer from tuberculosis, she could not be moved from the platform and a bench was screened off. She died two days later in the arms of her 16-year-old son.

On 23 May 1858, not yet 19 years of age, Buller was commissioned as ensign in the 60th Kings Royal Rifle Corps. Because of his tendency to speak in a way that suggested judgment had been passed—and no doubt his temper might have had something to do with "leaving" Harrow—he acquired the nickname *the Judge*. Two years later he received his first taste of fighting during an expedition to China. It was probably as traumatic an experience as the death of his mother. While taking part in the occupation of Peking (Beijing), he almost drowned, and when dragged from the water he was believed dead.

Buller recovered but then had the misfortune of being kicked in the face by a horse, losing several of his teeth. It was a tough price to pay for being awarded the medal and clasp—especially since he saw little fighting—because the incident altered the way he spoke for the rest of his life. He refused to wear the medal anyway, believing the war had been unjust. (Such blatant morality during mid-Victorian empire-building was rather unusual.) Later that year (9 December 1862), he was promoted to lieutenant and joined the 4th Battalion at Quebec. Buller was now a seasoned soldier known for speaking his mind and enjoying his drink.

It was during this tour of duty that he came under the influence of Colonel Robert Beaufoy Hawley, commander of the 4th Battalion of the 60th Rifles. Chisholm writes that Hawley was "acknowledged in his day as one of the finest regimental commanders in the British army," and the *DNB* notes that "Buller afterwards said he owed all that he knew of soldiering" to Hawley. Indeed, Buller continued a correspondence with Hawley up to the older gentleman's death, and referred to him in letters as "My dear Colonel," even though Hawley had long been made a general.

Buller became Hawley's adjutant in 1868 and the next year the battalion returned to England. On 28 May 1870, Buller was back in Canada as part of the Red River expedition, which traveled 600 miles from Lake Superior to Fort Garry. Sir Garnet Joseph Wolseley was the Commander-in-Chief of the treacherous trek by boat, and Buller quickly made an impression on him. The *DNB*: "[According to Wolseley, Buller] was a thorough soldier, a practised woodman, a skillful boatman in the most terrifying of rapids, and a man of great physical strength and endurance." Here was the making of John Bull incarnate, and Buller now became identified with Wolseley's *ring* of officers known for their bravery in battle or their new approaches to warfare. This association would hurt him later in life.

By the end of 1871, Buller, now 32, entered the Staff College. He passed through it quickly, and in the summer of 1873, Wolseley summoned him to be his chief intelligence officer in the British protectorate of Ashanti in western Africa (now a region in central Ghana). The Ashanti wars brought Buller into battle again, where he was slightly wounded at Ordashu because of his forward position in the fight. (Talk about a thick-skinned "John Bull" Victorian—he also took a bullet at Essaman, but it didn't penetrate his skin!) Lieutenant Redvers Buller was always out in front, leading his men and exhibiting a superb horsemanship, both of which became his trademark.

A pregnant pause for a paragraph might be in order before continuing this discussion of a Victorian career military man that ended up with a pub named after him. Most Americans are twice-removed from this kind of life that Redvers Buller led. They would have difficulty imagining the mind-set of owning an empire around the world—despite U.S. "imperialistic" leanings so menacingly articulated by the former Soviet Union. And most Americans cannot fathom making a career of engaging in warfare wherever there are hotbeds of battle. True, we have veterans who fought in the few military ground actions the U.S. has undertaken in the last half century: World War II, Korea, Vietnam, Granada (so to speak), Panama (so to whisper), Desert Storm, perhaps Somalia. And a few of these "lifers" have fought with stars in their eyes in order to get stripes on their lapels and epaulettes. But Americans do not think of their country as a power *immersed in battles* worldwide to protect and occupy interests they claim to be theirs. Nor do they view such battles as gallant, righteous or necessary for careerists climbing the brass flagpole to the top, although some in the military might disagree. That's because the United States is not the 19th century British Empire. Lieutenant Redvers Henry Bullers was in the thick of it.

Wolseley was further impressed with Buller, who now received the medal with clasp for his part in Ashanti—such "hardware" being the means to help military brass climb that flagpole. Now a brevet-major,

Buller served in the adjutant-general's department from 1874 to early 1878 and accompanied General Thesiger (later Lord Chelmsford) as a special service officer. One of the many Kaffir wars was raging, and Buller was viewed as a strong leader who could rally the men to success. Chelmsford later wrote of Buller's "untiring energy and dogged perseverance," and by the end of 1878 he was made brevet lieutenant-colonel.[*]

It was now, while following Buller's bravery and rising career in various sources after my return to the U.S. beginning in the summer of 1992, that I discovered a brief era of recent history—recent to me!—that I was familiar with thanks to a movie with Stanley Baker and Michael Caine. (?) Let me explain with a now-familiar literary device: a digression.

One of my all-time favorite movies is *Zulu*, a cult film based on a true event wondrously told in a book by Donald R. Morris called *The Washing of the Spears* (1965). Stanley Baker, whose first major movie role was as Henry VII, conqueror of Richard III (quite a coincidence for me!), both produced and starred in *Zulu*. He enlisted the voice of Richard Burton to kick off the movie. Stanley also gambled on a young new actor for the co-lead, Michael Caine.

Flag at Rorke's Drift, 22 Jan 1879, Brecon Museum, Wales

Zulu is the story of what we can call a Famous Last Stand, only we are not talking hotdogs or newspaper kiosks. The 300 Spartans, Hannibal's outnumbered engagements, the Alamo—these are battles where the self-proclaimed good guys (usually of the white male variety) face ridiculous odds, usually of the

* Kaffirs were Bantu-speaking tribesmen who fought against the rival Zulus when they weren't fighting the British.

"there's-5,000-of-them-and-only-12-of-us,-Sir" kind. Americans are familiar with Custer's Last Stand in 1876, when the Sioux nation came pouring down on George Armstrong Custer's 7th Cavalry—or rather pouring *up* if you visit what is now called the Little Big Horn Battlefield in Montana. (It used to be called "Custer Battlefield"—See? White males were the winners, even when they lost.) Custer's Last Stand marked a Pyrrhic victory for an indigenous population (the Sioux) against rapacious foreigners (the descendants of expansionist immigrants). And to show how white expansionism was all the rage in the 19th century, at about the same time the native American Indians were gasping out their last efforts at halting a steamroller that would not stop, the native Zulu tribes of Africa were trying to fend off the encroachment of covetous immigrants and their foreign armies, namely the British and the Dutch.

For the Zulus and the British, the Last Stand was in 1879 at Rorke's Drift. Only in this instance, three years after the Little Big Horn, "Custer" won.

The movie begins with a devastation scene: British soldiers lying dead, massacred by an unseen retreating enemy that were the Zulu warriors. Richard Burton narrates a letter from Lord Chelmsford, which tersely notes that on 22 January 1879, the camp at Isandhlwana—which by noon on that day numbered almost 1,800 European and Natal Kaffir soldiers—was virtually wiped out within hours.

According to author Morris, by late evening only 55 Europeans were still alive; maybe 300 Natal Kaffirs. Many of the survivors were hunted down and slain by Zulus. Morris thinks that perhaps 2,000 Zulus died. The movie then shifts to the central theme, the defense of nearby Rorke's Drift mission by a little over one hundred British soldiers against the thousands of Zulus coming to destroy it after the massacre at Isandhlwana. Eleven Victoria Crosses were awarded to the defenders of Rorke's Drift, who successfully held off the Zulus. When the Zulu wars finally ended, 8,000 warriors had died, along with 76 British officers and 1,007 men killed in action. Disease took more on both sides. It was the demise of Zulu life as it had been known for centuries. For the British, it was but another chapter in their Book of Empire.

And so I had a slight familiarity of the *scene* I was about to encounter in the source material when, in January 1879, Lord Chelmsford entered Zululand with a special service officer named Redvers Buller. It was Buller who remained in charge of the volunteer Frontier Light Horse after his successes with that group, and he now joined Colonel Evelyn Wood's force in Natal because of a threatened invasion by the Zulus.

The Light Horse were gallant-looking in their black corduroy uniforms with red stripes down the trousers, but they were not destined to remain clean for long. News came of the massacre at Isandhlwana, forcing Wood to halt his advance and make diversionary attacks. Buller took his Light Horse and two battalions and attempted to seize strategic terrain by dismounting part of his forces along a ridge and sending a group of army irregulars to force cattle into the western end of a plateau. He then hand-picked several officers to accompany him to the front for a better look at the enemy. The Zulu proved to be too much and a retreat was ordered. When one soldier scrambled away from several of his fallen compatriots without a horse, he was suddenly halted in mid-flight. Morris describes the situation:

> As (the soldier) rose to his feet, an iron hand gripped his shoulder and a tremendous clout landed on his ear. "Where's your horse?" someone yelled. He looked up into Buller's contorted face, and pointed back at the upper plateau. "Go back and get him," Buller shouted. "Don't leave him again." (The soldier) dutifully started back up, dodging the bodies that hurtled by and edging out into the rocks as he neared the top.

The soldier did, in fact, retrieve his horse.

According to the *DNB*, "The ground was very rough and steep, and many of his men were cut off; out of 400 Europeans, 92 were killed. At great personal risk Buller rescued two officers and a trooper, and on Wood's recommendation he received the Victoria Cross on 17 June 1879." Buller was 39 years old. One of several heroes in 1879, he was not the perfect human being, although he might have been viewed as the epitome of the Victorian soldier. While his drinking had not become the problem it would escalate to in later years, he did possess a rough temper and had little tolerance for civilians. News reporters especially annoyed him: a military posture familiar a century later. Moreover, there were signs of indecisiveness in his behavior despite an ability to make tough decisions in the face of battle. All these attributes would serve him ill in the future.

Nevertheless, for now Buller was a known quantity and a rising star. Morris paints the best portrait of the man:

> (Buller) possessed a very high order of personal leadership. He based his command on the pure force of his personality; he was stern without unjust harshness, and his demands were high but never more than he was giving himself. His enthusiasm was infectious, and he was one of the few Imperial officers who could squeeze out of irregular volunteers the performance and reliability expected of the professional troops. He was, in fact, one of that small and fabled band of leaders men cheerfully follow to hell.

For Redvers Henry Buller, V.C., hell was 20 years and 20 miles down the road.

Chapter 16

General Sir Redvers Buller, V.C.

FINISHING MY NOTES IN GLENDARAH HOUSE after the encounter with Captain and Company in the pub, I knew absolutely nothing about Buller and his exploits. The name Ladysmith had surfaced more than once, and I assumed it had something to do with the Boer War and a success credited to Buller—hence his fame, memorials and a pub in Chagford. And there was something else. While I didn't expect people in Chagford to openly talk about Buller and his exploits—any more than a New Yorker talks, or would even know, about Andrew Carnegie when visiting Carnegie Hall—I had this unwarranted feeling that the villagers of Chagford didn't know much about their pub namesake beyond a heroic feat that brought him national and local fame. Then again, if Keith were a good example, memories lingered about something less-than-noble occurring because of, or in spite of, Buller. If they did know about the Boer War, they probably weren't talking. For his fame in Chagford wasn't connected with his Victoria Cross, but with a later war that history would not look upon kindly as the 20th century progressed.

Perspective is important. What will people remember about John F. Kennedy in the year 2044, roughly the same time frame from Buller's death to my first visit to the pub? Will it be just a few tossed-out memories, like the Bay of Pigs fiasco or the Cuban Missile Crisis? Will it be only a murky recall of a momentary pause in history, the day he was killed in 1963? Will the memories center more on his personal life, reducing his brief stay in the White House to a series of liaisons with a movie star and the out-of-wedlock trysts prior to his election as the 34th President of the United States? What will my children tell their children's children, who will occupy that future time frame? And how accurate will it be, since the last *living witnesses* to the era of JFK in our family—my wife and I—will most likely be gone and barely a memory ourselves to our great-grandchildren?

As has been described, Buller did indeed have a past prior to his blip on the oscilloscope of history that was the Boer War. After receiving the Victoria Cross in 1879, a fatigued and exhausted brevet Lieutenant-Colonel with more clasps and things to come returned home. He was viewed as both a hero and an exemplar of the *new* military man. One dispatch that summer noted that "the action of General Wood and Buller had destroyed the prejudice of the colonists against the strict dis-cipline of regular military service and their distrust of the ability of Her Majesty's officers general to conduct operations against the Kaffirs." *Translation:* a belief came into being that British colonists, and colonists in general, were now putting up with the antics and bellicose behavior of Victoria's warriors, and actually put some faith in their capabilities.

Buller was briefly on staff in Scotland before being transferred in July 1880 to Aldershot outside London. In early 1881, he was back in South Africa as chief of staff to Sir Evelyn Wood. By then, the first Boer War had ended at Majuba—we'll run into that shortly—and Buller received the local rank of major-general at the end of March. He was back in England soon after, but in the summer of the next year he was chosen to head Sir Garnet Wolseley's intelligence staff in Egypt. Buller saw action at the battle of Tel-el-Kebir, received more hardware, including the bronze star, and was knighted by the end of the year.

By 1884, he commanded the first infantry brigade under Sir Gerald Graham and saw heavy action against armies of tribesmen. Buller ral-lied his men against the enemy, and Graham's final despatch of the engagement noted that his infantry commander's "coolness in action, his knowledge of soldiers, and experience in the field, combined with his personal ascendancy over officers and men." Buller was promoted to full major-general for distinguished service.

Downes Manor, Devon — Home of General Buller

I should rest your militarily-glazed eyes for a moment—or at least for a paragraph—to let you know that it wasn't all fun and games for Sir Redvers. On 10 August 1882, he took the day off and married Lady Audrey Jane Charlotte, daughter of the 4th Marquis Townshend and widow of Greville Howard, son of the 17th earl of Suffolk—yes, another Howard. They had one daughter, she of the "altar frontal of primrose and daffodil flowers" mentioned earlier. In 1900, an article in the *North American Review* described Buller as "a genial country gentleman and a man of refined intellectual culture." Besides his *noblesse oblige* in the county—he sold land in 1890 for a women's hospital and in 1907 he opened a boys' school—the good general also spent time with the right groups and the proper clubs. The latter included the Army and Navy, Naval and Military, Brooks's, Athenæum and United Service, according to *Who's Who* of 1908 (London). It should therefore be made clear that Buller wasn't merely getting clasps and barking orders day in and day out.

His last appearance in the field of battle before the Boer War was a momentous one in British history: the relief of Khartoum. Appointed chief of staff on 26 August 1884, he commanded a desert column which was to attack the garrison of the Mahdi, a nomadic messiah that gave the British lots of grief.[*] Buller quickly realized that a disaster was

---

[*] If this present book means you will never again jump into Victorian military history, literarily speaking, but you are curious about Khartoum and all that, rent the movie starring a post-Moses Charleton Heston as Lord Kitchener and Sir Laurence Olivier as the Mahdi. It's kitschy stuff, but probably more entertaining than the gaggle of history books written about it.

brewing in North Africa, and that if he didn't figure out a quick retreat he might see his troops massacred. Much like Dunkirk of a future era, Buller successfully avoided disaster and received more commendations and coatpins for the effort. (His success at "retreats" would be remembered decades later.) He stayed through much of 1885 before leaving, and his military lifestyle now became notable among military and civilian observers alike. Never one to avoid the comforts of home, Buller often traveled with sufficient provisions and wine stocks to see him through the weariest of campaigns. One officer, who was not in Wolseley's "ring" of up-and-coming military men, sneered that Buller's personal baggage was carried on 40 camels!

Major-General Sir Redvers Buller, V.C. was now heading into a phase of his life that eschewed the wild charges of tribesmen or the volley of cannon for the glory of the Empire. In August, 1886, he was sent to the black hole of the Empire—Ireland—to restore order in county Kerry. According to the *DNB*, the prime minister, Lord Salisbury, was in need of a "fresh, vigorous mind, accustomed to strict discipline," and Buller was the man of the hour. Apparently he did a credible job, for he was made undersecretary for Ireland and a member of the Irish Privy Council.

I stopped a moment upon reading this part of Buller's life to think about Julie and her Irish heritage. Here was a Victorian general put in charge of keeping the peace between the ancestors of Julie and his own English immigrants in Ireland, the latter going back to those adventurous 12th century Normans who were *invited* over to quell a local dispute. I wondered what Julie would think of sipping her lemoned drink in a pub named for the British enforcer in Ireland a century earlier? I also wondered what she'd have thought of Buller's own view of the situation as he found it. For I was to learn that the general was quite sympathetic to the Irish peasantry, and loathed enforcing the evictions of Irishmen his government prosecuted with such vigor. Sir Redvers was to leave this all behind him, spending the next 10 years at the war office. How he is viewed by the Irish I do not know. I would guess, however, that Julie would not hold his tenure in Ireland against him and boycott Bullers Arms. She might even give his portrait one of her illuminating smiles, along with a toast for being one of the few British military higher-ups who felt that something was wrong with the Empire's behavior in Ireland.

His war office years allowed Buller to exhibit a little *thinking* about the Queen's armies. He spent considerable time addressing ways to improve the condition of the ordinary soldier, especially in the areas of supply and transport—Her Majesty's warriors often found themselves far from ports and stores. The *DNB* states that Buller, unlike most of his contemporaries, was a military man concerned with spending—as in how to be more *frugal*—and both liberal and conservative secretaries of state liked him for it. At one point, it looked as if Buller was in line to succeed the Duke of Cambridge as commander-in-chief of the army in 1895, but politics got in the way and it was Buller's mentor, Lord Wolseley, who received the appointment. Two years earlier, Buller had turned down the post of commander-in-chief in India. By this time, more awards had flowed to the "soldiers' general"—lieutenant-general (1891), honorary colonel of the 1st Volunteer Battalion of the Devonshire Regiment (1892), colonel commandant of the King's Royal Rifle Corps (1895), and, on 24 June 1896, the rank of general.

An innocent paragraph in the *DNB* related what would prove to be Buller's greatest challenge, if not the Empire's. Furthermore, it would portend not only the *meaning* of Bullers Arms to me, but the legacy of a man...and a village. It began this way:

> On 9 Oct. 1898 Buller succeeded the Duke of Connaught in the command of the troops at Aldershot [in England], but remained there only a year. On 14 Oct. 1899 he embarked for South Africa to enforce the British demands on the Transvaal

republic, at the head of 70,000 men, the largest army which England had ever sent abroad.

"The largest army." Larger than the one that lost the American Colonies. Larger than the armies that battled Napoleon, or those against Philip IV of France during the onslaught of the Hundred Years War beginning in the 1330s. What General Sir Redvers Buller, V.C. couldn't have known in the days and weeks before the end of the 19th century was that he was leading 70,000 men into a quagmire, into the Transvaal of southern Africa, into his own personal, political and military quicksand for which there would be no escape.

Buller would get a pub named after him in Chagford, but only after his prosecution of "the British demands on the Transvaal republic." Those demands were the Boer War, and his men would follow him, perhaps not cheerfully, into hell for it.

And for the general from Devon, not far from Chagford, there would be hell to pay.

Chapter 17

The Glendarah Decision

IT WAS NOW ALMOST MIDNIGHT in my room at Glendarah House as I stared down at my note pad and tried to decipher the hastily-scribbled notes that suffered illegibility—beyond my normal scrawl—due to that second serving of cider. I was throwing questions out in my mind, in second person no less, that were usually reserved for severely-pained realists and lovelorn teenagers on first dates. It was a one-way conversation: 'Should you stay another day and see Julie & Company at the dart tournament? Did she and Chirpy want you to stay, or were they just being polite? Hadn't you already satisfied your curiosity, and wouldn't it just be better to *Let It Be* (with apologies to Paul McCartney and the Other Three)? Why not just leave Chagford in your mind as the quintessential spot on earth for the *simple life* and come back to visit it in a few years? After all, you can't LIVE HERE! What would you do, walk up and down the main road from the church to Bullers Arms cooing "Ah, how simple it all is?" And who would *pay* for that stroll? Did you forget your family, too? Reality check. You—your conscience, that is—know that you are restless and life at home is complex and doesn't get any easier, but why not leave this *ideal* exactly where it is in your mind tonight...as an ideal?

'Why muck it up by snooping a little too closely?'

Makes you wonder how self-imposed conversations like these can materialize when you are tired, confused and still in shock at meeting up with a fantasy. I mean, I had just returned to Bullers Arms, saw the same people I remembered 30 months earlier—even *talked* with a few, including the intriguing Captain. And although I only had random scraps of information about the village, the people and the general, Sir Redvers himself, it should have been more than enough to head for home with a smile on my face.

Or *was* it enough? It wasn't, according to the fastly-growing impertinent part of my brain that nonetheless refused to tell the rest of my gray matter to shut up and go to sleep. I closed the note pad and walked over to the large window and looked out on the road heading into town, with its surprise speed bumps that no doubt ensured a steady flow of business to the local car repair. I thought about a Persian cat my wife and I bought soon after we were married. We named her Lysistrata just to confuse her. (In ancient times, Greeks and Persians were not the best of friends.) Lysistrata was the exemplar of curiosity for a feline. If you put three cardboard boxes on the floor, empty-side down, and then turned over two, she would check those out before heading towards the last one. Naturally, it was the inaccessible box she would concentrate on, ignoring the other two 'easy solutions.'

Apparently Lysistrata had rubbed off on me, and more than just her fur. I had opened up a mysterious box—some villagers in an ancient village. Then a second box, a pub where many of them congregated to share their lives and adhere to a lifestyle that, to me, seemed to be serene and simple. But it was that third box—the one hiding the stories about Julie and the general of the Boer War—that I could not quite leave alone.

And as I sat down on the bed and removed my shoes, I knew that I was going to stay. Question was, what would I do until the dart tournament tomorrow night? No immediate answer surfaced from the part of my brain that was still conscious and making the inquiry. So I jumped to a non sequitur—I do that frequently—and recalled that Chirpy mentioned the place where the tournament was going to be held, the Jubilee Hall up the street past the church as you walked away from Bullers Arms and the market square. I now remembered I had grinned when learning that piece of information. Although the hall was built in 1935 to commemorate the Jubilee (25 years) of King George V, it now honored Queen Elizabeth II's Jubilee Year: 1977. It was the year my wife and I lived in England and I became hooked for life on digging up the past of this fascinating country. Here was another little piece of information in Chagford—Jubilee Hall—that reminded me of my own ties to the country and the experiences I had had at other times.

I looked through my maps and my travel Outline. Ah yes, "The Outline." Now don't laugh or think that there's something rather anal-retentive at work here. I like to research the place or places I intend to visit, and I write down a *wish list* of things to see. In fact, friends often ask for them when traveling to a place I have visited—they're too lazy to do their own! The list usually runs a page or two and, if properly pursued, would take several years to accomplish. No matter. It gave me choices and was, I think, a direct result of an experience I had in Italy with a new wife and four rich brats. (Digression time, but just one paragraph.)

When we was first married, the "young couple" did the sensible thing most married couples do when starting out on that joint road to Life Companionship that parallels the Slippery Sidewalk of Life— we sold everything we had, Barb quit her job (I was a starving grad-uate student) and we joyously bummed through Europe for two months. Since I was "the historian" and she was the "art historian and artist," we almost didn't care what countries or cities we happened to stumble into, since there was so much to see that we had read about and studied. So in Rome one day, deciding whether to first hit St. Peter Advincula (Peter-in-chains) to see Michelangelo's *Moses*, horn and all, or take a trek out to St. Callisto and St. Sebastiano catacombs, we were stopped by four American "young people" in designer jeans. Now mind you, we were in our early 20s, so "young" here simply meant 18 or 19-year-old college kids. But these American Youth had a dilemma and they came to us for advice: "Say, can you tell us what there is to see around here? We've been in Rome for four days, man, and there's not much to do!"

Apparently I need another paragraph to vent. My wife could see my face contort into what probably looked like someone possessed by the devil and about to spout a healthy flow of avocado dip. (Ref. *The Exorcist*) At any rate, I used all my inner strength to control myself and simply told the Poor Little Rich Kids who were sent to Europe by Mummy and Daddy—unlike the poor starving couple they were confronting—that they might try starting at the Vatican ("You know, where the little old man with the pointed hat and staff lives—he's got a nice collection of *stuff* and an old ceiling with pictures on it") and then check out one of the hundred or so museums and churches within a two-mile radius, perhaps ending with a stroll from the Palazzio Venezia ("Where Mussolini gave his famous speech. You know Mussolini? Played for the Chicago White Sox? Third base?") up past the forums of the Caesars and Trajan's Column to the Coliseum. I then walked away, fuming.

But I also made sure that on subsequent trips anywhere, I read up on the less obvious places to visit so I could round out the trip. Places like Grimspound and Spinsters' Rock and the Clapper Bridge at Postbridge. Places I have mentioned earlier, and which turned out to be wondrous and virtually unknown to the Typical Tourist of the USA Type. Places that led me to a village called Chagford.

So I consulted my Outline and a few things popped out. Lydford Castle was one. Trethevy Quoit was another, also known as Arthur's Quoit. There was a small piece of paper clipped to the Outline on my "If You Get To Devon" page. It had to do with relatives of my neighbor, Jeannie Fowler. I think I'd better start a new paragraph...

Jeannie and Jim Fowler were our next door neighbors and they are lots of fun. Jim occasionally travels abroad on business, and when in England always gets stuck in an industrial town, giving him a warped view of my favorite island. ("C'mon, Mark. There aren't any *trees* in

England. *I know.* I've just been to Manchester!") Jeannie works for a mega-corporation in the legal department, and her maiden name is Renfree or Renfrew, spelling optional—a good Cornish name. Her Dad and other relatives come from Gunnislake, the first village on the Cornwall side of a bridge that separates the county from Devon. I visited her Uncle George and his wife a few years ago and took a picture of them for Jeannie. Now, camcorder in hand, I had the chance to tape them, if they were still alive. George would be pushing 90.

There were other things on the Outline that sounded interesting or unusual, including a return visit to the village of Minions to see a large Celtic cross. 'Looks like you've got yourself a day,' a barely-conscious brain was communicating while I stumbled down the hall to hit the loo and return to the sink in my room.

Ever try taking out contact lenses after midnight when you're half-asleep and your brain has for all intents and purposes shut down for the evening? I stuck myself in the eye three times and one contact splatted in the sink and almost departed down the drain—I had forgotten to cover it with the little white plug on the end of the chain! Travel is tough business.

My brain continued lecturing me. 'You'll need to tell the owner of Glendarah that you require the room another night. Can you remember that?' My reply: 'Remember *what*?' The conversation died out while I flipped off the light switch on the Barbie-doll size lamp near the twin bed and fell into a vortex of thick black swirl that was sleep.

But I was not alone. Spinning in that vortex were images of Julie and Chirpy and the Properly Attireds and the pub's Three Musketeers, laughing with each other, then turning their faces to look and laugh at me. It was very surreal—all I needed were a few Salvadore Dali clocks dripping off the walls. The last thing I remembered was a voice calling to me—perhaps Julie's voice, I'm not sure. It was calling 'Mark. It's really quite simple. Really it is. Quite simple. Simple.'

As I have already hinted throughout this journey, I was to discover that simplicity is in the eyes of the beholder, and that what I would eventually behold was not all that simple. At this particular moment, I didn't know that. Just as well. I was enjoying the laughter and the faces in my mind as the eastern side of midnight set in and I fell into a deep sleep.

It does boggle the mind how things turn out when you look back, though. For in 24 hours there would be no laughter in my room or in my mind. Just sadness. Sadness and a determination to seek out Redvers Buller, wherever I might find him. The General would become the key to unraveling the mystery of the simple life of Chagford, because the story of the Captain would now see the light of day. My day. The very next day.

Chapter 18

Castle and Prison

I AWOKE EARLY TO THE SOUNDS of lawnmowers moving in and out of the village. Those little cars really got up and going, and round about the eighth lawnmower I sat up in bed and wanted to remove my head and place it in a huge bowl of ice, maybe next to the boiled shrimp and cocktail sauce. I think I mentioned that I am a cheap drunk. If I didn't, suffice it to say that going to college in a town known for free-flowing alcohol and wall-to-wall bars—New Orleans—can be disconcerting for the person who gets high when the doctor rubs alcohol on his arm prior to being vaccinated. That's me, and I was paying for it in hearts and spades early in the morning in Chagford.

The smell of coffee eventually helped me sway out of bed, and the cold shower down the hall—the "hot" water knob wasn't responding to my pleas—at least brought me up several levels of consciousness. I descended the stairway and bumped into the owner.

"Breakfast is in the room over there."

"Uh, thanks. Say, would it be all right if I stayed an extra night? I don't know how crowded you are, but I was hoping you might have a room."

"That would be fine. You can stay in the room you're in. Will you be having tea or coffee?"

"Tea."

The transaction done, I marveled at my mouth calling for tea when the house wafted coffee aroma. When traveling in England, Scotland or Wales, I always order tea in the morning. In fact, each day the British consume 187 million cups of the stuff—I read that in a small tea brochure, so it must be true. Thing is, when I drink it I'm usually always sober. Coffee seemed to be the hangover elixir of choice for most people. Apparently my brain fought the temptation and remained in English mode. 'Tea,' my mouth said, so tea it would be.

The dining room was large with an enormously high ceiling. My watch said 8:05 but it was obvious that a few visitors had already eaten. At the moment, I was the only guest in the room, and as I sat down the proprietor brought me a tray holding a small pot of tea and a smaller pot of hot water. We settled on a meal—I was foregoing the bacon but a scrambled egg, toast and a sausage sounded like it might go down without ill report. Toast was to be wheat; the topping was orange marmalade. Although boxes of cereal were available for consumption, I skipped those as well. My brain still had distilled apples floating about, and if it weren't for the fact that I was somehow hungry and hopeful for a new day of adventure, I'd have crawled back up the stairs and under the twin bed where I couldn't be disturbed by humans or whining lawnmowers.

Tonight it was one apple cider or die!

Naturally I had my note pad with me, and I jotted down a few random thoughts—which was easy, since everything flying through my brain at the moment was random.

The tea tastes great. (Deep statement. Hemingway move over!) Think I'll drive to Lydford first and check out the castle. Then head to Gunnislake to see if Uncle George is alive and able to withstand the strains and annoyance of being videotaped for Jeannie. I believe I then have to drive to Liskeard in Cornwall to snoop around for some of the ancient things described on my Outline.

Toast is good, too. Can't believe I'm hungry. What did I do to burn off the stroganoff? Walk 100 yards to the car? Must have been the furious note-taking in the pub.

After breakfast, I deftly drove over the calm-inducing speed bumps into town and circled the market square twice. There was no real reason;

I was just in a good mood as the effects of the cider dissipated and a full stomach meant I could concentrate on the day before me. Although still relatively early, people were moving about and the little lawnmowers continued zipping through the village. I rolled down the window and pulled up next to the Market House. Then I turned off the engine and just watched.

It was a wonderful show. Call it "Chagford Waking Up," but for me it was a joyous occasion, observing the residents of an ancient village go about their day as their ancestors had done all the way back to Roman times, if not before. Indeed, the residents at nearby Grimspound—remember the Bronze Age stone huts Conan Doyle used in *The Hound?*—were herding their animals and braving the winds and storms of Dartmoor long before there were even Romans, let alone an empire. Since much of my study of English history concentrated on the late medieval period, say around 1450 on up through the death of Good Queen Bess (1603), it was not difficult to imagine sitting in Chagford as it looked 500 years ago. I had little doubt that little would be different—except for the damn lawnmowers!

Can you imagine *crisp*? I don't mean like a potato chip—or crisps, as they are called in England. You would be closer if you thought of a stalk of fresh celery about to be snapped in half. My senses were picking up *crisp*—footfalls of people walking on wet stone pavement that gave clear, staccato-like sounds with each step; doors opening and closing to discrete, crystal-like clinks at different pitches; the church bells peeling half-past eight. Even the air was crisp and fresh. It was the difference between a cacophony of sounds that blended into waves of noise, and the distinct, clear impulses of sound that combined to create a total picture. That picture was Chagford.

I decided I would take a long walk around the village upon my return, and that exploration by car was now in the offing. I started the engine—which I realized to my horror was only a buzz or two above lawnmower quality—and left the village for Lydford. Heading

northwest on 382, I reached the divided highway (30) at Whiddon
Down—you may recall the Whiddons?—and turned left towards
Okehampton. I was tempted to pull off at South Zeal, a little village
tucked into a valley, but I didn't. South Zeal boasted the Oxenham
Arms, a 12th century stone building erected over an ancient monolith
of unknown age or depth. I spent the night there once and published a
brief travel article about it.[*]

I kept driving, then remembered from my trusty Outline that there
was a castle at Okehampton I had never seen. Okehampton isn't terribly interesting but at least worth a paragraph. It was first settled by
Baldwin de Brionne around 1086, Brionne being one of the invaders
who helped William the Conqueror subdue the Saxons. You could buy
a wife in Okehampton—remember the wife-seller from Chagford?
Well, until the 18th century there was a market for it in Okehampton as
well. One Anne Frise was sold by her husband for two shillings and six-
pence—perhaps not a bad deal for her husband, but Anne was very
probably not too serene about the whole thing.

Most of the medieval flavor of the town is gone, but along the river
and to the south is Okehampton Castle. It started out as a Norman keep
(stone, probably 12th century) around which a later castle was built in
the 1370s. It was used as a prison for at least one French soldier during
the Hundred Years War (1337–1453), for there is still graffiti of someone
whose name began with a V and who wanted us to know he was held
captive during the war. (*Hic V—fuit captivus belli.*) There is also a ghost
from the ubiquitous Howard family. According to the *County
Companion* guide for Devon,

---

[*] Since the original building was of a religious nature, it is not unlikely that the site was
picked for its already magical qualities, i.e., the monolith. Christian missionaries were
marketing mavens when it came to selling their religion, and they were not beyond
picking a place for a Christian church that was right smack in the middle of an ancient
Celtic religious site. Think about it. Isn't it easier to sell your religion by saying it's simply
an updated version of the old one?

Lady Howard (is) said to have survived four husbands, all of whom she probably murdered. Eventually she was burned as a witch on Gibbet Hill, and her ghost made to bring grass from Okehampton Castle to Tavistock, where she once lived at Fitzford House. She rides each night in a coach drawn by a headless horse driven by a headless coachman with a black hound running alongside. On the return journey it carries in its mouth one blade of grass.

I did a lot of snooping in and around the castle, but came up empty-handed on both counts: I couldn't find the graffiti, and no ghost. (I have always fallen victim to rotten luck with ghosts.) The castle ruins nonetheless were very imposing and it was not difficult to envision the original Norman keep and how the castle was expanded to include it. It was also easy to imagine how the inhabitants of the castle felt: cold! A wind was blowing and I was beginning to frost up, helped little by the humidity coming off the river. Much as the hopeless romantic in me wanted to go back in time and be a king or lord over lands and castles such as this one, I was ever reminded that central heating was not top-of-mind in 1370, or even 1570. You either needed lots of firewood, lots of blankets or lots of close, understanding friends.

After leaving Okehampton I took the left fork on 386 south to a small lane that led west and south to Lydford. And understand that we are not talking great distances here. As that weary flying crow will attest, a straight line from Chagford to Lydford is about 24 miles. My commute from a south suburb to downtown Chicago is 30 miles as the express-way clogs. Okehampton is even closer, so exploring the Dartmoor region is quick skips in the car followed by some serious trekking to wherever you want to wander. At the moment, I was wandering into what was once an important village on the edge of Dartmoor.

Lydford is a very old mining town. King Ethelred II, one of the last Saxon kings, established a mint here for the kingdom's coinage. Coins of the Danish sort also have been found in Lydford, suggesting that the Danes—who conquered a good portion of England by the 11th century—made it to this remote part of the island. A century after the Norman Conquest of 1066, local tinners began to meet nearby on the moor discussing business. Over the years, Lydford Law became notorious for its harshness—the poet Browne wrote "first hang and draw and then hear the cause, is Lydford Law."

Lydford Keep became synonymous with the dreary, horrible prisons of medieval times. Indeed, during the reign of Henry VIII (died 1547) it was written that Lydford prison was "one of the most contagious and detestable places within this realm." The prison also had a role in changing Parliamentary rules. When the local Member of Parliament, Richard Strode, supported an unpopular bill, the people of Lydford seized him and threw him in the prison. This event led to the rule of Parliamentary Privilege, meaning that M.P.s could do all kinds of unpopular and awful things and not get tossed in the clink for it. This ominous decision has found its way into U. S. law, for better *and* worse.

It was in front of the keep, or Lydford Castle, that I now pulled up, and it was impressive. This was an *old* building! While known as a prison in late medieval times, it may have originally been built for that purpose when the Norman keep went up in 1195, and not merely as a castle. It sat atop a large mound that was covered with grass, and the massive stone let you know that it was going to be around a lot longer than the curious visitor who chanced upon it. I got out of the car and walked over to a sign that told me about the place.

I went inside the keep and looked around. If the word "solid" needed a graphic illustration of its definition, this was it. The stones that made up the walls were going nowhere, and that included the entrances and window casements built into the walls.

Welcome to
Lydford Castle

Lydford Castle was probably built about 1195 to serve as a prison. It took the form of a freestanding tower of at least two storeys. Some time in the thirteenth century a thorough rebuilding was undertaken. A ditch was dug around the tower and the soil piled up against the ground-floor walls. The upper storeys were completely rebuilt and the interior of the ground floor was filled in, apart from the pit-like room to the left of the entrance. The filling has now been removed. The earthwork bailey to the north-west was constructed at the same time.

English Heritage
Historic Buildings & Monuments Commission for England

I sat down in the bottom of the keep, leaned against the wall and decided to have myself a *thunk*. Thunks are my personal description of long thinking sessions that are supposed to come to some conclusion or resolution. This particular thunk related to Chagford and *Time* magazine. I began thinking about this incredible survivor of the past that I was leaning up against, wondering if the occupants of the keep—the good guys and the bad guys—had thought that their lives were simple and meaningful. Chagford today seemed that way to me, simple and meaningful. *Time* magazine had told its society that it was the simple life everyone was now striving for, at all costs even—implying that Americans did not believe their lives were simple, let alone fulfilling. Much of that desire seemed to suggest a quiet return to the past: the corner grocery store, the market place, the farm, the small town— things that had been around the block a few times and proved to be serene and rewarding. Yet here I was, my back against some *real past*, pondering how those who inhabited the structure might have viewed their lives when Lydford keep was in *their present*, centuries ago to us.

Now don't go crossing your eyes on me. This isn't deep stuff, just some thinking about how the simple life is perceived at any given time. Put another way, what we view as simple today may have been rather complex and unrewarding to other people of another era in the same environment. (I may or may not have found that "pit" described on the sign, but I'll bet it wasn't part of the simple life for any number of occupants!) None of this is surprising, of course. Working in a lighthouse a century ago was not fun or stressless. Living in one today—one that no longer functioned but provided beautiful scenery, tranquillity and solace—clearly conjures up a different set of emotions and perspectives.

I stood up and decided I had had a lousy thunk. It didn't solve anything. The reason was plain enough: Lydford Castle was empty. No one lived here anymore. No one wanted to. Probably few remembered what the place was even about. Chagford, however, was well-lived, occupied, busy, warm. These stones were cold, as cold as the memories they hid. My answers for the simple life I believed I had discovered still lay with two people, one very much alive, one long dead. Lydford and its law were of no help.

Chapter 19

Quoit and Cross

AND SO I MOVED ON, rejoining 386 south until I entered Tavistock. I couldn't believe it was already lunchtime—hadn't I just downed three cups of tea and marmaladed my toast to death? (Which reminded me it was also time to find a Public Convenience before I became very *inconvenienced!*) Tavistock was another old, pre-Conquest habitat, brought to us in part by the Russells, who were the earls and dukes of Bedford and who did a lot of building here. The town's most famous Russell was Lord John Russell, twice prime minister in the 19th century and the grandfather of the philosopher Bertrand Russell. (We ran into Bertrand in a footnote.) Tavistock was also one of the four Stannary Towns, along with Ashburton, Plympton and Chagford.

I located both the public loos and a pub serving a scrumptious Plowman's Lunch: fresh brown bread, rich butter, a little lettuce, tomatoes, watercress, pickled onions and a chunk of white cheddar cheese. Heaven!—if you're not a health nut. I washed it down with a soft drink, then walked up the main street awhile to peek into shops while letting the sun warm me. A sunny day in Devon is a terrific image to behold, especially if you have spent time on the moor where it can be rainy, dreary and downright inhospitable. Tavistock recharged my batteries—which were still low after my overimbibing at Bullers Arms.

On my stroll back to the car, I wondered if Julie and her villagers felt the sun the way I was feeling it. Having momentarily escaped from civilization as I knew it, warm sunlight accompanying a walk along medieval streets and old buildings was a thing of beauty for me. Not that Lydford or Okehampton castles were not—although "warmth" was clearly not the operative word when viewing each. They had their own beauty, their own history about them that made me humble just at the thought of the centuries that passed under their stone towers. You could sense the ghosts of the past lurking about, wanting desperately to tell their tales to anyone who would listen—anyone except *me*, of course! The Tavistocks and Chagfords of the world were still alive. Their ghosts were harder to find, obscured by daily life.

And then I realized it was the *longing* for something warm and simple that brought me these feelings. Julie and crew had no such longing—they *lived* the life I was seeking. Where there is no quest, there is no longing. It almost put King Arthur and the boys out of business until the Grail quest popped up. Einstein was right, wasn't he? It's all relative. If Julie and I walked down the street in Tavistock, our feelings—and how our senses perceived our surroundings—would be very different. This was home to Julie. It was new to me.

I decided that Philosophy 101 required much more study and shelved the whole discourse in my mind, preferring to consult the map and head out on 390 west to Gunnislake and the border of Devon and Cornwall. It was only a few miles before I saw the bridge that separated the two shires by traversing the Tamar River and Tamar valley. I crossed the bridge, entered the tiny town and remembered the left turn I had to take to find the bungalow of Uncle George.

I found it and was soon grabbing both my camcorder and some wishful thinking that old Uncle George would still be with us and willing to undergo the modern form of preservation known as *videotaping*. To my happy surprise, his wife answered the door and brought me in to see Uncle George, all of 90 and nearly blind, and lucid enough to remember my first visit. I respectfully declined any nourishment—the pickled onions were doing a number—and besides, his wife had heart trouble and I didn't want to add to it. We chatted a few minutes about their relative, my neighbor Jeannie; then they let me videotape them. Saying our farewells, I felt rather good about the whole thing. 'Imagine, 90 years old,' I thought. 'The rugged moors and windswept weather of Devon and Cornwall didn't hurt him at all. And I complain when the air-conditioner in the car needs freon! Wimp!' I returned to the car and prepared for new adventure.

Now these mini-sojourns may not seem like much of an adventure to the reader familiar with Sir Edmund Percival Hillary's conquest of Mt. Everest or Madonna's book *SEX*. But an adventure is only as adventurous as the dreams and desires and energy you bring to it. When I visited something it was on many levels: what it is today, what it was yesterday, how it fit into the past and the present, and what happened during its tenure on the planet. So a visit to Canterbury Cathedral may give the visitor a few "Aahs" and "Awws" before departure. For me, I could stay at the cathedral a lifetime, reliving the *history* that took place there, from St. Augustine's building of a little church after becoming the first Archbishop of Canterbury in 597 A.D., through a certain "murder in the cathedral" late in 1170, to the translation of the 100th Archbishop of Canterbury late in our century. See? It depends on what you bring to the moment. When it came to sites and sights and history, my bags are packed.

So now I was off to visit what some might call 'a bunch of old stones' but what I call centuries upon centuries of hidden memories. There were two stops and I will be merciful and spend only one paragraph on each. (For those who are interested, check out some books on ancient monuments and monoliths. Also, write to Her Majesty's Stationery Office—or H.M.S.O.—49 High Holborn, London WC1V 6HB, ENGLAND, and tell them you are keen on books dealing with Bronze Age burial tombs and stone circles in Britain.)

Trethevy Quoit, St. Cleer, Cornwall

First, Trethevy Quoit. By heading southeast on 390 out of Tavistock, you can pick up 3254 north just outside of Liskeard and follow the signs to St. Cleer. Finding the church, you drive down the lane beside it, past the Public Conveniences (I didn't pass them up, however), down a steep hill to the bottom. Turn left and go *round* the road as it carries you to the right and a sign for Darite and Trethevy Quoit. You are now on your own, but you will find it off a dirt road. There are hundreds of quoits in Britain and northern Europe, and they are also called cromlechs: burial chambers with several upright stones topped by an enormous capstone and often covered with dirt to make a mound. Spinsters' Rock is a quoit. Trethevy is of the same species, only slightly built up on a mound. It is sometimes referred to as Arthur's Quoit, most likely because Cornwall is "Arthur Country" and his name pops up everywhere and then some. It's awe-inspiring when a quoit stands alone, and not among standing stones and circles that make it part of a larger prehistoric project. Trethevy Quoit was alone in a field near a farmhouse. I circled it several times, slowly, wondering who was buried here, how long it took to build, and all that must have gone on over the last few millennia or so while the quoit stood alone, silent and vigilantly protecting its occupants.

I spent some time at Trethevy Quoit, then hopped into the car and followed the map as it took me past Darite to Minions, which was more a group of houses than a village. Here on the right side of the road was a large Celtic cross, one of many that dotted the landscape in Devon and Cornwall. It was a burial marker, a signpost for traveling, a holy

site…any and all number of things. No one left us the user's manual—
we just don't know. But as the afternoon wore on and I stood next to the
cross, I made up my own stories about who walked past this enormous
standing stone. They were Christian. They were farmers and knights
and sheriffs and soldiers…and maybe a wandering Frenchman, recently
escaped from Lydford or Okehampton, maybe even as far away as
Moretonhampstead, where some of his compatriots died and were
buried. Across the road and up a dirt path were The Hurlers, two stone
circles of the smallish variety. More stories entered my head. More
walking, pondering, imagining.

As I returned to the car it became clearer and clearer to me that the
late-20th century person-who-works needs to dream more, have a
thunk or two and not be afraid to slither off the Slippery Sidewalk of
Life, if only for a brief time. I especially address the male of the species
because I think females are ahead of the game, which is why they live
longer, smile more and don't have trouble being affectionate or
romantic. Face it, American males are stuck with two opposing sex
chromosomes—a female Y and a male X—and they don't know if
they're coming or going emotionally. Males want a simple life, but they
want *power and authority* (read "complex life"). They want quality time,
but they want *financial success* (read "no time at all"). They want to
experiment and create, but they want to *survive and get ahead* (read "no
risks"). It is why they prolong adolescence well into their 30s—much
easier than growing up!

Yes, I know. A digression far off the road to Chagford, the simple life,
Julie, Sir Redvers, the Boer War, concentration camps and a few other
things I promised to get to in due course, including Churchill and the
media. But this is all part of the same landscape. If you think you know
where you want to go, you have to know where you're coming from. My
"coming from" involved a disillusionment with Corporate America and
the self-imposed stress to be successful, whatever that means. (It's not
really *dress* for success, but *stress* for success. You read it here first!)

It wasn't so much that I was looking to live a different kind of life. I just wanted to know that one *existed*. I had heard *ad nauseam* from friends and acquaintances the standard "Just-give-me-a-little-shop-in-a-little-town-and-I'll-be-happy" line, but I was never convinced that they were serious. What did they think they were leaving? And what did they think they would find? I was asking the questions that these people seemed to shun. Now, on my way back to Chagford and Bullers Arms, I was prepared to find some answers.

Chapter 20

A Walk Around Chagford

BEFORE RETURNING TO GLENDARAH House to wash up, I drove the car into a rare open parking space in the market square and glanced at my watch. It was late afternoon, which would give me enough time for something I had wanted to do since first visiting Chagford in 1989: take a snoop around the village by foot. Now don't concern yourself that the following footfalls are going to regress into a boring travelogue of "And on the left we have the little shop where those cosmic cookies are baked" and all the rest. Indeed, I dislike most travel articles that give you the Visit-Westminster Abbey-The Tower-Big Ben pabulum lifted from a brochure, followed by a couple of places to eat and sleep, often as a quid pro quo for a free meal or night's lodging for the travel writer. Many years ago I hawked a weekly travel column to newspaper syndicates that related the *history* of a particular place, so that travelers could 'travel back in time' as well as travel through the present—a nifty way to take a vacation because it involved a quest, and it would be memorable once they returned home. (One sample article was a walk around the old wall of Old Jerusalem, with quick stories or references to historical happenings taking place at each nook and corner.) None of the syndicates bit, so there you have it. But I won't give in to current travel writing styles. Obstinate.

Rather, if you've made it this far I think it makes sense to give you a *feel* for the environs of the simple life as I believed it to be on that sunny,

late-afternoon in Dartmoor. And in true travel article iconoclasm, the
descriptions will not take any particular route or order.

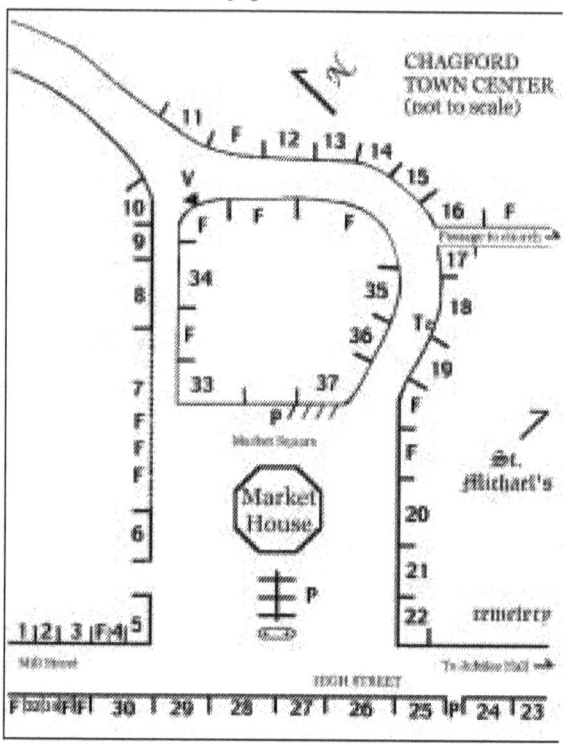

All buildings are two-story; some are three.

F=flats P=car park	T=telephone	V=Victorian fountain
1 Methodist church	14 Jeweler	27 Ring O' Bells
2 Ladysmith house	15 Clothing	28 General Store
3 Bullers Arms	16 Arts/Crafts	29 Hardware
4 Craft shop	17 Food store	30 Outfitting store
5 Bank	18 Solicitors	31 Dentist
6 Grocery store	19 Post Office	32 Bakeshop
7 Vet/Surgery	20 Antiques	33 Bank
8 Fabrics/Gifts	21 Hair salon	34 Antiques
9 Radio/TV	22 Accessories	35 Chemists
10 Country store	23 Endicott house	36 Butcher
11 Bank	24 3 Crowns Inn	37 News Agents
12 Tea Room	25 Clothing store	
13 Dairy	26 Wine/Spirits	

The octagonal Market House you have already heard about easily stands out as the symbol and heart of the village. Sometimes referred to as Pepperpot, it was torn down in July, 1862, and replaced with the present structure the same year. (If you look closely you can find the 'bishop's mark' where it was consecrated.) Each of the eight sides measures about 22 feet—I'm not sure because I paced it off—and includes loos for men and women, an antique shop and, on the second floor, an office for Chagford's policeman. You can walk around it in 30 seconds, unless you decide to sit upon each of several benches fronting it. That quick little trek around the perimeter will allow you to see shops on three sides; the fourth side has room to park six cars—mine now being one.

Beyond the car park is the main road. If you stand with your back to the car park and the Market House, you will see a bank on the corner to your right, a pub (Ring O' Bells) straight ahead and the beginnings of the Three Crowns Inn on the far left. Turn the corner of the Lloyds bank on the right—where the main street is called Mill Street—and you bump into Bullers Arms at 7 Mill Street. Turn to the left of the Square and you walk along High Street to the old stone edifice of the Three Crowns with a raised cemetery just across the street from it. The cemetery leads to the parish church of St. Michael's.

Back to the Market House and the three sides of shops. There are two lanes that run downhill at the corners of the three sides, with shops and dwellings along each lane. The right and left lanes join up and carry on down and to the right to the kidney-loosening speed bumps and Glendarah House just beyond.

I walked up one lane and down the other, up the main road to the right of the bank and beyond Bullers Arms, and back past the market square on to the Three Crowns and St. Michael's. I went inside the church and chatted with two ladies who were cleaning near the chancel. Exiting the church I could see a building that would later turn out to be Jubilee Hall. I entered the 16th century coffee shop next to the Three

Crowns to have a look, especially since they proffered a Devon Cream Tea, which I could witness in progress.[*] I walked back to the market square and entered the news-and-goodies shop to buy newspapers and forage for little gifts for my kids back home.

Then I turned the corner and followed the right lane downhill, past the butcher and chemist, around a flat or two, until I linked up with the left-hand lane that met at a 19th century fountain. I crossed the street to peep through the window of another tea room, then walked back up the lane I came by only on the opposite side. When I reached an arts and crafts shop, I noticed a passage leading to the cemetery. I entered it through a gate and looked at the old tombstones, including several Lyddons, probably related to the owners of Bullers Arms at the turn of the century. I also found the "Roman altar," believed to be an ancient altar of the church, perhaps belonging to Saxon times or early Norman. Some have suggested it was a tomb and actually dates back to the Roman occupation.

Now it is much harder to describe how this all felt, and why it was different from similar experiences I have encountered in small towns. After all, I have visited some pretty diminutive ones in Vermont— Newfane and Rockingham are ones I recall with fond memory—and many more in Louisiana, Illinois, California, Arizona, Florida, Massachusetts, Montana, and other states. Even small towns in Quebec and Ontario, to say nothing of villages in parts of France, Italy, Spain, Austria, Israel, etc. (Hopeless romantics travel a lot, to the detriment of their savings accounts.)

---

[*] Time to talk briefly about clotted cream, which I believe is cooked up in a pan and comes as thick as poured concrete. It is applied to bread, scones and any number of desserts. It makes butter seem thin and non-descript! Devon is known for it, and Whiddons—the Tea Shop in Chagford built when John Whiddon was still around—serves an afternoon Olde English Tea or a Devon Cream Tea. The difference: both have home-made scones, strawberry jam, Devon clotted cream and a pot of tea (choice of three blends). Olde English includes freshly cut cucumber sandwiches on whole meal bread. There—now you know.

Some have beautiful mountains as backdrops; others possess lakes or rivers, deserts or grasslands. Chagford is very, very different...to me. Quaint is too trite and misses the mark by miles—especially *this* Mark. Same with uncommon, baroque, charming, picturesque: the thesaurus can't help this one. There is something...something *familiar and safe* about Chagford and its winding medieval lanes and buildings and market square and pubs and houses and cottages and flats and shops and B&Bs. Something comforting and very, very safe, like your grandmother's lap or a 200-year-old tree to lean against. Very old, and therefore somehow safe. Something protective—a promise of security for the senses. You could trust your eyes and ears and the smells in the air and the tastes of the local food and drink. You could trust the touch of the old stones, the tombs in the church, the walls of the Three Crowns Inn.

It was trust and the promise of a good life, a simple life. Not a financially-rich life, not a materially-rewarding life or a constantly-active life, although you might be surprised at how the village remains awash in culture, as alluded to earlier.

We are talking a quiet, safe, simple life.[*]

I realized then, while taking a last walk around the market square, that the people I saw in Bullers Arms in 1989 had come to represent these feelings that now were so hard to articulate. This return in 1992 only confirmed the reasons for my emotional attachment to Chagford. In my mind, I saw villagers living their lives in a very old

[*] At a conference of the American Planning Association, author Randall Arendt, who is also vice president of conservation programs with the National Lands Trust in Pennsylvania, told his audience that "village-style development"—not conventional zoning—was needed if the United States hoped to cease its creation of suburban sprawl, which at present is replete with strip malls and subdivisions that do little to promote a feeling of community. "We're planning backwards," he said. "The trees are down and the signs are up." He called for village-style developments of narrow streets arched by tall trees, smaller lot sizes, village greens and mixed use shopping areas that face streets. (See where this is going yet?) Why village-style development? Arendt says it will create a more heightened sense of community and more pleasant surroundings. In other words, it's time to progress to medieval villages like Chagford.

village without a cause to push, an ax to grind, or a memory to lay to rest. (I was wrong on this last count.)

In America, when the male reaches 40 a silent cry fills the air—the cry of acknowledgment that certain goals haven't been attained, certain dreams still remained but dreams, certain hopes stood mute and, well, hopeless. In Chagford, 40 would be a celebration of a special day followed by another day. Bullers Arms would open its arms to all ages and all situations in life. The farmer and the shopkeeper and the landowner and the factory-worker and the housewife and the soccer player and the taxi driver and dart queen.

The Gates of Hell, as Dante described them, had an ominous welcoming sign that alerted new arrivals to ABANDON ALL HOPE YE WHO ENTER HERE. At Bullers Arms, the sign would have said WELCOME ALL WHO HOPE FOR ANOTHER DAY.

And so, despite my trepidations about the unknown stories that lay behind Julie and General Sir Redvers V.C., I returned to my car and headed down the hill towards Glendarah House, confirmed in my belief that this was what I had been looking for, and that 77 million Americans would agree that, at this moment, I was a "Discoverer." One could live here and leave the past behind, the worries of the world, the grind of modern civilization. All I needed to see was a bicycle and an old pair of boots and I could take a picture and send it to *Time*.

I parked the car to one side of Glendarah and got out to search for a stick to clean the mud from my boots. Then I opened the front door and walked up the stairs to my room. I was feeling sated and excited. It was a fun day, the only regret being that I couldn't share it with someone. It's always been that way for me: a struggle between the occasional desire to be alone to collect thoughts and take a reading of my life, and the need to share experiences with others. I suspect I am not singular in this, but I still believe people need to take more solitary time to reflect and have a good *thunk*.

The current source of my excitement was the upcoming dart tournament. Now this hardly seems like something an American would jump up and down about, but since you have ridden along with me this far you can understand where I was coming from. If I was correct that Chagford represented the simple life of a people who led fulfilling lives, maintained a realistic perspective of what life was all about and truly knew how to enjoy each other's company without pretense or plasticity, I would see an example of it at the Jubilee Hall this evening. Moreover, I would get to see the Captain in action—from a safe distance—along with her brother and perhaps some of the other characters of Bullers Arms.

I strolled down the hallway to take a shower, returned and dressed, then decided to relax, catch up on what "home" news I could glean from the newspapers, check the maps for tomorrow's drive...then head for dinner at Bullers Arms, followed by the tournament at Jubilee Hall. Much of the news centered on the Royal Family, mainly the offspring and their marital woes. People today of course do not realize the problems royal kids have given the British monarchy for centuries—from William the Conqueror's strange brood (did young Henry, the third son, have anything to do with his older regal brother's hunting 'accident' in 1100, since an arrow in the back looks dreadfully deliberate and Henry quickly became *Henry I* ?); to Henry II (died 1189) and his troublesome warring boys; to Prince Hal (later Henry V, died 1422) and his cavorting with vagabonds and sidewalk hostesses; to Henry VIII's sister Margaret, who unabashedly and secretly married for love, and not for her royal brother's political needs in the early 16th century; to a variety of scandals among the royal families of the 18th and early 19th century Hanoverian Georges (I, II and III) right up to Victoria's house of horror (from the son and heir chasing practically every skirt in the court to perhaps one nephew's ripping up of prostitutes in London); to Edward VIII's 1936 abdication for the woman he loved and required for mothering.

Whew! To me, the present pick of princes and princesses are small potatoes compared to the bizarre vegetation that has been cultivated in the Garden Royal of ages past.

I glanced at my watch. It was 6:50 PM and my stomach was starting to rumble. I decided to bring my note pad with—hell, practically everyone in Chagford knew I had it by now! I also wanted to bring the camcorder to see if I could tape some of the tournament. I didn't want to be obvious. The hope was to just rest it on my lap and take in a minute or two of the noise, the smoke that would no doubt rise from the cigarettes of the villagers and the atmosphere of a village at play.

With everything packed up and ready, I descended the staircase and entered Glendarah's courtyard. Then I got into the car and slowly advanced into Chagford—those speed bumps had really made a cautious, "calm" driver out of me.

As I past the bumps and started to drive up the hill toward the market square, I spied Gwen—she of the pub—walking uphill. Without thinking that I was a stranger in a strange land (with all due respect to the Bible and Robert A. Heinlein), I quickly pulled up alongside her, rolled down the window and asked if she needed a lift. She stopped and looked at me, and for an instant I felt the fool—she didn't know me from a quoit! Why would she hop into a foreigner's car? Happily, a smile came to her face as she recognized who it was, and said "Why thank you." Although a short ride, we chatted.

"This is very kind of you."

"My pleasure. So you've got this climb up the hill each day to the pub?"

"Yes, but you get used to it." Gwen was not a small woman, and I could guess that the walk wouldn't get any easier with time.

"Will you be going to the dart tournament?" I asked, as we entered the market square.

"I don't think so. I'll be at the pub."

"What time does it start?"

"About half-past seven, I should think. Here we are. Do you want to park over there?"

"No, let me drop you off in front of the pub first."

I did, she got out and thanked me again and I told her I would see her shortly for dinner. I then parked on one of the three sides of the square, just up from the post office, and set the emergency brake after turning the wheel into the curb: the hills were deceptive, and I didn't want to watch my rented car take a solo flight down the medieval lane. I got out, closed the door and looked around. It was still a clear day, now turning to evening and surprisingly light outside for almost 7:00. Most of the shops were closed; one or two were just closing up, and people were walking about while occasional "lawnmowers" zoomed by in all directions.

The air smelled really good to me, and I tried to imagine myself living here, closing up *my* shop before meeting friends just a few feet away at the pub for dinner on a Friday night with other friends popping in at intervals. It was a puff-of-smoke of a daydream, quickly vanishing as I began to walk across the square toward Bullers Arms. 'Don't delude yourself, alien being,' the brain was relaying to all parts conscious. 'Your kind of life is light-years away from this life you are witnessing in Chagford. Just take it in as an observer. Don't start hurting yourself. It's not worth it.'

Nevertheless, as I saw the pub in sight I still wanted to believe that I could live here—that I *had* lived here my whole life, without the influences that had shaped me to be an American growing up in the last half of the 20th century. Influences such as the need to succeed, to make lots of money, to keep up with the Joneses, to be busy, to have plans, to push your kids to excel…and so on. Quentin Crisp once said something like "Never keep up with the Joneses. Drag them down to your level. It's cheaper." Not a bad concept. I prefer just leaving the Joneses alone and doing my own thing. Many people I know didn't think that way.

I wondered what it would have been like for me to grow up here, without the "American" 60's, the Vietnam war, the drugs, the riots, the Me Generation, the greedy 80s—the latter stamped with approval by the government. It was a useless wonder to pursue. There were 77 million of us who had lived through all that and more, who were shaped by it to the point where we were now creations of it, like it or not. Chagford was another game in another country. I had to play the hand I was dealt, and simply watch the villagers play theirs.

I reached the portico to the pub and began to feel all warm inside...and also famished! Castle-and-quoit hunting gets your appetite up, and if Bullers Arms was ready for me, I was ready for it. I opened the door, then the inner door and stepped into the pub. The table I had occupied lay before me, as did the familiarity of the wall hangings, the pub bar and the service area straight ahead.

Activity to the left caught my eye, and as I turned I saw Julie's brother, Nick, throwing darts at the dart board. I took a step further inside and spied Gwen behind the bar, busying herself. Then I looked back at Nick and observed his face, frozen in sheer concentration as he aimed one dart, then another. Besides a few people seated at the bar and a small group to the right at a table, there was no one else in Bullers Arms. I watched as Nick seemed to guide the darts with phenomenal precision to exactly where he wanted them to stick. Then he would walk over to the dart board, remove them, turn and walk back to throw more.

And it now became clear that although I was watching Nick, he didn't see me. Or put another way, Nick the brother of the Captain didn't *want* to see this interloper to Bullers Arms who had spent some time talking with his sister. He threw his last dart and stared for a brief second at the board, an incredibly intense glare that bordered on anger. I wondered if the stare was for the board, or for me.

Chapter 21

Last Night at the Pub

RATHER THAN STAND THERE like John Wayne waiting for the other guy to draw his gun (dart?), I entered the pub and sat down at my small, round table. Funny how I thought of it as *my* table, but as I have said, there was a comfort level with Bullers Arms that let me enter and exit without a forethought or an afterthought...indeed, without much thought at all. Never mind that I knew almost no one, and that no one knew me or what I was about or what I thought or what I did (except Julie, who learned only superficially about the guy with the note pad). So while sitting at *my* table, I carefully scrutinized the overhead chalkboard with its listing of food items, only to decide that it was going to be another mushroom stroganoff kind of evening.

Young Brunette instantly appeared from behind the larder to ask my preference. It was now 7:05, giving me plenty of time to chow down, sip a *single* cider and stroll over to Jubilee Hall for the night's festivities. I told her I wanted the stroganoff and would be happy to await its arrival with a half-pint of medium apple cider as a distraction...well, not exactly those words. She gave me a warm smile and glided over to the bar, where Keith prepared my liquid request while waving to me. I also observed another gentleman behind the bar, who I was to learn worked the pub as co-owner and Keith's brother-in-law, Bob Lewis-Jones. Young Brunette floated back to my table and deposited the cider and one of those little napkins that couldn't absorb a dewdrop. Then she was off to the kitchen, order in hand. It appeared that Young Blonde had the night off.

"My" table, Bullers Arms

I was preparing to jot down a few more impressions of the pub while I waited, but Keith came over.

"Have you seen the other portrait of Buller, over there?" he asked, pointing near the counter where food magically appeared.

"No, I haven't."

We walked over and Keith showed me Sir Redvers, bullish look and all. He truly was a caricature of the John Bull of British Empire lore, a true representation of an empire-building era long gone. I told Keith I really needed to look into the general's life, and he suddenly remembered he wanted to give me something related to Buller. I walked back to my table to sip the cider and Keith came over with a blank receipt check. It had the name and address of Bullers Arms on it, along with a place for the date, a column for the cost of food and drink and a listing of various pubs offerings for patrons:

• FREE HOUSE • LARGE RANGE OF BEERS •
• EXTENSIVE RESTAURANT MENU •
• BAR MEALS • BEER GARDEN •
BOOKINGS TAKEN

For pub initiates, a "free house" simply means that beers under several labels can be served, and not simply the label or labels of one brewery that may, in fact, own the pub or lay some fiduciary claim to it.

Keith, however, was not showing me a blank check to gloat over how he billed customers. In the left corner was a coat of arms—the arms of Redvers Buller. They were rather simple in design, but Keith was anxious for me to look at the motto.

I squinted to make out the words—contact lenses on near-sighted humans tend to blur reality inside of six inches.

"I think the first word is 'aquila,' for eagle. Then it looks like 'non capit.' Don't capture. I can't make out the last word."

"It's 'muscas.' His motto was 'Eagles do not capture flies.'" Keith smiled.

"Hmm. Pretty profound, huh?" I observed. "Sort of a twisted 19th century version of Leona Helmsley's 'Only the little people pay taxes.'"

"I'm afraid I don't understand. Who is Leona Helmsley?"

Keith was perplexed and I should have known better.

"Uh, she's an elderly owner of hotels and property who doesn't bother with the activities of those beneath her, specifically people who work for a living."

"Does she live in one of her hotels?"

I smiled. "Actually, at the moment she resides as a guest in one of our government's special living quarters—the ones reserved for people who hear the words 'we find the defendant guilty' in a court of law. I'm sorry I brought the whole thing up, Keith. Can I keep this?"

"Of course. Oh, here comes your dinner. See you later."

Keith retreated behind the bar as Young Brunette delivered dinner with a smile. I thanked her and she asked if I needed anything else. I have always been enamored of the politeness exhibited through a British accent: you almost feel guilty being asked if there's something else that can be done on your behalf. I declined, thanked her again for the receipt of dinner and dug in.

And while I ate I listened to Gwen and Keith and the few patrons sitting at the bar. Gwen was in self-deprecating mode: "I went into Plymouth and they don't have large sizes for me. I guess large women don't live in Plymouth!" Her audience chuckled, including Keith, who didn't miss a stroke serving brew and coordinating the movement of glasses and shillings. From the corner of my eye I saw Nick, still throwing darts, still silent in his preoccupation.

I decided to put a few scratches in the note pad:

It's 7:11 PM Chagford time and the stroganoff was delivered piping hot and is very good. I'm starting to mellow out a tad, in part from a tiring day of trekking through the countryside, in part from the cider which is shutting down brain activity at a slow but steady pace. I hear someone coming in.... Well, if it isn't Chirpy, who I see give an acknowledging nod to Nick. Chirp then moves past me to the bar. I think he notices me but there is no recognition.

I must remind myself I'm the outsider. Worse, an outsider with a pad of paper and too many questions.

My attention now moved to a group of five at one of the two tables that could hold six people. Three women and two men perused the table. Several were smoking and all had drinks. Before I could focus on the gathering a good-looking female redhead entered the pub, age about 20—maybe less—and had her say with Bob at the bar. She then walked over to the two women at the Group-of-Five enclave, said hello and promptly exited Bullers Arms.

You would think the pub was setting up some Shakespearean tragedy before my eyes, introducing character after character until the poor bard has to begin killing them off just to clear more room on the stage. (Hamlet comes to mind. Messy stuff.) But no, this was a pub in the center of a village in the heart of a moor where people come and go with ease and with purpose. It was a sight to behold.

It's now 7:15. Again I'm writing down times for no apparent reason. Nick now leaves the pub with three other men I hadn't noticed before. Presumably they are off to Jubilee Hall for the tournament. Chirpy yells out that he'll be along shortly. I'd better put the pen down and empty the plate. I see Young Brunette eyeing me in case it's time to swoop in and take up the tableware. Wonder if she'll be at the tournament or if she is destined to serve out the evening.

7:22. Three more young women now walk in. They wear skirts which are very short and very tight. Given the, er, pronouncement of the outline they cut in their clothing, I venture to say that sexual harassment must be in full bloom around here, although the villagers don't see it that way. If this were the States, plaintiff's attorneys could fill up their mutual funds on the lawsuits generated from words passing between males and females. Of course, in Chagford that wouldn't happen.

7:24. Chirpy has just come over to me, quite unexpectedly, and said "See you later." "At the Jubilee Hall?" I queried, which was more of demonstrating my mastery at the obvious than anything else. "Right," came the patient reply. "I'll look for you," I said as he retreated. Chirp smiled and left the pub.

I forgot to write down one tidbit gleaned from a question I tossed at Keith. Gwen, as it turns out, is not related to Chirpy's family, but is sort of the uncrowned queen of Chagford pubs, having worked in Bullers Arms for five years and for 27 years before that at Ring O' Bells. Duly recorded.

7:33. I am leaving for Jubilee Hall but need to dash this off quickly as I down my last drops of cider. I never had the opportunity to tip Young Blonde last night amid the chaos of the conquering soccer heroes and my nerve-shredding encounter with Captain. So a moment ago I walked over to Young Brunette and discovered that, in fact, Young Blonde would not be in this evening. My thought was to leave Young Brunette a tip for herself and a tip for Young Blonde, figuring that 20 percent for each would work well even in the old U S of A, let alone for penurious (and often fiscally-wasted) me. Then I realized that it would come out to a pound each—about $1.80—not enough to buy a pint of beer! "Damn inflated prices!" I thought. So I gave Young Brunette four pounds, "two for you and two for your colleague." She smiled warmly, almost surprised, and thanked me. If she made it to the tournament that night, I never saw her.

Chapter 22

Jubilee Hall

I WAVED GOOD-BYE TO KEITH, who waved back, then went through the doors of Bullers Arms and out into the cool air of evening. I was still having a hard time believing that my return to Chagford was for real, not just an ongoing wish never quite reaching fulfillment. As I walked up Mill Street toward the Market House, then past the square as the Three Crowns Inn loomed on my right, I had to keep reminding myself what had actually occurred to me over time. It was an interesting summary of events, presented on the overhead projector in my mind, in bullet form no less:

- Stumbled into Chagford and Bullers Arms in November 1989
- Witnessed a 'simple life,' punctuated by almost losing own life twice
- Characters in pub characterized and memorized during dart tournament
- Especial note taken of lady mindfully dubbed The Captain
- Returned Stateside to 30 months of changes, turns and twists euphemistically known as 'living'
- Through a sequence of events—perhaps induced or encouraged by either the odds or the gods—returned to Bullers Arms in May 1992

- Revisited the characters of 1989, including Captain, and met a few
- Now preparing to revisit the venue that began it all: a dart tournament

I stopped at the porch of the Three Crowns, entered it and unknowingly sat where Little Sid caught a bullet, or rather straddled it. Perhaps his ghost could have explained to me how I felt, how I marveled at a place I didn't want to relinquish for a departing airplane a few hours away. Like Carter's King Tut discovery, I was astonished at what I had uncovered—in this case the simple life—yet cursed from that very encounter with the unknown. As I might have guessed, Sid didn't make an appearance for me yet again.

I also thirsted to know more—more about Julie as the epitome of a life so many burned-out Boomers could only fantasize about. And, almost reluctantly now, I could not put aside the growing obsession of learning about General Buller, to see if he also stood as the symbol of something imbued in the simple life of Chagford, or something perhaps more dark than I cared to confront. Was he a tall, proud figure for the villagers of Chagford to admire, a George Washington of the moor, worthy of a pub named after him? Or was Buller representative of a national tragedy, a disgrace haunting the aggregate consciences or dim memories of a nation, much as Vietnam continues to haunt 77 million Americans?

Cut to the chase and stop the brooding, right? I had unearthed a way of life I felt many would envy. That was that and it was time to remeet the Captain in action. As for Sir Redvers, V.C., his story would have to wait. (Of course, we have already seen a glimpse of him—authors have the incredible power to screw up chronology when telling a story just to make things work out for the best...or so they hope.)

I walked past the Three Crowns Inn toward the beginning of the village proper, with St. Michael's church staying in view to my left. Its tall tower seemed to follow me, moving with my gait and looming eerily in the lightly illuminated sky. I zipped up my jacket as a breeze picked up slightly. It was very quiet.

Soon I could see a few people milling about a large building to the side of where the main street converged with a perpendicular one: Jubilee Hall. I crossed the street and strode up to the entranceway, where bodies were bustling in and out of the door. I took a deep breath, oddly nervous. What was I worried about? 'True, you're not *among friends*, as it were,' I thought. 'But you are among friendly people, most of whom have kept you fascinated with their way of life for two and a half years! And Julie doesn't look like she bites! Quite the contrary.'

I told my mind to leave me alone, exhaled and walked into Jubilee Hall. It consisted of one enormous rectangular room, with tables lining the two long sides of the building running from the front to the back. Green metal chairs were arranged in a large backward L, with the dart board on the third side at the front of the room facing opposite the entranceway and chairs for contestants on the fourth. The dart board was surrounded by what looked like a large white tire. At the very front of the room behind the dart board was a stage concealed by a red curtain. Above it high on the wall was a cut-out sign that said "1977: The Queen's Silver Jubilee." 'Interesting,' I told myself. 'The year I lived in London.'

Upon entering Jubilee Hall I saw Chirpy, pint in hand, chirping away with friends at one of the tables lining the right side of the room as you faced the front. He didn't see me, which was fine at the moment since I was trying to acclimate myself to new surroundings in an old village. Immediately to my right was a concession stand where villagers were stepping up to the window counter and filling up on liquid fare to the jingle of pound coins with change. It was smoky and noisy and very, very busy.

I slowly started walking up the center of the room, keeping the dart board in sight. As I reached the first row of chairs, I saw Julie and Nick, teamed up against another couple. To their right was a large, multi-tiered display of trophies—dozens and dozens of them, all shapes and sizes—glittering like the hardware in Elizabeth's jewelry vault…Taylor, that is. I froze in my tracks as Julie stepped up to a designated spot. She was dressed in a T-shirt and pants, and her hair bobbed as she quickly flicked three darts at the target. Although they weren't thrown hard and seemed to amble through the air, it was indisputable that they landed basically where she wanted them to go. Lots of people cheered.

I looked at the chalkboard where a scorekeeper was cryptically notching numbers. It was divided into two columns, one headed "J&N," the other "J&E." I looked back to see Nick step up, hesitate for a moment, and then with great purpose throw his darts one by one, mechanically. They must have accomplished his mission for the crowd cheered, the J&N column's last number was stricken through and Julie patted Nick's arm. After someone from the J&E team took their turn, Julie stepped up, flicked away, louder cheers emerged and the score-keeper crossed out a number and put down the chalk.

They had won…I think. How, what and why remains a complete mystery to this day.

Chirpy suddenly was standing next to me, holding a piece of paper. Our conversation was pleasant and extremely helpful for the American with the clueless expression on his face.

"Thought you might like a look at the teams for tonight. Here's how they ranked during the year." He handed me a photocopy of the team listings.

"Thanks, Chirpy. Say, what exactly did Julie and Nick just win?"

Chirpy smiled. "The Under & Over. That's Under & Over-40 pairs. Nick's under, Julie's over. She's 42."

"Hey, so am I," as if that were relevant to the formation of the Cosmos. "So they won a trophy?"

"Right. They'll hand them out later. After the raffle."

"Raffle?" See how helpless I was in the land of the Simple Life?

"See the table over there?" Chirpy pointed. To the left of the room was a table filled with bottles of wine, fruit baskets, four-packs of ale and other retail items.

"Yeah." The cider still had control of my elocution.

"We all bought tickets for a raffle. To win prizes. See you later."

	CHAGFORD DARTS LEAGUE FINAL TEAM POSITIONS		
		POINTS	BEER LEGS
1)	GLOBE 'B'	86	21
2)	POST INN	69	14
3)	GLOBE 'C'	63	13
4)	BULLERS 'A'	62	15
5)	BULLERS 'C'	57	18
6)	R.O.B. 'B'	49	10
7)	T. CROWNS 'A'	42	11
8)	GLOBE 'A'	39	9
9)	NORTHMORE	36	13
10)	BULLERS 'B'	35	4
11)	T. CROWNS 'B'	33	7
12)	R.O.B. 'A'	31	9
13)	R.O.B. 'C'	27	7

Chirpy pushed off to greener, and probably more interesting, pastures. I remained standing, looking at the fruit baskets. I probably would have been shocked to learn at that moment that, later in the evening, I would be responsible for awarding one of those prizes...to Julie's best friend!

For the record, here is what I gazed upon, while intermittently looking up to see if Julie and I could make eye contact. (We didn't.) It is reproduced faithfully from the original, showing the rankings of the 13 pub teams making up the Chagford Darts League. As I was now to understand, some pubs sponsored as many as three different teams.

I stared down at the paper trying to make sense of it all. It looked like The Globe did okay during the year, holding 1st, 3rd and 8th places. Old General Sir Redvers might not have hooted too loudly over his teams' rankings, but at least they eschewed the bottom of the barrel where two of the Ring O' Bells' teams dwelled. Unconsciously, I continued reading while slowly easing myself into one of the green chairs about four rows from the back. The beer legs were an enigma, although I assumed they had something to do with winning, losing and buying beer. (Legs are rounds, as in when both teams complete a round of throwing darts.) I suddenly was reminded of Julie's recent victory and looked up to find her. She was nowhere to be seen and other teams of people were now throwing darts and tallying up numbers.

So I watched the villagers of Chagford play darts. You may recall I promised to get back to all this earlier. Well, here's the paragraph. While no doubt there are many Americans familiar with darts and, perchance, skillful in the art of dart-throwing, I was simply in shock at how deftly Chagfordians could send a dart into flight on its way to a carefully-calculated pinpoint on a confusing and crowded target. The goal apparently was to reduce your score from, say 501, as rapidly as possible, until you hit the target on the exact number to clear your side of the chalkboard altogether. It had nothing to do with hitting the bulls-eye; rather, it was careful addition and subtraction, and more careful aiming at a particular number required to obtain the desirable score. (The inner bull—or bull's eye—is worth 50, or double the outer bull's value of 25.) The distance from the dart board to the throwing line was between 7'9" and 8'0". Numbers could be doubled, and the game usually had to be won on a double. Others were purposefully avoided. It amounted to a fast-paced game of skill that left little time for contemplation or planning. The strategy was in the mind as the dart was in the air.

I gleaned much of this from observation and was engrossed in the whole process when a quiet "Hello" entered my right ear. I looked over my shoulder and it was Julie, glowing in her smile and gleaming eyes, fresh from the victory of battle at center stage. She was leaning on the back of the chair next to me, so I half-turned to see her.

"So what do you think?" she asked. Had I known the *traditional* Chagford greeting and how close she was to saying it, I would have rolled my eyes in disbelief. Of course she was asking about the tournament, not the town.

"I think this is wonderful! Sort of a larger version of the tournament at Bullers Arms I saw in 1989, only there's more room to move—"

"—And less chance of being hit by a wayward dart!"

She was quick with words as well as darts. Julie laughed and I couldn't help but join in. I had made so much of my near brush with death at the hands—and wheel—of Captain that it was both funny and embarrassing to have it thrown back at me, figuratively of course. Then Julie saw the piece of paper Chirpy gave me and asked if I understood what was taking place.

"In a way. What I don't understand is how the teams are formed. And do you have to pay to join?"

Julie got comfortable—meaning she shifted her weight while leaning against the chair back. "The league this year consists of 13 teams within Chagford. Bullers has three teams. Each player pays a signing-on fee of 30 pence and there are eight players to a team. Each week the players pay 50 pence, which goes toward the cost of the trophies at the end of the season—the ones over there. We also donate a lot of the money to various organizations, which we'll do in a ceremony later tonight. Each team chooses whom the money should go to."

Before I could ask seven other questions, we were interrupted yet again, this time by a jolly type of woman who entered my aisle, walked over to my seat and turned to hug Julie, who now stood upright. It was Ann, whom Julie was later to tell me was her best friend. I rose from my seat and Julie introduced me. Then Julie said she had to return to the competition and Ann sat down next to me.

"Did you see Julie and Nick?"

"I sure did. They seemed rather confident in their play."

"Yes. Nick is an incredible dart player. The best in Chagford, if not Devon. Julie is very good, too. They're both playing in several competitions tonight."

I now learned of the competitions—10 in all. They were (not in order):

Under and Over (just completed)	*Men's Pairs*
Sixes	*Captains*
Ladies Singles	*Mixed Pairs*
Fours	*Ladies Pairs*
Threes	*Men's Singles*

I decided to do a two-minute videotaping of the room and the competition, and noticed through the eye-piece that Julie was up and at it again. Ann was delightful, filling me in on what was going on, the various teams, who was good, always with a return to Julie and her prowess with darts.

"She's such a wonderful person," Ann concluded.

I stopped taping. It had been accomplished by resting the camcorder on my lap and looking through the viewfinder at a 90-degree angle, hoping to be less conspicuous. I now decided it time to jot a few things down. It required only a brief explanation to Ann, who readily accepted it. We were soon joined by her husband and the three of us sat and watched amid the comings and goings of people, the sloshing of beer and intake of cigarette smoke and the deep laughter of villagers having a genuinely good time.

It's 7:49 PM—hey, why stop the timekeeping at this point! A new competition has begun between Globe B and Globe C teams. I know I look like a cub reporter, and that people are studying me as much as I am observing them. But I don't want to just rely on memory. Especially in my

*delicate state of slowly-diminishing sobriety. Maybe I should stop drinking
that stuff altogether.*

*Julie's friend, Ann, has told me a little about Julie and her life. I hope I
can follow up on some of it with Julie. Chirpy will also be a good source to
corner, if he's in the cornering mood. And damn!—I've got to remember to
ask if he wore some sort of badge or coat of arms on a sportscoat when I
was here two and one-half years ago. My memory's usually pretty accurate,
although drinking cider seems to reduce my neurological input capabilities
considerably.*

*Julie is flinging her darts and puffing away on cigarettes. I also notice
that she returns to a chair to pick up a small glass of something—probably
the same thing she was sipping in Bullers Arms. Her occasional laughs and
snickers during the competition are obviously catching to those around her.
Although it is her time to shine among her dart peers and villagers, she is
not caught up in any celebrity posturing. True, this isn't exactly the Final
Four NCAA tournament, but for Chagford it is. 'Enjoyment' and 'sharing'
are the operative words here tonight. It's great fun.*

I looked at my watch and it was almost 8:00. The smoke was starting
to get to me, so I asked Ann to save my seat and withdrew toward the
back of Jubilee Hall. I saw Chirpy talking to several fellow villagers and
smiled his way. When he made eye contact, he quickly jumped to his
feet—almost spilling his drink—and excuse himself to come over to
me. It was a wonderful gesture and between Julie, Ann and Chirpy, in a
matter of minutes I actually felt as if I were a little part of this tradition
of villager-gatherings that were centuries old, if not millennia.

Chirpy and I chatted a few minutes, about Julie and her life, about
the tournament, and a very little concerning his life as a farmer. While
the thought of asking about his coat of arms escaped my mind at the
moment, a glance to see Julie near Ann reminded me of a politeness
Chirpy exhibited at Bullers Arms that I now wanted to emulate.

"Say Chirp. What is it Julie drinks? You seem to have that one
down pat."

He took a slurp of whatever he was slurping before answering.

"She drinks tonic, with a piece of lemon in it."

Tonic and lemon. How about that. She puffed cigarettes like a chimney—the American Tobacco Institute could honor her and her neighbors with Lifetime Achievement Awards—and threw darts with the best of them. But Captain drank tonic and lemon. Wonder why?

Chirpy was suddenly involved in a three-way conversation with two other gents—I'm not quite sure how it happened, but I wasn't surprised—so I wandered over to the concession stand and ordered a tonic and lemon. After paying for it, I cautiously pushed through the crowd of people at the back of the hall and moved toward Julie, who was bending over talking to Ann. As I got closer, she noticed me coming, stood up and the cat eyes flashed me a warm smile. I held out the glass as I came closer to her and she extended her arm to accept it.

"That's very kind of you, Mark. How did you know?"

An interesting question, causing me pause for a moment. How did I know she wanted a drink? Or how was it I knew what she drank? Did it matter? Was there something I *shouldn't* know? I read into everything.

This time, however, the reading wasn't far off the dime. Or pence.

She took a sip and despite my desire to get some fresh air I hung around to talk with Ann, Ann's husband and Julie, mostly me listening about some local situation or happening. There was no pettiness in the conversation, no neighbor-bashing or one-upmanship. Just a discussion about *village things* that actually kept me interested and, dare I say, intrigued. Part of my mind sat back and marveled at how different, how refreshing this all was compared to my University of Chicago days of intellectual windmill-tilting, or my Corporate America days of character assassination and wheeling-and-dealing. Even in the suburb I called home, conversation inevitably traveled down the path to *ad hominem* remarks, social climbing, libel, slander and not a little flinging of the mud. It couldn't be helped. America is the land of the peeved and the home of the outraged. I was witnessing a friendlier, simpler way of addressing life. I liked it. George Bush's kinder, gentler nation never happened. Rodney King happened instead. And the Oklahoma City bombing. And Columbine.

Much as I wanted to stay and watch Julie be Julie before her next performance, I needed some fresh air and, it now appeared, a little time for a thunk. I knew that, much as I didn't want the night to end too quickly it nonetheless would. I had to collect my thoughts, get some perspective…and try not to become hung up on leaving both a village I was becoming attached to in body as well as in spirit, and an intriguing woman who, I was now learning this evening, had a long, checkered personal history.

Yes, I have been holding out. For besides watching the dart tournament and taking notes and video, there were moments when I talked with various villagers about all sorts of things. And don't you know but when the subject turned to Julie, all kinds of images appeared for my mind to pin to its Wall of Learning. Oh, I was learning, all right. But what exactly was it? Regrettably, I think I knew.

I left Jubilee Hall, crossed the road and jumped up on the stone wall that holds back the grass and tombstones of the churchyard from the sidewalk. The church bell was now pealing eight rings. I was glad for the fresh air—Devon has cubic miles of the stuff—after the stuffiness of the hall. It remained curious to me how the sun could still light the skies and the birds could still be singing. It was light enough to jot…so I did.

Bell Tower, St. Michael's, Chagford

Only an occasional "lawnmower" goes by as I sit here. The air continues to cool but the ever-so-slight tepid breeze prevents it from becoming chilly. I have learned a few more things about Julie, with the promise of even more from people I now know are familiar with her. Even Nick is moving into a range of understanding. I am slowly, methodically coming to terms with a fact I refused to believe existed before this night in Chagford. When I reenter Jubilee Hall, I will of course try to confirm 'the fact,' but it is unsettling and it has forced me to a thunk I have avoided thinking since first coming to this ancient village to seek out the simple life.

It is a fact I don't much like: Julie's life isn't so simple. Never was.

I look at the lofty tower of St. Michael's behind me and it peers back at me, cold, old stones and all, as if to console and comfort a sojourner who has betrayed his own fantasy with frozen, stark reality. If the tower could talk, it might say to me 'You have made a fundamental error, my son. Believe me, I have seen it all through the course of centuries. Remember, I share one of the dreams you humans spin: the dream of spiritual contentment amid a very temporal, unsettling world. Your error is common. You seek what you cannot find, yet you never cease in trying to locate it. Worse, you became attached to a picture you saw on the cover of *Time* magazine. Bummer, dude.'

Apparently this particular church steeple modernized itself along the way. The message is the same. I feel I'm about to get shoved back onto the Slippery Sidewalk of Life, without training wheels or a prayer. Yet I can't sit here all night contemplating my proverbial navel. Time to face the music.

God, I wonder what I'm going to find out about General Sir Redvers Buller, V.C.....

I pushed myself off the retaining wall. It was 8:10 and I slowly reentered Jubilee Hall. It seemed even more crowded near the back, if that were possible. Drinks and cigarettes frolicked to and fro from hand to mouth and I could see Ann and her husband, and the vacant seat they reserved for me. I retook my seat and Ann filled me in. Julie's team lost in the Three's (three players per side) but she picked up a Second Place trophy. She was now playing Mixed Pairs with her brother. We continued chatting, then I roved around and chatted some more. By the time I returned to my seat, Julie and Nick had already won the Mixed Pairs and other teams were going at it, with the scoreboard keeper tallying away at breakneck speed.

And now my mind started to put together the pieces that were Julie, from things she told me and things that others had mentioned in passing. It was a strange exercise in synthesis. I had not asked people about Julie; I simply listened to them talk and when I mentioned my 1989 story of Julie-and-the-dart and Julie-and-the-taxi, words and images were put forth. She was an admired lady, a hard-working lady, a fun lady...and a lady with a story.

A story about a very different life than the one I made up for her.

Chapter 23

A Simple Life

HERS WAS A SIMPLE LIFE, growing up in an ancient village in the post-World War II years, surrounded by the spirits of millennia past that haunted the moor, the monoliths and the gorse growing wild. She entered the world in the sunshine and fresh air of the countryside, safe and secure, few luxuries but no wants. Security of family. Stability of mother and father. Tragedy was not known, nor was stress or great anxiety. Money was adequate, opportunity available. Friends and neighbors mirrored her own existence. Her country had a proud past, without any national blight or disgrace to mar her own well-being, her own pride in the actions of her nation. Ah yes, a simple life.

This was not Julie's story, much as I might have wanted it to be. No, my symbol for the simple life was Mark-made, as I should have expected. When you find yourself in the middle of a pack of 77 million money-earning, stress-churning, simplicity-yearning Americans, you want to believe in something better. In the case of most of us, that something was supposed to be simple. Supposed to be. And when I first saw Captain darting away in Bullers Arms, I instantly transformed her into an icon of the life I wanted to have and to share with others. No problems. No worries. No national calamity whose memory constantly erupts at odd times during one's life. But it was not to be.

Florence Mary Grace Brown was born in 1921 in North Bovey, just a few miles from Chagford. In 1937, when she was a teen, a Mr. Thomas Joseph O'Reilly arrived from Ireland to work at the Fernworthy

Reservoir near Chagford. Reilly (he dropped the O) did not particularly like the English, but the War Years brought people together, and Anglo-Irish animosities—at least in Devon—were not prevalent. The Irishman met the Devonian lady and they were married. In February, 1949, the couple moved into a newly-built house in Chagford; three months later, on 29 May, Julia Mary Reilly entered the world.

Julia was to be the sixth of eight children in the Reilly family. She began her education at the local primary school (now a private residence) in Chagford. Julie, as she was called, then went on to Modern Secondary School across the road from Glendarah House. She was raised a Catholic, but her father withdrew his religious support of the church and his daughter probably followed suit.

The eighth and last Reilly born into her family was Nicholas.

Sounds uncomplicated and simple enough. But tragedy has a way of convoluting the normal and the acceptable. In 1962, Julie's father died in a traffic accident in Moretonhampstead, leaving behind a widow and eight children, including ten-month old Nick. Julie was 13 years old.

Florence Reilly was now a widow on a low income, which dramatically changed the directions her children would take with their lives. Julie left school at 15 to help support the family, without any chance of further education. The other children pitched in as well. As the children grew up, several of them remained in Chagford, living near their mother—three still do today, including Julie, and only one lives out of the country.

Life was not completely bleak, despite the sudden loss of their father, although Julie got her share of hand-me-downs. Nor should it be believed that it was dreary. But clearly the eight children did not have many of their wants or needs fulfilled. For Julie, one happy event occurred during a coach ride to a Speedway meeting. (She loved the sport.) While on the coach, she met Alan Jefferies, who was born in Oxford and whose father ran the coach. Julie and Alan were married in

1970. The Speedway outings ceased after Julie became pregnant with her daughter, Joanne.

Growing up without a father can cause youth to bring all kinds of psychological baggage to adulthood. While I am far from even pretending to understand the workings of the mind, it is not hard to imagine the difficulty of a 10-month old son losing a father and, therefore, never knowing him. Nick grew up very close to his sister, Julie, twelve years his senior, and no doubt received a lot of comfort and nurturing from her. While I guessed that he might have obtained his tattoos in the national service—I figured the earring was a more recent addition—he in fact did not serve, picking them up when tattoos were a big fad among English boys. (And, yes, tattoos seem to be decorating American hominids of both sexes today at a fast clip.) Nick spent much of his youth honing a skill at darts that appears second to none in all of Dartmoor, if not Devon or beyond. He had also become a mean football (soccer) player, playing for the Chagford First Team. He currently plays on the Globe B darts team, which helps explain their first place standing.

It was interesting to learn that Nick once worked for the Fernworthy National Rivers Authority, not dissimilar to the Fernworthy employment of his father. Today, he works for the Water Board.

If I thought him an angry young man—younger looking than his current 30 years—I could now understand why, having been robbed of a father he never knew. I could also see why he would be so protective of his sister. Keeping out of his way was something I needed to consider seriously.

Employment was, and still is, hard to come by in the West Country if you are not a property-owner—although such ownership in Devon at the beginning of the new century doesn't ensure a steady income and probably brings times of little income. As a young woman and then mother, Julie continued to work, holding a job at a general grocery store (now the sports shop). The store was owned by a man who also ran the local taxi business, and for the last 18 years Julie has been a taxi driver. Her husband drives heavy plant machines and often is away from home, going where the work is to be found. They are both fortunate to be working as Britain's recession in the early-1990s caused greater economic and social upheavals than in the United States.

Simple life....

Tragedy was not to end with the premature death of Julie's father. Her mother remarried later on, only to lose her second husband to a heart attack. Then six years ago, Julie's sister Ruth, age 46, died, leaving two children[*]. Although Julie never told me this, it seems that Ruth may have had a drinking problem that may or may not have contributed to her death. Suffice it to say that since Ruth's death, Julie's drink has been tonic and lemon.

Julie lost her father while young. Redvers Buller lost his mother while young. Anything to make of it? Only that simplicity is in the eyes of the molder. Ignore the simple truth, and it is easy to make things simple. That could no longer be the case for the Captain. As I was to discover, neither would it be for the General, or the people of Chagford.

Later on, after my return from the village to the States, I would learn that life in Chagford is far from simple. For example, Chirpy—a sheep farmer—suffered through depressed lamb and wool prices in 1992. The post-Thatcher government of 1992 appeared paralyzed, and economic hardship had become a way of life in villages large and small.

Then there is that dreadful plague that can infect and weaken the simplest of lives: crime. A survey of English youth found that 67 percent of them "think it likely they will be mugged or beaten up." One out of three girls believes there is a strong chance she will be raped or sexually assaulted. And 33 percent of all teens personally know of someone who has committed a burglary. Perhaps more worrisome is the fact that more than half are "not bothered" by shoplifting or other minor crimes. Sounds a little like the situation in their former Colonies....

[*] I would learn in April, 1993, that Ruth's husband died of cancer.

What about crime in Chagford? Since the survey showed a correlation between negative responses and working class urban youngsters, how could a remote village in Dartmoor succumb to the ravages of late-20th century crime? Well, it has, perhaps underscoring the truth that isolation is relative and that if the telephone can come to a far away place, so can crime. Here is a news item from *The Western*, a regional newspaper, dated 6 February 1987:

> "A spate of burglaries from unoccupied houses at Chagford
> has led to a police appeal to be extra vigilant.
> "The two latest incidents have led to the theft of almost
> £1000 of property from an isolated bungalow and a
> detached house."

No, a "spate of burglaries" in 1987 does not constitute a crime wave. But things are not as peaceful as they look. St. Michael's church, I learned first-hand, locks its doors to the choir screen that provides access to the altar and the resting places of John and Mary Whiddon, respectively. (I had to get permission—and a volunteer escort—to gain admission to see their stone monuments.) Even the Prouz coat of arms in the church became a victim of crime. It was recently stolen: the one I saw was a reproduction.

And the Trinity Church in Buckfastleigh on Dartmoor where Sir Arthur Conan Doyle and I visited the tomb of Richard Cabell—on separate occasions, of course—burned down in the summer of 1992. It was the work of vandals.

No, Julie's life and world were not simple—the simple I wanted so desperately to exist in Chagford. It was enough to make me want to tear up a certain issue of *Time*.

Chapter 24

Pieces That Fit

WOULD YOU LIKE SOMETHING TO DRINK, Mark? Mark?" I must have been in a daze, thinking about Julie. It was Ann's voice, and as I turned to look at her she gave me a big smile.

"Sorry, I didn't think you heard me. Can we get you something to drink?"

"No thanks, Ann. Not just yet. I'm fine."

I slowly surfaced. The crowd actually seemed a little larger, although the size of the room allowed for lots of breathing space between the individual huddles of people chatting, drinking and laughing. I noticed that dart play was still in progress. Ann and her husband excused themselves, saying they would be back in a few minutes. I smiled and resumed watching the tournament.

Suddenly a tap on the right shoulder. A turn to see the smiling face.

"Gets a bit tiring, do you think?"

Julie was sipping a drink—I suspected one or more refills since my earlier offering. I turned and looked at her directly.

"Not really. Do I look tired?"

"A little."

"I think I was zoned out. Too much excitement at once." We both smiled. "Where have you been?"

"Hmm, it *must* be exciting for you. I just competed in the Ladies Pairs."

I felt stupid. "Uh, I guess I missed it. How did you do?"

She sipped her drink. "We won."

It wasn't a cocky reply or an answer full of braggadocio. Just a statement of fact. Neither of us, apparently, were surprised with the outcome of the Ladies Pairs. The rocket-armed pitcher Dizzy Dean once said 'It ain't braggin' if you can do it.' Dizzy could do it. So could Julie.

I now wondered what the night was like for the Captain. "I assume none of this is tiring for you. But tell me, Julie, are *you* enjoying yourself?"

She paused a moment, looking past me. Then she returned her gaze and smiled.

"Yes I am. And I suppose you mean more than just the tournament."

"In a way."

"To some it must look a very mundane life," she began, staring at her glass. "And to some very boring. But for all of it, I'm a very contented person and wouldn't want it any differently."

She must have seen my face change expression, for her eyebrows went up into her bangs as if to ask what was the matter.

"I kind of viewed your life—and life in Chagford—as a very simple, rewarding life. Personally rewarding. But it's not free of its hardships and hard times, is it? It's not…it's not all that simple."

She thought a moment. "No. No, I wouldn't see Chagford as free of problems. In fact, I suspect many are similar to yours, but perhaps on a smaller scale. Still, there is a lot of caring and a lot of support among the people who live here."

She took a sip and swallowed quickly. Then another smile.

We now heard some cheering at the front of the room where the tournament was in progress. I squinted to see what was happening.

"What's the cheering about?"

"See that chap throwing darts? He has to hit a 'double one' to win."

I saw him slowly extend his arm back, staring intently at the dart board. The front part of the room became very quiet. It was obviously an impossible shot…to me. Although I was a distance away, I whispered to Julie "Do you think he'll make it?"

She turned and gave me a big grin. "Yes."

He did. We spend millions and billions on guidance systems that can't hit a barn in an empty field—didn't all but a few of our Patriot missiles miss what they were aimed at during the Gulf War? And here some bloke from an ancient village nails down an uncanny shot *because he had to.* I want my tax dollars refunded!

I looked at Julie and was hit with the desire to ask her about the pictures that had run through my mind, the ones about the little girl born in Chagford five months before my birth in Chicago; the little girl growing up in an environment completely foreign to my own. But those Celtic gods were determined not to make it easy for me, despite their spasmodic lapses into kindness. Someone called to her and she acknowledged that she would be right there.

"It's Chirp. I'll be right back."

"Okay."

She stopped in her retreat and looked back at me. "Oh by the way. I asked Chirp if he owned some kind of jacket or sports coat with an insignia or heraldry on it. He said you have a good memory. He does have one, and he's worn it to the pub."

I must have grinned from ear to ear. "Is it his family coat of arms?"

"Chirpy with a coat of arms? No. Chirp's a Buffalo. You know your Masons?"

I nodded affirmative.

"This is a step down." Julie turned and left.

Her words about Chagfordians supporting each other stayed with me, and I wondered if my knowledge about Julie's less-than-simple life had totally brought me down about the village and my quest. So I looked around, then stood up and walked back to the concession window. I ordered a tonic and lemon.

As I walked along the sides of the room I picked up conversations, especially between young and old, which were not infrequent. There was a lot of wisdom being imparted here—wisdom from ages past, exchange between those who knew and those who needed to know.

When I approached the dart-playing area, I also saw encouragement from old to young, from the pros who could hit "double ones" without flinching, to the novices missing terribly and letting their teammates down...at least, that's how they wanted to feel.

But what was it that I heard yelled out as players tried their best? The phrase was "Good Darts." Regardless of the score or where the darts landed, everyone was part of the whole, and they were constantly reminded of that fact. There was a togetherness, keeping the traditions of the village going and flowing, from generation to generation. It wasn't important what you did for a living. Work was but a means to the end of the day. And performance wasn't what counted. It was contact, being, participating. In a word, Chagford.

It was also cooperation. Remember my mentioning those narrow lanes throughout Dartmoor that can barely fit one car? So what happens when another car approaches from the opposite direction? In the States, we might call our insurance agents, police officers and lawyers. In Dartmoor, each driver looks to see who is closest to one of many slight outcroppings of road in the lane constructed at odd intervals for just such occurrences. The closest driver backs up or pulls forward to it, allowing the other drive to pass. As the eyes of the drivers meet— they always do—each tips a hand or forefinger to the other in mutual thanks. Without such cooperation, people could not get about their lives in Dartmoor.

People here, I realized, took time to care. There was comforting and encouragement and support in this old, old village. It *was* a different kind of life from what many Americans experienced. I was surrounded by it in Chagford; I just forgot to remind myself that it was there.

I suddenly found myself in the company of Ann, who stood next to me and started to point something out.

"See those two men? They're farmers. Good men."

"Like Chirpy."

"Yes. They put in long days, you know. And they're always late."

"What do you mean?"

"Just that they're late for events and things. You have to tell them to come one-half hour before they're due, or they won't make it on time. Did you see Julie's Threes team?"

"Yes I did."

"Well, her two partners are farmers. They almost didn't make it on time."

We laughed and I now saw Nick step up for a competition. Ann told me it was the Men's Singles, and that Nick was expected to win. A thought popped into my head as I watched the men begin their competition.

"Nick's married, isn't he Ann?"

"Yes. He was married about three years ago. Amanda."

"Is she here?"

Ann looked around. "I don't see her."

Curious. I would have thought that when you're married to the fastest dart-slinger in the West Country, the least you could do is show up for the Men's Singles. As it happened, Amanda did arrive right before Nick won the event. Amanda is a naturally-permed blonde, I think. I would learn later that her sister, Vicki, married Pierre the Canadian, whose wedding was the cause for the party at Bullers Arms where I saw many of the same characters from my 1989 visit, including Julie.

Although Amanda and Nick made eye contact, there wasn't much verbal exchange between them after he was declared the champ. I wondered how difficult it would be to get to know Nick. Who knows, maybe Amanda has been wondering that for some time.

Ann and I returned to our seats and I checked my watch. It was 10:55 PM. Incredible! I thought I had come back from my thunk outside just minutes ago, not almost three hours. A gentleman now walked to the front of the room to get everyone's attention, which took a minute or so. He then began handing out checks for money raised by the 13 darts teams: £225 to the Recreational Trust; £225 to the Health Center; £150 to the Football Club; and £75 to the Playschool. It fit right in with all that I had observed in Chagford since bumping into Bullers Arms 30 months ago. Lots of caring. Lots of helping. Lots of taking time for others. No one had much money, but you gave what you could…because that's what it meant to be a Chagfordian.

This took all of five minutes. Then there was a stir in the room, as if the Second Coming was on stand-by while our television stations identified themselves…well, maybe not quite that dramatic. But when Ann bent over to tell me it was 'raffle time,' I felt I really wasn't that far off on the Enthusiasm Scale. Numbered tickets were drawn from a basket or hat—I couldn't quite tell—and the Mistress of Ceremonies announced lots of winners, who started claiming those fruit baskets and four-packs of ale. Meanwhile, Julie came over to join us, sitting behind me, raffle tickets in hand.

A dilemma developed when a number was called and no one had a ticket for it. What to do. As I sat there, all innocent and wide-eyed, the Mistress apparently eyed *moi*, walked over to me and asked me to pick a new winner. I hadn't felt this nervous since awaiting the baton in the 4-man relay in my high school conference track meet. That bad! To make matters worse, Julie said to me in a low voice "Make it a yellow ticket with MY number." Well, fair is fair, and I did close my eyes the split second I reached in and grabbed a ticket. It was, in fact, yellow. But when Mistress called out the number, I was almost greeted with a coronary as Ann, seated right next to me, shouted out "That's me!"

It sure looked like the fix was in, but neither hugs and kisses nor accusations were forthcoming. Ann won a tin of pipe tobacco.

It was now time to give out the trophies for the year, and I decided it was a good point to pop out the old note pad.

I'm still in shock that all 10 competitions are over already. A village elder of sorts is now getting ready to hand out the hardware to the winners. As he does so, Julie comes over to Ann and me, asking if we can reserve a chair for the trophies. No problem. I didn't turn down Michael Jordan when he asked me for a chair for his two gold Olympic medals, MVP awards, NCAA and NBA championship rings et al—or at least I wouldn't have if he'd requested it.

Globe B—Nick's team—cleaned up. Nick and Julie are now called to the front to receive their first place trophies for the Under-and-Over. By the collection of awards on the multilevel table, I can tell it's going to be a long ceremony. I'll just keep this short.

Nick bagged numerous trophies, including that first place for Men's Singles. He brought them over to the chair—no, he didn't look at me— walking past Amanda on the way. Julie won three first place trophies: Under and Over, Mixed Pairs and Ladies Pairs. Also that second place for Threes. (Wonder if the farmers on Julie's Threes team had been tired out from trying to get to Jubilee Hall on time.) The trophies were now overflowing the seat and placed on the floor. I felt like the Keeper of the Crown Jewels.

Now that the trophies are gone...

I stopped writing. The watch said 11:28 PM. We all stood up and I helped Julie collect the booty. Ann then shook my hand and said good-bye; I didn't get to say good-bye to her husband. Nick was chatting further up from where we stood, and I presumed he would shortly retrieve the results of his skill this evening.

And then Julie kissed my cheek, said good-bye and wished me a fair journey the rest of the way. "I'll look forward to getting that from you," she said, referring to the notes I hoped to send her for correction and annotation. I said farewell as well, about as anticlimactic as ever a story envisioned by Margaret Mitchell! But what do you expect when you dream up a reality and then you face it, only to experience the anguish of separating the reality from the dream? I know, I know—that's easy for *me* to say.

So I departed Jubilee Hall, and I was not disappointed at my findings for the 24+ hours spent in and around Chagford. No, the simple life of Julie and her companion villagers was not that simple, from Nick's apparent marital strain and the deaths of a sister and of a father he never knew to Ann's second husband (as I later learned) to personal tragedy, personal need, lost opportunity and all the rest. But it was a good life here, based on the continual reaffirmation of friendship, togetherness and the realization that 'everyone was in this for the long haul.' As Americans turn inward to their multimedia existence of fax-phone-TV-radio-CD-DVD-VCR-Request movies-Nintendo-internet-and God-knows-what-else being invented while this is being written, Chagford still looked outward, to its people.*

In this respect it was simple, and desirable. My burned-out generation would not be disappointed with this village in the moor...unless they conjured the dream I dreamed and aimed for perfection. Dangerous things, dreams. Fortunately for me, certain pieces of my dream fit well in Chagford.

---

* Hard as it is for me to believe, American households now watch over 7 hours of television a day. That's an incredible amount of non-verbal activity, on par with sleeping (and perhaps just as productive). The internet will rob more time, leaving very little for actual, personal contact between people. In fact, a concentrated study by Carnegie Mellon University concluded that frequent internet users experienced high levels of depression and loneliness, witnessed a decline of interaction with family members and a reduction in their circle of friends, and became more and more involved in "building shallow relationships, leading to an overall decline in feeling of connection to other people."

Chapter 25

The March into Hell

NOW THAT MY VISIT WAS AT AN END, I realized my efforts to unravel the "simple life" in Chagford would necessarily shift to the general, whose pub was up the road. After all, if Julie and her village could no longer represent that pristine, perfect symbol of the life I had dreamed up, it meant that, more likely than not, the people of Chagford were connected to a past that defied simplicity as well—an albatross necktie not dissimilar to the Vietnam Syndrome most Boomers are reminded of at odd intervals.* Of course the village's past had no such notoriety, as I would learn later on, unless an occasional wife purchase or the collapse of a building carried scars for generations, which I thought unlikely. No, it would have to be something on a national level that nonetheless found representation in Chagford. And I think I knew where to find it.

So as I walked back to the market square I decided to stroll up to the pub bearing the general's name. Bullers Arms. The moon was in the wrong place for illuminating the old building, and the dark letters announcing the pub's name blended into the dark shadow of night. I leaned against the

---

* As mentioned earlier, the Vietnam War would continue to haunt non-participant President Clinton and, therefore, his generation. Thousands of Vietnam veterans wrote Clinton requesting he not attend a Memorial Day service at the Vietnam wall memorial because it would be "hypocritical." Other vets disagreed, saying the wall is a place of healing, not anger. None of the Boomers will ever fully heal. Bosnia, as was noted, has also been referred to as a 'potential Vietnam.' The same fear was raised about possible troop deployment to Kosovo.

building across the street from the pub and let the breeze blow against my face. It was a cold breeze now, and I faintly sensed the salty sea in the air, carried over the moor from the English Channel.

It was the cold Channel air that greeted General Sir Redvers Buller as he stood on the deck of the *Dunottar Castle* in Southampton Docks on a fateful Saturday: 14 October 1899. His train had arrived at 4:00 PM from Waterloo station in London, and the general, who was now 60 years old, had walked up the gang-plank to the cheers and well wishes of the crowds of English men and women who had come to see him off with his army. According to Thomas Pakenham, whose definitive study of the Boer War makes for fascinating reading, Buller wore a long dark overcoat and felt hat and his "red face with the bulldog jowl, and the sprig of Devonshire violets in his button-hole" made an impressive sight for the crowd and the primitive movie cameras recording the event. Parts of the crowd sang 'Rule, Britannia' and similar patriotic songs; others yelled out 'Give it to the Boers!', 'Bring back a piece of Kruger's whiskers!', and 'Remember Majuba!' Accompanying the general were a cadre of war correspondents, not unlike the wars of today.

One of them was a bold, young, reckless upstart named Winston Churchill.

Buller must have had a lot on his mind. He was well aware of the mission in his charge, of the history of the conflict, of his trepidations about how to proceed, or even if to proceed at all. He might have wondered why his life had come to this—this expedition that would end up being a last gasp of empire for Great Britain. Buller had warned his superiors, had pleaded with the government not to undertake what he was now being ordered to do. One can only speculate how he would have felt if he knew that all the accomplishments, glory and success of a lifetime would be compromised and dashed to pieces in 118 days. Might that stiff upper lip have quivered just a little?

It was this journey into what was to become a hell for many that I would begin to learn about after returning to Chicago from Chagford.

Had I stopped with Buller's life after the Khartoum campaign, I could have fitted his pub into my mind as merely a symbol of a British hero, nothing more, nothing less. But a clue and my curiosity prevented me from *covering up* what might lurk behind the story of the general. For in wondering if the people of Chagford had a ghost of sorts like my generation's Vietnam, the name *Ladysmith* stuck in my mind since its first mention by Keith, proprietor of the pub. He said it like a war-minded World War II soldier might say Tobruk or Normandy or the Battle of the Bulge. Or, for the Baby Boomers, maybe the Tet Offensive or the DMZ or Saigon: phrases and places that were all too familiar to millions of Americans, young and old, during the Vietnam war. Ladysmith— what was Ladysmith?

In order to answer that question in a meaningful way—much as an explanation of Vietnam would require more than a passing paragraph—I needed to understand the mindset of the British government in 1899 and why they would send a hero of the Zulu wars back to South Africa with the largest army they ever mustered. Clearly, the reasoning originated from the same source of grief plaguing Americans who cringe when they see the black marble monument to the American dead of Vietnam in Washington, D.C.: *historical baggage*, never unpacked, always ready to travel wherever you go. For the British, that baggage was marked HOLLAND.

I promise to spare you the many thousands of pages written on the Boer War—not a few of which I explored and borrowed freely from one summer.[*] Rather, a few pointed paragraphs—14, to be exact—will allow an explanation of why General Buller set sail in mid-October to begin a war that, for all intents and purposes, *had* to begin. And as I have come

---

[*] There are several good books on the Boer War. The aforementioned one by Thomas Pakenham lays out the whole tragedy in fascinating detail, and includes information never used before. (Pakenham, eldest son of the Earl and Countess of Longford, discovered letters written by Buller hidden under the billiard table at the general's house in Downes in Devon.) Other books of interest are Ladysmith by Ruari Chisholm, and The Boer War by Denis Judd.

to learn about most wars, the roots of this one lay in fear and in economic rivalry. For Vietnam, the fear was communism and the economics seem to point to oil and gas reserves and a military-industrial complex in need of revenues, although it is more complex than that. For the Boer War, try imperial supremacy, ethnic hatred, diamonds and gold.

American students receive a brief basting of colonial history in school, with the Dutch squeaking into the lesson as fairly good navigators and the founders of a shipping station at the Cape of Good Hope in South Africa in 1652. But there's much more. As time passed, the Dutch settlers at the Cape came to resent the ever-encroaching Europeans, perhaps as the American colonists grew less fond of the British. These Dutch began to call themselves *Afrikaners*, with the poorest of them tending to be itinerant farmers called trekboers, or simply *Boers.* They also weren't too happy with British complaints that the Boers treated the native Africans poorly.[*] Then in 1834—almost 30 years before Honest Abe's emancipation speech in America—the British ordered the slaves of the Dutch settlers freed.

This policy—which arguably could be viewed as hypocrisy by an empire that enslaved whole continents for gain and power—set into motion a series of events that would lead to General Buller's departure from Southampton at the end of the century. In 1835, the Great Trek of some 5,000 Boers and as many black Africans began. Over a two year period, the Boers moved beyond the outskirts of Cape Colony and founded a new one: Natal, which the British soon seized. However, the British recognized the independence of two newer Boer republics, Transvaal and the Orange Free State. It might have stayed that way short-term, with all four entities coexisting, if not for two discoveries: diamonds and gold.

---

[*] It need hardly be stated that several parallels emerge between the current story and U.S. history just from this initial plunge into the colonial waters of South African history. Much as the British were sanctimonious about Dutch treatment of blacks, they had little qualms about mistreating and abusing the Dutch! Keep reading....

In 1870, a Diamond Rush commenced in and around Kimberley on
the borders of the Cape Colony and into the Orange Free State. The
Rush made millionaires out of several British speculators, including
Cecil Rhodes. The British, never at a loss for ways to hang onto an
investment, quickly incorporated the diamond-laden Free State into the
Cape Colony. Meanwhile, Rhodes helped found a new colony north of
Transvaal, Rhodesia. Rhodes—he of Rhodes Scholarship renown—had
an ego the size of Cheop's pyramid and then some.

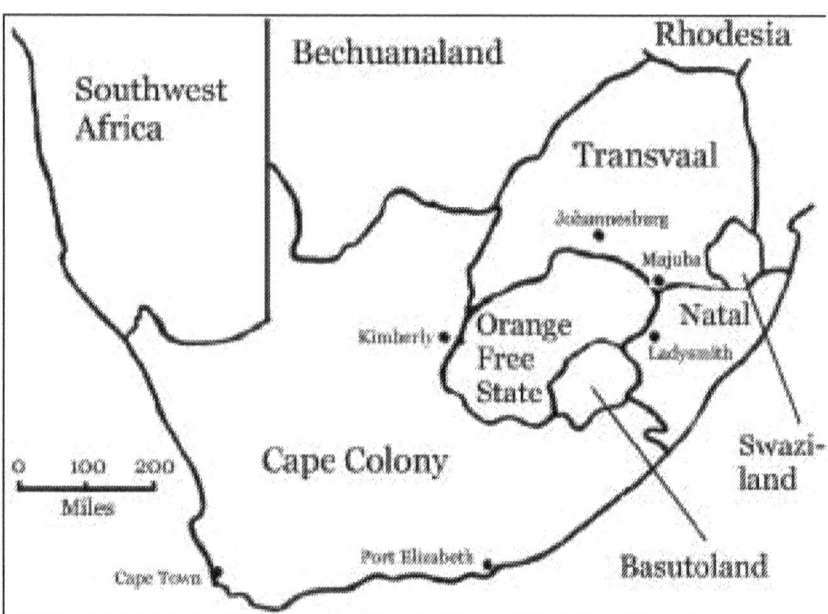

All these colonies may seem confusing, so you might want to take a
peek at the map. I kept it simple.

The British laid off for awhile to enlist the help of the Boers in fighting
a common enemy: the Zulu. Thus began the Zulu Wars in 1879, along
with a debate in Britain led by Prime Minister William Gladstone's
government over the wisdom of continuing to pay for colonial rule. The

Boers, however, cared little for debates, and in 1880 revolted against the British occupation of the Transvaal. There now began warfare between a colonizing empire (Britain) and the descendants of colonists from a minuscule but obstinate rival (Holland).

Then in 1881, the British received a shock: their armies were defeated by the Boers at Majuba. The Boers retained their independence—Britain still ran foreign policy for the colony—and two years later Transvaal named a president: Paul Kruger. Majuba was a defeat akin to the Alamo for Americans, and the British had long memories.

In 1886, a Gold Rush now superseded diamond fever, with a major discovery in the Transvaal hills called the Rand. (Yes, the origins of the Krugerrand!) The new wealth-seekers to the region were adventurous British immigrants and some Australian and European prospectors, collectively called *Uitlanders*, who now clashed with the Boers in Transvaal while looking for gold. The British government again began to consider seizing Transvaal from the Boers…considered, and waffled. By 1895, Rhodes and the British High Commissioner for South Africa, Sir Alfred Milner, quietly started lobbying for war. Milner was also the Lt. Governor of Cape Colony, and he saw a successful war as a means to establish Britain firmly in South Africa and in full control of the area's riches.

Nothing happened. The "nothing" lasted all through 1895, to the dismay and anger of Rhodes. Not one to take things lying down, he now supported a secret raid into the city of Johannesburg in Transvaal, both to take it from the Boers with the help of the Australian and European Uitlanders living there, and to provoke a war between Britain and the Dutch colonists.

On 29 December 1895, a surreptitious raid into Johannesburg took place, led by a surprised adventurer named Dr. Jameson—surprised because when he entered the city with several hundred men on horseback, no Uitlanders rose in revolt to support him. Instead, the raiders were greeted by Boer soldiers, who captured Jameson and his men. Now began a *cover up* similar to those during the Vietnam War and the later scandals of Watergate and Iran-Contra. For though Rhodes supported Jameson's Raid with full government knowledge and acquiescence, Her Majesty's ministers now distanced themselves from the affair. During the trials of the raiders in Victorian courts, Rhodes actually endeavored to get Jameson to take the whole blame! Britain now saw its power wane in South Africa and Rhodes, who had been Cape Prime Minister, was forced to resign.

Her Majesty's Government were not amused, much as they were appalled at Majuba 14 years earlier. British troops continued to prod parts of Transvaal in the years after Jameson's Raid until it came to a head on 10 October 1899. President Kruger now demanded the removal of all British soldiers from Transvaal or war would commence. Kruger gave the British 24 hours to act. The British didn't. On 11 October, the deadline expired. On 12 October, the Boers invaded Natal with 23,000 men. Kruger was but the leader at a point in time when, given preceding historical events, war was inevitable.

There were 10,000 soldiers under the command of the British in South Africa, along with 5,000 reserves. All they required was a directive from Queen Victoria's government and a leader to take charge. Both would materialize in less than 48 hours when General Sir Redvers Buller set sail from Southampton to Capetown.

The British people—bolstered by the media—viewed the beginning of the Boer conflict as a just cause. The buzzword in late-Victorian England was *Imperial Unity*, and Buller possessed the broad shoulders required to get the job done and bring order to the region. Much like the United States and its early view of the enemy in Vietnam, the British had a low opinion of the Boers. True, the Boers had kicked their bums at Majuba almost 20 years earlier—the French, we might recall, were unceremoniously tossed out of Vietnam in the mid-1950s. But that was then, this is now and those in defeat later forget. The British expected the "war" to be over in a matter of weeks. After all, we're talking Great Britain, ruler of the waves.

The media agreed. Winston Churchill, standing near the general on the deck of the ship, wrote "Absolute tranquillity lapped the peaceful ship and Buller trod the deck each day with sphinx-like calm." At 25, Churchill had wangled a £250/month job as war correspondent for the *Morning Post*. (Buller, as general and Commander-In-Chief, earned £200/month!) The reporter would now feed the angst of his nation, which expected valor, excitement and a quick end to the struggle for British superiority. Well, perhaps not too quickly: Churchill did order several crates of wine for what he told his editor would be about a four-month stint in Africa. Maybe the extended timetable was a way to justify a large quantity of spirits. Or perhaps he believed that hostilities wouldn't break out in earnest until after Christmas.

Whether Buller agreed with the media or his compatriots, he surely was not equipped for a quick sweep. He had bad maps, absolutely no strategy and Winston Churchill on board—not a good sign for a major undertaking. A British staff member in South Africa, who later would be under siege by the Boers, wrote of the British mentality about the whole affair: "They speak of a British brigade being able to take on five times their number in Boers, which is silly rot." Indeed, when it was all over, even the ultra-jingoistic Rudyard Kipling painfully noted the war gave the British "no end of a lesson." And yet the papers and the public felt that the "Crisis of the Transvaal" would be over by Christmas.

If Buller enjoyed his sea voyage or loathed the thought of what lay ahead, he would be helpless either way to do anything between his departure on the 14th and his arrival on the 31st. During that time, events would unfold that eventually sealed his fate, as well as the destiny of the British Empire. For while the general "trod the deck," battles and skirmishes were taking place in South Africa that would lead to Mournful Monday, so-called because on Monday, 30 October, the British would succumb to a new kind of warfare similar to what

American soldiers faced in Vietnam more than a half-century later. And on that Monday, the day before Buller arrived in South Africa to end the war by Christmas, many British soldiers would die, surrender and face a humiliating siege at a strategic town only 30 miles from Rorke's Drift and the region where Buller won his Victoria Cross 20 years earlier.

That strategic town, in Natal, was named after the Spanish bride of Sir Harry Smith, who seized the colony for the British in 1843. It was called Lady Smith. It was the name I had heard in Bullers Arms. It would be the name that led to the decline and fall of Sir Redvers Buller and the creation of a nation's ghost.

Chapter 26

Ladysmith

IF A PARALLEL IS TO BE MADE between the Boer War and Vietnam, it is important to follow the events of the former, especially since they are virtually unknown to American Baby Boomers and those on both demographic sides of that prodigious group. True, the story of lessons learned in Chagford will be momentarily interrupted. But to understand the 'symbol' of Buller and his pub as a national tragedy that can haunt a culture as Vietnam does in America, we must accompany the general and put ourselves in the thick of it, if only briefly. In this way, we shall emerge fully equipped to make a final assessment of the simple life and what it might mean.

Now before you start to think "Uh oh, these upcoming pages look suspiciously like chapters in a history book—'Oh—my—God, I HATE history'", take a quick cleansing breath. This is not history as most of us know it, the stuff boringly taught and written about by historians who cloud the fact that history is fascinating all by itself. This is a story. It is the story of a man whose fate was caught up in events beyond his control. The same thing happened to 77 million Baby Boomers, who as well got caught up in something they did not seek out nor ask for: Vietnam. And remember: we take the word 'history' from the Greek word *historia*, or inquiry. We are about to make a momentous inquiry.

Let's begin unconventionally: The very first Bulls basketball game I attended reaffirmed a lesson in how to study events that were previously unknown to me. As I lined up to turn in my ticket and find a seat, I passed a table covered with neatly-stacked piles of game programs, listing the names of each player in the game that evening, their biographies, statistics and other information relevant to basketball. The man selling the programs boomed out a most compelling argument to acquire one: "Get your programs. They're just a bunch of tall guys running around the floor without a program." Too true. And too important to forget when jumping into past events and happenings without any familiarity of the names, dates or places.

If you've made it with me to this point, you should have a passing memory of Redvers Buller, V.C. and his background. It should also be clear that South Africa was the venue for his success, and I have hinted it will as well be the place of his undoing. Sir Alfred Milner was mentioned as the imperialistic Lt. Governor in the Cape Colony; other names such as Jameson were useful for the moment but can now be saved-to-disk or deleted from your neural RAM memory…at least for the purposes of the present journey. As with any major event, there are numerous players, places, plots and subplots. Since analyzing the Boer War in gross detail is (fortunately) not in the cards for either of us, suffice it to say that only a few more names will drop in for a short visit to explain what is happening. Perhaps why.

One that will recur, however—besides our friend, Winston—is General Sir George White. While Sir Redvers was winning his Victoria Cross in the Zulu Wars, Sir George picked up a V.C. during the Afghan War (1878–80). In October of 1899, with Buller on his way to jump into the fray that would become the Boer War, White found himself in the middle of it. White was in charge of the town of Ladysmith, which at this time had 21,500 mouths to feed, including 13,500 officers and men of the imperial army along with Natal volunteers, 5,500 white civilians, 2,500 Africans and Indians…and Buller's prospective chief-of-staff and all of the intelligence officers. When the Boers declared war on 12 October, White had sent out the cavalry from Ladysmith to meet the invading Boer armies. It was the beginning of the end for the town.

After the first two battles, both British and U.S. newspapers began writing about the brutality of the British, a "savagery" much as the Americans were sometimes accused of in Vietnam. Savage or not, through a series of blunders the British were forced to retreat back to Ladysmith, and the Boers now amassed an army around the town. On 30 October 1899—Mournful Monday as it was called in the press—the British army at Ladysmith tried to attack the Boers.

It was now that the British would learn about 20th century warfare. The Boers used commando tactics, which the British had never faced during their neat, proper, face-to-face warfare activities of the 19th century. One lieutenant at Ladysmith wrote to his father: "You don't know what it means shooting at a Boer. He is behind a rock and all you can see is his rifle sticking out." The British now faced something different—snipers and guerrilla warfare—as Americans did in the jungles and swamps of Vietnam. Many British died at the mercy of these Boer tactics, and by the end of the day 37 officers and 917 men surrendered to the Boers. General White accepted the blame and Ladysmith was under siege.

Under siege and in deep trouble. Those 21,500 people had only 50 days food supply, and only 30 days for the horses. Worse, Ladysmith had a 14-mile perimeter to be guarded. White's strategy was rather feeble: Survive the artillery bombardments from the Boers, try to hold off surrendering to the enemy...and wait for Buller. The Boers were of a slightly different mind. While they could have followed White's retreat back to Ladysmith and taken the town, the Boers feared it would have resulted in a great loss of life for both the British and themselves. Moreover, the Boers fully expected the British to surrender. Their strategy was thus to step up bombarding the town to facilitate an early defeat while attacking other British enclaves. It was a bombardment the British would experience again 40 years later from German airplanes and missiles, only in London, not Ladysmith.

Mournful Monday bolstered the Boer spirits. The next day, the Orange Free State surprised the British by also declaring war. Alfred Milner in the Cape Colony was now jumping up and down about a siege in Kimberly—where old Cecil Rhodes was demanding relief with the threat of doing his own negotiations with the Boers. Milner also feared a possible Boer uprising in his own colony. He was aware that one of the younger Boer generals, Louis Botha, didn't agree with the siege mentality of his peers at Ladysmith. Botha wanted quick victories; he wasn't going to wait long.

So General Buller walked down the gangplank at Capetown on 31 October and into a nightmare facing him in broad daylight. At least it would be a nightmare with frequent relief, for following him off the ship was his hip-bath, a full-sized bed and many bottles of champagne. When Buller met a visibly-broken Sir Alfred Milner, who dumped the whole situation on the general's lap, Buller replied "So now I am expected to conquer all South Africa—not just two small Boer republics." This would no doubt be a trick, since much of his army was tied up at Ladysmith along with his strategists and chief-of staff.

Buller needed more troops, and his only hope was that the Boers wouldn't press their advantage too quickly. Moreover, while the square jaw showed the world an emotionless, stern appearance often mistaken for arrogance, Buller could be emotional and deeply worried. Writing to his younger brother, he said "I am in the tightest place I have ever been in, and the worst of it is I think none of my creating."

We might want to digress long enough to move along young Winston, who was to become a literary John Wayne of sorts during the war. Churchill bounded off the ship with Buller on 31 October and immediately headed into Natal for "adventure." It didn't take long to locate. While on a train with 164 soldiers, he was ambushed by Louis Botha and his Boers, who rolled a large rock onto the tracks and began bombarding the train with artillery. Churchill loved it: "Nothing was so thrilling as this: to wait and struggle among those clanging, rending iron boxes, with the repeated explosion of the shells and the artillery." Not my idea of thrill, but that was Winston and this was the final chapter of the British Empire. Churchill, for all his enthusiasm, was captured and taken prisoner. He would escape several weeks later and eventually weasel his way back into Natal during the relief of Ladysmith. The Boers offered a small reward for his capture, almost as an afterthought. Winston would later be mentioned as a Victoria Cross candidate for his "bravery." The Boers referred to him as a "little bit of a newspaperman."

Some 21,000 troops embarked from England for Africa in early November, and by the end of the month 50,000 had arrived for battle. Because of the various fronts opened up by the Boers, plus pressure from a hysterical Sir Alfred who feared for imperial prestige and honor, Buller decided he had to split his troops to fight on several fronts, with the main force going to the relief of Ladysmith. On 7 November, he was 25 miles from the town. He set out on 22 November and said he would relieve it in two weeks.

It would take three months.

Meanwhile, General White and his troops at Ladysmith were hungry but not idle.[*] On 7 December, a British column slithered out of town undetected and climbed Gun Hill to take out two pieces of Boer artillery. Another raid took place four nights later. The next day, White received a message from Buller. The general was marching with 18,000 men and said he would avoid the Boer stronghold at Colenso and veer around it to go the 17 miles to Ladysmith. This kept with Buller's warning to the British government long before his departure that British troops should not go north of the Tugela River to Colenso to risk defeat at the hands of the Boers.

---

[*] Lord Wolseley, Buller's mentor and "ring" leader whom we met earlier, was of the opinion that General White's blunder—which led to the encirclement of Ladysmith—required White to be relieved of his post. Buller had reservations about sacking White upon first arriving in Capetown. But eventually he supported Wolseley, saying White should be relieved of duty only after Ladysmith was relieved.

Then on 13 December, Buller changed his mind. Why? Some specu-
lated that he would be farther from his supplies, and Buller was the soldier's soldier. There had also been reversals two days earlier by other
British generals who had engaged the Boers in battle. Others thought he
was concerned about losing communications. Regardless, Buller now
contradicted his own thinking and decided on a frontal assault. The
decision, added to his past reversals and several to come, would earn
him the moniker General *Reverse* Buller.

On 14 December, Buller moved out…and Louis Botha anticipated it.
Buller split his troops and as they began to cross the Tugela River they
were ambushed. Many of the British big guns were abandoned. Buller
was hurt in the ribs from a shell explosion. He may also have been
deeply demoralized, for he fired off a telegram to White at Ladysmith
telling him to make "the best terms you can" if Buller couldn't relieve
the town in a reasonable time. This telegram later would be taken out
of context and used by the media and his enemies to suggest that Buller
wanted Ladysmith to surrender, contributing to his decline and fall at
the end of the war.

Colenso was an unmitigated disaster and Her Majesty's government
once again were not amused. The toll: 1,100 British soldiers killed or
wounded and the loss of 10 guns. Dr. Kay, one of the residents at
Ladysmith during the siege and later an avowed enemy of Buller,
recorded "there was heavy firing Colenso way; it turns out Buller was
repulsed and lost ten guns. Very serious for us, as no one knows when
we shall be relieved. No one believes in our generals. If what the
Russians said about our armies in the Crimea [1848] was true, we are
an army of lions led by asses."

On 18 December, Buller was relieved of his supreme command in
South Africa by Lord Roberts, V.C. (It should be noted that Lord
Robert's son, Captain F.H.S. "Freddy" Roberts, was among those killed
at Colenso, trying to save the British guns.) Roberts' chief-of-staff
would be Lt.-General Horatio Herbert Kitchener of Khartoum fame. At

the same time, Queen Victoria announced to the world "We are not interested in the possibilities of defeat; they do not exist."

The Boers were not interested in what the irritated English Queen had to say. Beginning on 16 December, they commenced the steady bombardment of Ladysmith in earnest, and many British casualties resulted. On Christmas Day, however, the Boers filled their shells with Christmas puddings and a note "With the Compliments of the Seasons." And all the while, the world media played up either a David-and-Goliath theme of the British against the Dutch or a 'Britain must win' chant, fostering both pro-war and anti-war sentiment globally. It was not unlike the Vietnam War.

Churchill, newly escaped from the Boers and now on a ship sailing to Durban, was of the pro-war party that believed in victory first, negotiation second. In a report he cabled to the *Morning Post,* he said "There is plenty of work here for a quarter of a million men, and South Africa is well worth the cost in blood and money." He ridiculed his fellow countrymen for not lending more support. "Are the gentlemen of England all fox-hunting?" he asked. "Why not an English Light Horse? For the sake of our manhood, our devastated Colonists, and our dead soldiers, we must persevere with the war."

The Crimean War fought with a British "army of lions led by asses." "Why not an English Light Horse?" Lots of irony in these two observations by a doctor under siege and a journalist under delusions of grandeur. For while Buller would take all the blame for the disasters befalling the relief of Ladysmith, there was something else operating that was reminiscent of the Crimean War and the foolish *Charge of the Light Brigade,* which brought death to so many young men of England. Buller was in command of an insufficient number of troops at the height of a continuing feud between the Lord Roberts' inner "ring" of officers and the Wolseley/Buller ring. St. John Brodrick, who became British War Minister in 1900, later compared the battles between Roberts and Buller to those between Lord Lucan and Lord Cardigan that led to the horrendous Charge of the Light Brigade. Historian Pakenham notes "Certainly this astonishing War Office feud [Roberts *vs.* Buller] at the end of the nineteenth century explains much that would otherwise be inexplicable in Britain's bungled preparations for [the Boer] war and her reversals during it. And in the end it was Buller, to his credit, who successfully hammered out the new tactics needed when a nineteenth-century army had to fight a twentieth-century war."

Unfortunately for the moment and for many years to come, no one in Britain knew that. Although replaced as Commander-in-Chief, Buller still commanded the Natal Front. He now took 25,000 men to a new base on the way to relieve Ladysmith. (He was to be joined by Winston Churchill, who was now a lieutenant—no surprise—in the South African Light Horse after receiving permission to join from Buller.) Sir Redvers wanted to wait until he was fully provisioned despite being only 16 miles from Ladysmith—always thinking of his soldiers, he saw a need for his men to be rested and well-fed before advancing. He also knew the Boers were hiding among ridges and hills, including a massive buttress known as Spion Kop, which was Dutch for 'Lookout Hill.'

Then on 16 January 1900, Buller gave his orders. Sir Charles Warren, who was no friend of Buller, was put in charge of the main operation. Warren was also not a bright commander. (He held dress rehearsals for the coming battle in full view of the Boers!) Buller wanted a left flank attack; Warren ignored it and refused to release the cavalry to surprise the Boers—unbeknownst to Buller, Warren had secret instructions from the War Office to succeed the general in the event Buller was killed! Buller was furious, but he and Warren patched up differences enough to agree on attacking Spion Kop directly during the early hours of 24 January.

It was too late. Any advantage was lost and the attack was disastrous, with the Boers, led by Louis Botha, bombarding the British with artillery from three sides. There was frequent hand-to-hand combat.

Buller couldn't get his communications through, his commanders did not coordinate their efforts and many British soldiers perished on their way up to the summit. One observer wrote "I shall always have it in my memory—that acre of massacre."*

Churchill decided to climb Spion Kop to get a better look, noting that he passed "about two hundred [corpses] while I was climbing up." It was a slaughter for the British and Churchill met with Buller to describe the scene. Buller blamed Warren, writing "If at sundown the defence of the summit had been taken regularly in hand, entrenchments laid out, gun emplacements prepared, the dead removed, the wounded collected, and in fact the whole place brought under regular military command...the hills would have been held I am sure." He also recognized he was partly to blame for not sacking Warren and taking over himself. Now it was over. Medics from both sides were allowed to pick up their dead: 500 soldiers and volunteers, which included 243 British.

One of the medics for the British was a young Indian lawyer named Gandhi, who would go on to seek more passive solutions to disputes in his native India.

The media went out of its way to crucify Buller. He would be blamed for Spion Kop—along with 1,750 soldiers killed, captured or wounded during the last 10 days—even though he had been undermined by Sir Charles Warren's refusal to a surprise attack which might have avoided the disaster. The passage of time without relieving Ladysmith was Buller's main enemy, and time meant further disgrace and ridicule. Buller would now take the whole affair upon himself—something he had never done in his entire military career. Churchill observed that the general was now "gripping the whole business in his strong hands."

* An unrelated but intriguing digression regarding Spion Kop: In the 1897 novel, Dracula, by Bram Stoker, the Count was shipwrecked off the seaside town of Whitby in North Yorkshire, England. Several memorable scenes in the novel take place around the two headlands that bisect the harbor, the East Cliff and the West Cliff. A wood-and-iron bench, fashioned in Victorian style, commemorates Dracula's visit to the area. It is found today on the West Cliff atop a grassy bluff called Spion Kop. Seems the name relates to a bloody event in both fact and fiction.

Meanwhile, the monody "Where's Buller?" continued to cry out in Ladysmith. Whisky in the beleaguered town now cost 120 shillings (it was 4 shillings in London), and the stores were running out of food, ammunition and artillery shells. The town's homemade journal, appropriately called the *Ladysmith Bombshell*, said in January, 1990, "Our lingering faith is growing small, 'Where's Buller?' is the weary call." The town inhabitants could hear the artillery being fired at Spion Kop and assumed it was Buller, defeating the Boers on his way to relieve Ladysmith. When they learned the truth—that Botha and his Boers had defeated Buller—it was decided to start eating the horses. Nonetheless, 12 people died each day from fever.

Ironically, one of those holed up in Ladysmith, suffering from the effects of typhoid, was Dr. Jameson, he of the Jameson Raid. It looked like he and his belligerent sponsor, Cecil Rhodes, got their war after all and then some.

On 5 February, Buller was in relatively good spirits despite Spion Kop and temperatures reaching 100° F in the shade. Orders then arrived that he was to take a hill which, he believed, could cost him 2,000 to 3,000 men: orders from his rivals to undermine his command. Buller telegraphed Lord Roberts—his nemesis—and asked if the relief of Ladysmith was worth it. Roberts replied "Ladysmith must be relieved, even at the loss you anticipate. Tell your troops that the honour of the Empire is in their hands and that I have no possible doubt of their being successful."

It is not beyond the realm of imagination that U.S. generals sent out similar replies to President Lyndon Johnson during the Vietnam War as he wondered the wisdom of trying to win that war. Buller reluctantly agreed. The subsequent attack proved another disaster for the British, ending in a withdrawal and a search for a new route to Ladysmith.

Chapter 27

Relief and Retribution

FROM 14 TO 18 FEBRUARY, THE BRITISH OCCUPIED several strategic hills and the Boers looked to be in retreat. Buller was feeling more confident that his relief of the city would be imminent, although White signaled him that the Boers were still around Ladysmith. Buller moved and suddenly the 11th Brigade was surprised by sniper fire. Some 500 casualties resulted and by 25 February the number had risen to 1,200.

Cynicism regarding Buller's leadership ability was now setting in. When he devised a new plan to relieve Ladysmith, Maj. Gen. Lyttleton wrote that it "appeared so sound that I doubted if the ideas were his own." Yet Buller had written his wife, Lady Audrey, a letter which may suggest otherwise. "We were fighting all last week," he wrote," but old Warren is a duffer and lost me a good chance. However, if I have the least luck I think I have at last found out how to get through these beastly mountains."

On 27 February, Buller feinted a withdrawal across the Tugela River, reerected a bridge and then crossed elsewhere to attack the Boers as one army in different strategic directions, not small groups split up as had been done historically. The plan worked. With 91 cannon providing cover, Buller's troops captured a key hill and then cleared a path, step by step, to Ladysmith. The next day—February 28—British troops began entering the town. Churchill recorded the event for the *Morning Post* as if inside the town, even though he was with the Light Horse several miles away. (Journalism's integrity has had its problems all century long!) Buller entered the next day and greeted General White. The relief of Ladysmith had cost the Empire 5,000 men.

On 1 March, the Prince of Wales (and future King Edward VII) sent Buller a telegram of congratulations. Imperial humiliation had been avoided. Buller, ever the humanitarian with his own troops, refused to pursue the retreating Boers from Ladysmith, perhaps living up to his family motto that, indeed, eagles do not capture flies.

For General Sir Redvers Buller, V.C., the war was almost over.[*] For the last visages of an empire, the Boer War would continue for two years. Lord Roberts had several victories after Ladysmith's relief, and he departed for England leaving Kitchener to win it and telling the public the war was "practically over." (Roberts was also made an earl by the Queen.) But it didn't work out that way. The gentlemanly Lord Kitchener would fight in a very non-gentlemanly guerrilla war that had no end in sight, and he perpetuated the 19th century thinking of Lord Roberts by leading quick assaults followed by long delays for regrouping—delays which gave the Boers ample time to advance or change strategy.

Like Vietnam later in the century, the government's thinking revolved around the concept that the only way to end a war was to win a war. And like Vietnam, when the lesson was learned that the Boer War could not be won, peace meetings began to develop. In both 1901 and 1902, conferences were held between the British and the Boer leadership while battles continued to be fought. Peace was finally achieved on 31 May 1902, and Kitchener was voted a £50,000 "victory grant" by parliament! And this was the man who wrote the War Minister in 1901 "I

---

[*] According to the DNB, "In May, after much discussion with Lord Roberts as to his line of advance, Buller moved on the Biggarsberg; and skillfully turning the Boer positions, which were not strongly held, he entered Dundee on 15 May." In August, Buller and 11,000 troops marched north and defeated Boer forces under Louis Botha. On 9 November, having received thanks from Lord Roberts, Sir Redvers landed at Southampton, almost 13 months after his departure.

don't want any incentive to do what is possible to finish...." Lapse in memory, I suppose.

Victory. The victory was more expensive than Kitchener's "grant." During the 33 months of fighting, the Boer War would cost Britain $500 million. In terms of life, it would cost 22,000 British lives, 25,000 Boer lives, and 12,000 African lives. The four-month Ladysmith siege was little more than a fiasco for the British: 22,000 Boers contained General White's force of some 14,000 inside Ladysmith while holding Buller's 28,000 soldiers at bay. It was a war waiting to happen, and the only thing it ended was the British Empire.

For General Sir Redvers Buller, V.C., it was formality, shame and retirement. Roberts' ring of officers, many of whom served under Buller to relieve Ladysmith, began a letter attack to discredit the hero of the Zulu Wars. One letter noted "Buller is no use." This whispering campaign spread to the British media, already stung by the loss of prestige for the Empire. (They would paraphrase and publish the secret "surrender" telegram from Buller to White at Ladysmith.) Buller became a scapegoat for failure even as the relief of Ladysmith was viewed as a crowning achievement. Here is a commonly-held assessment of Buller written by Denis Judd in his book on the Boer War:

> He was sixty-years-old in 1899, overweight, ponderous and self-indulgent; he later boasted that he consumed a pint of good champagne every day during his campaigning in South Africa—and there was certainly a good deal of evidence that his judgement had been impaired by heavy drinking. Equally serious, though unavoidable, was his complete lack of experience against European opponents; when he left for South Africa he had never commanded more than two thousand men at once, and even then against a variety of poorly armed indigenous people. He was undoubtedly brave, and had won the Victoria Cross at Hlobane during the Zulu War; he also took remarkable care

of his soldiers' welfare. Yet beneath the surface glitter he was painfully unsure of himself, and was soon to reveal considerable prowess as a military fumbler and ditherer, thus amply justifying a brother officer's description of him as 'a superb Major, a mediocre Colonel and an abysmally poor General.'

Harsh words, and they would echo throughout the late-Victorian world. Not totally accurate either, as if author Judd unwittingly slipped on a few War Office correspondence and fell head-first into Robert's ring.

The charge of alcoholism for a British general and officer might be tantamount to the charge of ego-satisfaction for U. S. Senators and Congressmen. True, Buller was a known imbiber…along with much of British society-at-large. But it is hardly necessary to blame his actions or inactions on alcoholic intake, especially since he was so often undercut by his superiors and his own officers, sober or not. As for his "complete lack of experience against European opponents," Buller had no such opponents in the Boer War, for the war was not conducted along 19th century European models. The Boers were much closer to the guerrillas of South America or Southeast Asia in the 20th century than anything the British military had encountered during their heyday of military successes. Despite all this, Buller would take the blame for the loss of life and failure to win the game on the first try. It just wasn't acceptable. "We are not amused," and all that.

Outwardly, the government eased Buller steadily toward obscurity. On 17 November 1900, he was the guest of Queen Victoria at Windsor Castle. Lord Roberts mentioned his "services" in official dispatches, and Her Majesty, while withholding an earldom or a cash bonus, awarded Buller with a few more clasps and another set of letters, GCMG, both of which came much cheaper.[*] In January, 1901, Sir Redvers resumed commanding the Aldershot division and he now headed up the combined 1st Army Corps. The media, however, was

---

[*] GCMG stands for Knight Grand Cross of St. Michael and St. George. The British snicker at the letters and honor, and have given them another meaning: God Calls Me God.

angered by the appointment, believing that only *future* war leaders should command armies. The government did not respond to the attacks, nor did it let Buller defend himself, which greatly agitated him. It was perhaps why he gave an "indiscreet" speech at a public luncheon at Westminster on 10 October, which the government renounced. The speech included the *actual* text of his telegram to White, the one the colluding War Office had refused to release. Eleven days later he was removed from his command, despite having two years left on his term. Buller had little support. A motion in the House of Commons denouncing the government's decision was defeated 236 to 98.

Thus the most experienced senior officer on guerrilla tactics and step-by-step warfare—the warfare of the 20th century—was relieved of his duty to Queen and country, giving way to those future generals who would bungle World War I so badly a little over a decade later and contribute to the deaths of an entire generation of young men.

Statue of General Buller, Exeter, Devon

Britain would continue its tradition of placing asses in front of lions.

Buller spent the rest of his life as a country gentleman and celebrity in his native Devon. In 1905, Captain Adrian Jones erected a statue to Buller in Exeter with the inscription "He saved Natal." Receptions continued for Sir Redvers until failing health limited his engagements. He died at his home at Downes on 2 June 1908 and was buried at Crediton with military honors. His grave is in a lonely corner of the church cemetery, along with members of his family, including his wife and daughter.

Sometime during his return and retirement—Keith would tell me it was in 1902—a pub called Bakers Arms in the village of Chagford was renamed Bullers Arms.

The Ladysmith campaign had cost Buller both his career and his self-esteem. Few would remember that it was Lord Roberts who took much of the army to fight the Boers elsewhere, leaving Buller with insufficient forces to orchestrate a '20th century war.' Few would remember Winston Churchill's words about Buller written during the thick of battle—words that the "little bit of a newspaperman" would later change to fit the prevailing conventional wisdom: "A great deal is incomprehensible," he wrote. "But it may be safely said that if Sir Redvers cannot relieve Ladysmith with his present force we do not know of any other officer in the British service who would be likely to succeed."

Perhaps the worst cost was the evil spirit rising from the events *within* the Boer War. For much as the Vietnam war questioned America's morality and justification for destroying most of a country and many of its people—as well as the lives of some 58,000 American soldiers and other personnel—the British would also be haunted by their country's behavior in the Boer War. It as well would become an albatross, one that has faded into dim memory, yet one that nonetheless can remind future generations of a moral lapse that pulled at a nation. Buller, near the end of his life, wrote to his wife "It will all be the same in 100 years." He was optimistic: Vietnam would begin some 60 years later, and would create its own evil spirit that continues to haunt a generation. As for the ghost of the Boer War, it would manifest itself just a third of a century later…in Nazi Germany.

Why? Because part of the haunting from the Boer War, unmentioned to this point but about to be disclosed, would provide the world with an example of cruelty from which dictators and repressive governments would take comfort and copious notes. In this respect, the haunting goes beyond the Boer War, rising from the South Africa of the 1900s over the Germany of the 1940s to Bosnia-Herzegovina and Kosovo of the 1990s. I would learn that, indeed, there was a ghost in Chagford, as well as the rest of the country. It was a ghost that quietly, unobtrusively haunted the big cities and the little villages of the island.

The villagers of Chagford were too far removed in time from this haunting—although Keith the pub proprietor retained a glimmer of it in his memory. But it served as a reminder that any hoped-for simple life on the moors of Devon could never be void of a past filled with ignominy and guilt, much as my generation suffered…and continued to suffer. The ghost would always be there, just up the main road past the Market House.

It dwelled in the pub with a general's name on it. Bullers Arms.

Chapter 28

The Haunting of the Past

"THE DEPORTATIONS…A BURNT-OUT POPULATION brought in by hundreds of convoys…deprived of clothes…the semi-starvation in the camps…the fever-stricken children lying…upon the bare earth…the appalling mortality…"

One could easily see these descriptions as the creations of a journalist first visiting an Auschwitz or a Dachau or a Treblinka—examples of numerous concentration camps liberated by conquering allies in 1945 at the close of World War II. But that is not the case here. The description came from Emily Hobhouse, Secretary of the Women's Branch of the South African Conciliation Committee, in 1901, as she described the camps set up by the British in South Africa to *concentrate* mainly Boer women and children. Her listener was the leader of the Liberal party, Sir Henry Campbell-Bannerman. And all he could say in response was "methods of barbarism," over and over. The media and much of the civilized world would soon pick up the chant.

Keith of Bullers Arms had dropped a little bomb about Buller, the Boer War and concentration camps while I was sipping cider in his pub. Yet unlike my subsequent research on Chagford and the environs of Dartmoor, it took very little digging to uncover what amounted to a large cover-up by the British government during and after the Boer War. Yes there were camps, set up during the summer of 1900 in the Orange Free State and the Transvaal, with several more in Natal and the Cape Colony. But Buller had nothing to do with them, although he may be forever linked to them because of his role in the Boer War. Ironically, it would be Lord Roberts who orchestrated the creation of the camps, and Lord Kitchener his minion who would enthusiastically fill them with Boers—two men who worked hard to disgrace Buller and who would live out their lives with the knowledge that atrocities in South Africa would one day be irrevocably attributed to them for all time, although it escaped the public mind of their era.

It began by proclamation. Lord Roberts ordered all buildings standing within 10 miles of any railway damaged by the Boers to be burned to the ground. The burning of buildings was nicely complemented by *farm-burning*, a useful weapon of terror happily employed by Kitchener much as General Sherman scorched the Southern earth from Atlanta to the sea during America's Civil War in the 1860s. It was a policy raised to a fine military art form in Vietnam when the U.S. dropped napalm and used Agent Orange to burn and defoliate good portions of the country. These activities in South Africa created homeless people, mainly Boer women and children, who were now rounded up and taken to a few camps previously established to house feuding Afrikaners, or so the British would say. Soon, the camps were expanded in number to include families of prisoners of war and all victims of farm-lootings and farm-burnings.

One British soldier recorded an incident involving a Boer family about to be transported to a camp:

> A small girl interrupted her preparation for departure to play indignantly [the Boer] National Anthem at us on an old piano. We were carting people off. It was raining hard and blowing—a miserable, hurried home-leaving; ransacked house...a distracted mother...pushing along her children to the ox-wagon outside, and this poor little wretch in the midst of it all pulling herself together to strum a final defiance.

As with all bureaucracies—civilian or military—once you turn the spigot on for what seems to be a strategic decision, it's hard to turn it off. As the camps increased in population—at their height, 160,000 people were situated in them—the army referred to them as "Refugee camps" and insisted they were voluntary and very habitable. Moreover, it suited the vindictive Kitchener just fine that the Boers were suffering at the hands of the British. This was the man who wrote when first arriving on the scene, "I think I hate the country, the people, the whole thing more every day." With Lord Robert's benign approval, Kitchener felt he could win the war by cutting off food supplies and military information through a policy of *cleansing the veld*—a phrase we "moderns" have accepted in a slightly different presentation: *ethnic cleansing*.

Kitchener and the army would not tolerate opposition to this program. When three editors in the Cape Colony criticized British treatment of the Boers, they were put on trial. It must have been difficult for Kitchener to swallow when two Members of Parliament, aghast at the situation in South Africa, compared the camps to the *reconcentrado* camps used by the Spanish against Cuban guerrillas. It was a name that stuck: concentration camps. Furthermore, in an imperial age of male chauvinism and female complacency, it must have irked him to no end to discover that women were now crusading against the use of camps and the appalling treatment of the Boers. This included the activities of Emily Hobhouse—whom Kitchener referred to as "that bloody woman"—and her politicizing of the camps with the help of men such as Campbell-Bannerman.

Emily had unearthed a monster both Kitchener and the government wished to keep entombed: atrocities were taking place and Boers were dying in concentration camps at a steady rate. She visited numerous camps and broadcast her findings to politicians and the media. The camps harbored unsanitary conditions. Diet was poor. Diseases ran rampant, including measles, typhoid, jaundice, malaria, bronchitis and pneumonia. One out of five children died in the camps, and there were rumors that British soldiers put ground glass in their food. On an annualized basis, one in three died in all the camps, and both the Boers and the British public were convinced that the British army was trying to exterminate a people. It led to Campbell-Bannerman's observation of "methods of barbarism." It moved David Lloyd George, leader of the Labour Party, to comment on why rations were withheld in the camps from women and children whose husbands and fathers had not surrendered: "It means that the remnant of the Boer army who are sacrificing everything for their idea of independence are to be tortured by the spectacle of their starving children into betraying their cause." Lloyd George felt that such treatment of the Boers would end British rule in Africa. Actually, it began the steady disintegration of the entire British Empire worldwide.

Emily fanned the flames of outrage, which had now spread beyond the British shores around the world. She told stories: at one camp, it took her great effort just to get British authorities to agree to provide one ounce of soap per person per week. She described the soldiers running the camps as possessing "crass male ignorance, stupidity, helplessness and muddling." She saw the results of Kitchener's burn-and-capture policy. On several occasions she witnessed railway stations jammed with open trucks overflowing with women and children, stuck in the cold rain and left in the trucks or railway sidings for days without food. She saw camps increase their numbers daily, and often watched as many as 20 to 25 people a day die. In June, 1901, Emily Hobhouse published a report on her findings and distributed it to Members of Parliament and the press. "[I saw] war in all its destructiveness, cruelty, stupidity and nakedness."

Important voices were raised louder than ever. Campbell-Bannerman of the Liberals, reluctant to rock the boat too greatly, now wondered aloud why the camps existed at all since the government had been telling the world either that the war was over or that it was now no longer a war but a mopping-up activity. Lloyd George of Labour now accused the government of "a policy of extermination" against women and children. He wanted to know why Great Britain was making war on women and children. "By every rule of civilized war [is that a contradiction in terms?] we were bound to treat the women and children as non-combatants." Clearly the raping-pillaging Serbs today are unaware of Lloyd George's rules; neither was the British army in 1901.

The government—as governments characteristically do when they are attacked—covered up the whole affair and basically lied about it. The War Office denied the camps were bad, indeed explained that they were necessary since women had been aiding Boer soldiers, although exactly how remained a mystery. The government said the camps were improving, even disputing Emily's figures to say that deaths were dropping in number. (They did by the end of the war—from 33 out of 100 to 7 out of 100—but, of course, if there had not *been* any camps, there would have been 0 deaths. Simple math.) A reporter at the London *Times* helped the cover-up by writing that the death rate was in fact decreasing, and should not be an issue.

Then there was Dr. Alec Kay, the gentleman we met briefly who had been holed up in Ladysmith pending rescue in early 1900 and who hated Buller. He began writing disapprovingly of the "agitation raised by a few unsexed and hysterical women who are prepared to sacrifice everything for notoriety." His defense of the camps in 1901 is frightening in its timelessness for the rest of the 20th century:

> The whole question of the camps is bound up with that of guerrilla warfare. If it is lawful and necessary to destroy such Boer houses and farms that are used as bases for warfare [like all buildings within 10 miles of a war-damaged railway?] is it not more humane to establish camps where women and children can be housed?.... All the misery, the burning and the camps are the result of war; it has always happened, and will happen again!"

He, of course, was right. And it was minds like his that made sure it would happen again.

Kay proffered a nice propaganda line similar to the ones created by the Nazis in their fictitious films about the deportation of the Jews to camps during World War II. Kay wrote:

> As far as the authorities are concerned, everything is done in the camps that can be done: good food, good clothing and blankets are provided and British soldiers are employed to keep the camps clean, carrying water, serving rations and assisting in every way. It is my firm belief that if the camps had not been established, sickness and mortality would have been far greater on the farms and villages, and even in the towns.

It is interesting to note that Kay failed to mention who it was that *destroyed* those farms, villages and towns! And if the camps were so clean and well-run, what caused one out of three to die? Boredom?

Both Campbell-Bannerman and Lloyd George hoped to use the camps as a means to bring down the government. But despite public outrage—much like the protests against the war in Vietnam—they knew they couldn't win a vote in Parliament without more ammunition, so to speak. This came in August, 1901: an accounting of the camps noted that there were 93,940 whites and 24,457 blacks in concentration camps. In May, 550 died; June, 782; July, 1,675. Deaths were on the rise and government opposition had a case...or so they thought. Unfortunately, Parliament now adjourned for a five-month holiday, allowing the pro-Imperial press to continue its support of the government's policy in South Africa.

Curiously, the banners of dissent continued to be waved by two unlikely sources. Remember Sir Alfred Milner, High Commissioner of South Africa and by-jingo Imperialist in the Cape Colony who actually pushed for the Boer War? Well, Sir Alfred apparently had a stomach, and it didn't like what his eyes were feeding it. The camps were now a liability to his quest for future investment in South Africa, especially with a prolonged war costing £1,250,000 a week and soon to be billed to the public, who would probably want nothing further to do with the region. Milner actually contacted Lord Roberts and floated the idea of perhaps moving Kitchener out of the way and over to India! He was also not thrilled with Kitchener's use of public executions to dampen Boer morale, a tactic used with flair and verve by the Nazis four decades later…and culminating in the now-famous picture of a North Vietnamese sympathizer being shot dead in the head in public during the Vietnam War. It didn't help that Kitchener released to the public the number of Boers killed, captured or surrendered each month, showing that the numbers were not great and that the war had no end in sight. [*]

Another woman jumped into the fray, the leader of the suffragette movement, Millicent Fawcett. Heading an all-female commission to South Africa to visit the camps, Millicent hoped to find out the real truth behind the alleged atrocities perpetrated by Her Majesty's government. If Kitchener and crew hoped the pro-Boer War Fawcett would rush to their cause, they were greatly mistaken, thanks in part to their own behavior. At one camp visit in August, 1901, Millicent warned the superintendent that unsanitary conditions would lead to a typhoid epidemic. He ignored her request for improvements, saying that only 40 had died since March. When she returned to the camp 90 days later, 400 were dying a month, many from typhoid!

---

[*] I remember all too well in the late 1960s watching Walter Cronkite of CBS News every Friday evening to hear the "body count" of North Vietnamese killed, then Americans and South Vietnamese. (The bad guys' numbers were always big; the good guys' numbers were always small.) I also remember a law student who claimed to have written down every tally since the numbers were released, only to determine that the American military had already killed the entire population of North Vietnam and then some. Like the initial numerical "successes" of Patriot missiles in the Gulf War (as mentioned before, most apparently missed their targets), the military has often been playful with numbers in order to keep the war wagon moving.

Women were leading the charge against atrocities, and they ferreted out the government cover-up. When several women saw a game of lawn tennis being played at one camp, they concluded it was being staged for their benefit—not unlike the string quartets put together at Hitler's death camps for the viewing pleasure of gullible Red Cross observers. Pressure was now on the government to end the camps and the war.

Kitchener now wanted more than the 250,000 soldiers he had in South Africa to seal a victory once and for all. And if the government had any doubts about his views on the Boers and the camps, they only had to look at a correspondence he sent the War Office in mid-October, 1901, when he wrote "Extermination...is a long and very tiring business." Events, however, were to alter his dreary workday. In October and November, General Sir Redvers Buller, V.C., was destroyed by the press. His downfall, however, did not satisfy the media feeding frenzy amid the prolonged death and destruction in South Africa, and now the target for doom became Kitchener. At the same time, the prime minister refused to let "K" institute a policy of mass Boer executions, which he had wanted to do. Meanwhile, the peace conferences trudged along and finally bore fruit in the spring of 1902. The war was officially over on 31 May, and like Germany in the coming world wars, Britain had to make war reparations to the Boers for the misery caused them.

Depending on the sources used, between 20,000 and 28,000 people died in the concentration camps housing Boers. Initially lost on the public mind was the toll on Black Africans who supported the Boers, for they were kept in separate camps, some 107,000 of them in all. Of that number, about 12,000 died. The Black Africans were caught in the middle. Many who supported the British were killed by the Boers, including a large number of unarmed civilians. The whites-against-blacks story of the Boer War is a legacy seen today in South Africa, most recently in Cecil Rhodes' old colony, now called Zimbabwe.

Kitchener and Roberts, despite their culpability in orchestrating concentration camps and their inability to win a war for the Empire, nonetheless survived as military heroes of sorts, with Roberts actually being retained for product endorsements! Buller we know went into retirement in his beloved Devon. As for Sir George White, V.C., who bungled his way into getting Ladysmith surrounded, he was made Governor of Chelsea Hospital, London, and became a symbol of courage and tenacity, especially every 28 February, which was now referred to as Ladysmith Day.

If we agree that historical baggage can bring about conflagrations requiring only a spark for ignition, it is easy to look into the eyes of General Buller, staring out from the wall in a pub in Chagford, and see beyond them to the camps of Kitchener and further into the future. The vision includes the German policy of *cleansing* the Fatherland of any non-Aryans—true, Hitler wasn't too blue-eyed or blonde-haired, but no one in Germany seemed anxious to tell him at the time. Just as the British began with looting and burning an age-old enemy, the Germans followed the looting-burning-concentration camp model against those who were not 'pure' Germans, especially the Jews—never mind that German Jews were more German than many of the Germans living in Germany! (Hitler, we may recall, wasn't a German at all.) The Nazis went a step further—total extermination of a people—but we might remind ourselves that had Kitchener been let loose to pursue his policies, Britain might have beaten Nazi Germany to the punch. For it seems that that's what "K" had in mind.

The Vietnam War could be viewed as an example of a nation trying to exterminate the people of another nation, although few Americans would admit to such a perspective. The U.S. methodically lashed out with everything short of atomic bombs to kill the Vietnamese enemy. It was also a war that, like the Boer War, divided a nation and caused it to question its own morality, its own beliefs and ethics.

Buller alluded to this as an old story that will happen again. He may have realized privately that it will *always* happen again. Even since Vietnam, we have had other "Boer Wars" and "Vietnams", two being the recent Bosnia-Herzegovina tragedy and the ethnic cleansing of Albanians in Kosovo. Baby Boomers in the U. S. have their Vietnam ghost, and they are reminded of it with each possible military intervention or reference to an era when a generation faced its society and didn't like what it saw.

Britain had its own Vietnam, further removed in time but vivid in its representation of a national guilt that will always be part of a proud, old nation. For the villagers of Chagford, they have only to round the corner past their Market House to glimpse at that ghost. It may not be clear; it may not be fully known or understood. But it's there.

Chapter 29

Hugh Griffith in my Mirror

I WOKE UP AT 7:15 AM AND TOOK a long shower before shaving, dressing and descending the stairs in Glendarah House for what would be my departure from Chagford. I went into the dining room, found my table—with a little Number 4 sign placed on it designating my room—and grabbed a coffee cup and filled it at the serving table. (I was going back to the U.S. Time to readjust to coffee again.) I also filled a bowl with fruit segments, returned to my table and doctored the coffee with sugar and cream—the whole thing is bad medicine for the body, but so was the cider of the previous night and I needed help. Other guests entered the dining room, including a Dutchman I vaguely remembered seeing at Bullers Arms prior to leaving for Jubilee Hall. He said "Good morning." I think my mouth replied in similar fashion and he asked me what I did last night.

"I went to the dart tournament."

"What dart tournament?"

"??????"

"There was a dart tournament?" he continued, truly surprised.

"Yes. The Chagford pubs competed."

"I didn't know. I was at the Ring O' Bells drinking beer."

"That's nice."

The proprietor came in and asked what I wanted for breakfast. This was going to be a toast-only morning, and I think he sensed that my undoubtedly morose outlook on the day stemmed from more than just being tired.

"Will you be leaving straight for home?" he inquired.

"No. I'm going to Ivybridge for awhile, then off to London and home."

"Were you at the dart tournament?"

"Yes."

"I heard Nick won the men's singles."

Word travels quickly around Chagford. Here we invent portable modems, palm computers and sophisticated voice mail and E-mail systems, and a medieval village can 'get the word out' in no time flat. No chance of the system crashing, either.

"Yeah, he was pretty impressive."

A pause first. "Yes, Nick is a great player. Some say he could have gone far."

I decided not to go there, and he left to put in my toast order. I was both depressed and confused. Depressed because I was leaving a village I had first created in my mind—one that many Americans hoped to locate—only to become aware that something was not quite right, not quite that simple. Confused about Buller, Julie, Chagford. There were stories I had to uncover, truths I had to confront, contradictions I had to make clear. My mind would not leave well enough alone. It had to know what wasn't simple about this simple life.

I packed up my car after paying the proprietor, then ventured into Chagford over the harrowing speed bumps I had learned to master with finesse. I parked across the street from Bullers Arms and took a picture of the pub. High up on the wall I noticed a set of initials and a date: JR 1823. Just then Keith came out to greet me, and when I pointed out the letters he said "Oh, I guess it *is* JR and not JB. Well, Baker *sounded* about right." I thanked him for his hospitality and we shook hands. "Come back again," he said, echoing off into the air as he retreated from me. I hoped I would.

The outfitting store was open and I suddenly had an idea. I went inside and asked the woman behind the counter for something suitable for "a female dart champion with a wicked flick of the wrist." If I had thought for a moment, I might have realized that she probably knew who I was talking about. She smiled and replied "We have darts and flights. Come this way."

I followed her along a narrow aisle past other tributaries and steps leading to an assortment of gear and things. We arrived at a small area where there were a few dart sets. Julie still used her brass ones, not the more gauche nickel creations, but I didn't know if she'd like them or become embarrassed at the thought of receiving such a gift from an outsider. Worse, they were a bit expensive, and although I'm far from rich, the price tag could also cause uneasiness with someone known to me only a few brief hours. Add to the possibility of her husband being less than enthusiastic about a stranger buying His Wife and Dart Champion a set of nickel darts, and the dilemma of a small gesture became complicated.

"She might like some flights, dear. The good players are always breaking them and needing new ones." Flights—or feathers to the unwashed. A voice from heaven, solving my earthly problem. The store lady was correct. Ann, the friend of Julie whom I met at the tournament, first told me that players often stuck one dart in the back of another one in the target. I found that hard to believe until, unbelievably, I saw several players do just that, sticking a dart dead-on in the base of another one. Until I actually witnessed it, I thought only Errol Flynn could accomplish the feat, as he did in the movie *Robin Hood.* (Yes I know, Kevin Costner recently did it, but he had special effects. I adamantly refuse to believe that Errol required such wimpy crutches. I mean, he was Errol Flynn!) Ann also said that such an occurrence didn't count: the dart stuck in the back of the first one got no points. "Hell," I told her, "I would have awarded the thrower a Nobel Prize in Physics!"

The bench on one side of Market House, Chagford

So I looked at the flights, really plastic fins for the back of the darts, and saw that they ran from bland to flashy to a set with a bunny rabbit on each flight. I bought her two sets: a flashy one and the bunnies. After paying, I marched over to the news store behind the Market House and bought a card of a beautiful sunset in England—no writing inside. I sat down on the bench against the House—the one I sat on seemingly eons ago—and wrote Julie a note:

I thanked her for sharing a little of "her story" with me, and asked her to accept the flights, choosing which ones she wanted to use on a whim. I also promised to write her, and I told her if boredom should ever set in—which I firmly doubted—she could always knock the unsuspecting tourist off the sidewalk, especially of the American variety: it worked before. I sealed the card with the flights and walked across the street to the Post Office. "Do you want to send it first or second class?" came the official question. I realized I probably could have just asked for directions to her street and dropped it off, but I didn't think that proper. Besides, she and Nick had a wedding to attend to this morning. I was now part of their history. My presence should no longer be present.

So I paid 24 pence for first class and the letter was on its way down (or up) the road. I walked outside the P.O., stared at the Market House and the people and cars circumscribing it all which ways, then decided to resume my seat on the bench and have a thunk.

I did not know the history of Chagford at that moment, or who Buller was or what the Boer War was about, or what ghosts lurked about

the village and the country. I had gained a brief outline of the life of
Captain, realizing that it had been far from simple for her in a village
that, I was now sure, reflected the same *unsimple* life for those who lived
in it, despite my machinations and mission to achieve the quest so
boldly announced on the cover of *Time*. And yet if I wanted to allow
myself to be depressed and discouraged, it didn't come to pass. For during that brief thunk on the bench in front of the Market House, I came
to understand that there were other qualities to the simple life besides
the outward trappings. It was always in front of me; I was just too
caught up in my own vision to see the one before me in Chagford.

I let my observations of the past two nights run through my mind. I
saw people content with their lives without a greater goal in mind—
something I had misconstrued as a lack of motivation or a competitive
nature...American perspectives. Nothing could be further from the
reality that was Chagford. These people worked hard, probably harder
than many Americans. They were also highly competitive, in sport and
in speaking. They wanted to win the game and they wanted to win the
argument. The only difference, perhaps, was that they wanted to do it
fairly and *squarely*—hardly a vision of Wall Street c. 1987 and attributes
sorely lacking in my late-20th century "competitive" society.

The villagers supported each other in many ways. They passed on the
traditions of the village to the next generation, including the boldness
that has helped a group of people survive for 2000 years. They supported each other financially by shopping at each other's stores and
farms...even taking an occasional taxi when it wasn't booked for
tourists. They gave to their local charities, volunteered of their time,
bought each other drinks, kept the support going from emotional to
financial to personal to collective.

And they wanted their lives to remain the way it has since ages past.
In 1981, a questionnaire was sent out to the villagers of Chagford asking them about the future. Know what the majority of them replied
regarding their village? They wanted the population to remain the

same, and they were against further development. Perhaps they saw just enough television to see what *change* can do.

When First Lady Hillary Rodham Clinton told an audience "we lack at some core level meaning in our individual lives and meaning collectively," she was talking about an American society very different from the inhabitants of Chagford. If she could sneak into the village quietly, dark glasses and scarf, she would witness what I had seen regarding how a life could be lived. She might even share my feelings: envy, admiration and awe at how it's supposed to be, or at least how we believe we'd like it to be. She would encounter words and laughter, both representative of the human condition—the need to communicate, the need to laugh. I sometimes feel we have lost both in the States, with much of our laughter at the expense of others and a falling off of communication as we retreat inward to our monitors and mail order lives.

I stood up from my thunk and headed toward the car with a decision in my mind. I decided I wanted to talk, to laugh, to care, to make an effort with people much as it was done effortlessly in a very old village. If this was the true meaning of that one-shot deal we call "life," it would be a waste at the very least to ignore what I was feeling at the moment. I would practice despite the hazards found along the Slippery Sidewalk of Life. Not at the local bar—we don't have pubs, although we may think we do. I would try to emulate a group of villagers, if that were possible.

Here I thought my life was pretty much defined: work hard, work harder, send the kids to college, hopefully put money away, look for a little breathing space at the tail-end of my life to do a little lecturing and traveling and writing and thinking, with the occasional thunk until the breath was no longer there. (I realize that ended a bit morbid. But no one said reality was supposed to have a happy ending.) That could never be the case now. I had discovered another *way*, and it meant involvement and caring beyond the confines of four walls, be they office or home or the barriers and borders we build each day. It could be as simple as I wanted it to be. Perhaps.

And some day I would return to Chagford, and to Bullers Arms.

After taking a final picture of the pub, I slowly, almost reluctantly got into my car and headed out of the village the way I had entered. My depression had passed. I was feeling good, almost optimistic. It was while approaching the speed bumps that I suddenly spied "Hugh Griffith" of my 1989 encounter, cap on head, walking slowly and solemnly toward me up the hill to town, the same hill Gwen had to conquer each day on her way to Bullers Arms. Just as I was about to pass him, I saw Hugh break into a smile as he recognized a familiar face and began talking to a man walking in the opposite direction. It was just an instant and then it was gone.

I looked in my rearview mirror, watching Hugh and his friend slowly grow smaller—with one brief moment of shaking as I hit the speed bumps a little too fast. The two men got smaller and smaller until I made a turn and they disappeared from my mirror, replaced by trees and a few scattered dwellings on the outskirts of a village once owned by a Saxon named Dodo. He would recognize it still.

Going Back: A Postscript

NOT UNTIL I HAD RESEARCHED CHAGFORD and Sir Redvers did I decide that it would be worthwhile to put together a literary journey involving a quest for the "simple life," from past to present, beginning with Bullers Arms and what I had witnessed during my two visits to the pub. I conducted the research at the University of Chicago while updating my lecture for the U of C publishing program where I gave a seminar periodically. I also wrote out a series of notes and questions organized in outline form and sent them to Julie...and waited while I pondered exactly what to do with the information I had pulled together. Waited and went back to work, for there was a lot of work to do in the coming months. The real world does that to you.

Julie did respond, answering my questions about her life and those of people I had met, along with tidbits she felt may or may not be useful. Thus commenced a correspondence between the Captain and the American, talking about each other's lives, activities and views of the world. We couldn't be farther apart in our backgrounds and upbringings, and couldn't be closer in our desire to learn from each other.

And all this began with two threats on my life in the middle of Dartmoor...and perhaps a little intervention by the local gods who never quite departed the scene. Interesting.

As the months rolled along and the decade confirmed what it was going to be all about, I tried desperately to scratch out a few hours here and there to put the story to words. And all the while the world continued to zip along its axis, with its "intelligent" inhabitants busying themselves with events: a new President that began with hope and flipped and flopped about because he didn't know how to work with the other powers-that be; continued wars and brutality, with even Cuba getting into the act by shooting down planes;[*] increased instability within Russia and with its neighbors; a switch from aiding starving Somalis to killing a few to stop warlords and other snags in the humanitarian mission. (After this book was researched, we had a worldwide distraction which did little to promote the American ideal of justice, summed up by the two letters "O.J." And later on, of course, Bill Clinton eventually undid himself by frequently undoing his zipper in front of a White House intern.) Beyond O.J. and Bill and the myth of dotcom companies and Elian Gonzalez and a little stock market crash, it continued to get worse right into the new millennia. (See Appendix I, if you held off this long.)

Julie would write me snippets of village happenings, but only a few personal stories. One event that I suspected was in the offing reached fruition when I learned Nick had separated from his wife. To my mind, they already appeared that way, but one never knows and a dart tournament is hardly a group therapy session...or is it?

In April of 1993, when I started writing this journey in earnest, I decided to mortgage my future lecture money and go back to Chagford to begin filling in the missing blanks in the story. I called Julie—after a mini-adventure of sorts trying to get her phone number—and told her I would attempt to be in Chagford near the end of May. I hoped to catch her for a chat, but I didn't want to push. Our worlds were still different, and I was the outsider looking in. People might not like that, especially a husband away from home or a brother with a deadly aim.

---

[*] At least 30 regions of the world were involved in "major armed conflicts" in 1993, according to the Stockholm International Peace Research Institute. While some places improved, the new locations of nastiness were Azerbaijan, India-Pakistan, Laos, Tajikistan, Kosovo and Bosnia-Herzegovina. It won't get much better. Since 1988, 200,000 Kurds have reportedly been slain in Iraq, which may be low. And in an almost unknown war in Nagorno-Karabakh east of Armenia, 15,000 people have been killed and a million more turned into refugees. Rwanda may have a million deaths or more. By the end of the century, the number of estimated wars in progress had risen to 71.

As I booked the final reservations, I looked over everything I had read and written to date, and marveled at the whole affair. A simple life. It all started with a lifelong quest for a simple life shared by 77 million questors with varying degrees of hope or despair. How this large group would play out their lives only time would tell, but I felt more certain than ever that each and every one of them needed a night at a Bullers Arms. For ghosts or no ghosts, it was an experience that could only bring about a positive attitude toward life on this spinning, dizzying planet. It could help the Boomers avoid the temptation to become what Michael Eisner, head of Walt Disney Co., calls "housebound zombies." Or as Eisner has said quite bluntly, "cocooning becomes a form of self-burial." The people in Bullers Arms were alive, as they reminded themselves each night. The Boomers needed reminding as well.

P.S.

May 26, 1993
9:46 PM Chicago time (3:46 AM Chagford time). I am watching the BBC Sports Report on a British Airways 747 heading toward Heathrow Airport, London. This exercise in trying to figure out the mind-boggling cricket news is most painful. Here—try a couple out, with phony names substituted to protect the culprits: "Norfolk paceman Will Wobham's three runs off Kenny Cogham's final delivery forced a tie in a Lords thriller." *(Not THE Lord, but a famous place where they play, although many view cricket as a religious experience...God knows why.)* "Earlier, Mick Plickett's pugnacious 91—including a six and 10 fours—had lifted the home county to 247-7 against the League front-runners."

Try another one, apparently a real heartbreaker: "A career-best 5–26 by Avonshire's Roy Gilley counted for nothing as the match against Shropshire was abandoned." *I just don't get it.*

This torturous trek through the cricket sports news follows a conversation I had with an egg farmer, who occupied the aisle seat. I am in the window seat and we have established the middle seat as a Demilitarized Zone of sorts, since we'd both like to kill for more room. The plane is overbooked so we are thankful for one of the few overlooked overbooked seats that remains vacant. Whatever.

The egg farmer was interesting. (Then again, like I had a choice?) He owns seven farms in Iowa and Indiana and he supplies eggs to the Midwest. Those seven farms, I was told, have 11 million chickens laying between seven and eight million eggs a day. There's more! Did you know that from chicken to store, an egg hangs around from five to seven days? That an egg can stay refrigerated six months? That medium eggs—which come from younger chickens—are lower in cholesterol? I didn't know that!

Long flight. . . .

The Sports Report just ended, with no word about what happened to the Bulls last night. Ah, but it's déjà vu all over again. . .again! First, I must report that the Chicago Black Hawks made it to the Stanley Cup hockey playoffs and were unceremoniously trounced four games to zip. (Seems I read that somewhere at the beginning of this book, only it was a year earlier. See—nothing changes!) As for the Bullies, having cruised through the 1993 opening playoff rounds by sweeping Atlanta three games to nothing and then Cleveland 4–0, they marched into Madison Square Garden, NY, and were blown off their feet by their perennial enemy, the Knicks, in the first game of the National Basketball Association's Eastern Conference Finals. This unhappy event occurred in part because Michael Jordan left his cape in Chicago (the one the temporarily-deceased Superman wore); in part because the rest of his teammates started believing their press clippings about being invincible and therefore didn't bother to play. Then last night, Michael retrieved his cape and scored 36 points, but the Bulls still lost. Now they're down 2–0 in a best-of-seven game series. Doesn't look good for a third championship in a row.[*] But I probably won't learn about it until I get back to Chicago from Chagford.

---

[*] The Bulls, of course, won a third championship in a row. Then Michael retired, played baseball, came back, and the Bulls won three more championships. The more things change. . . .

Grave of Gen. Redvers Buller, VC, Crediton churchyard, Devon

Chagford. You see, I'm on my way to Chagford. I called Glendarah House— the House in the Valley of the Oak—and booked Thursday and Friday nights. I might stay there Saturday and Sunday as well, before leaving Monday for home. I have a lot of snooping to do, mainly to suss out places where the General visited, or earned a memorial, or in the case of Crediton, was buried in a lonely corner of the churchyard. These I will incorporate into this little journey, which is now over. Or is it?

It is perhaps fitting that this journey ends with a journey. I'm going back. Not to a simple life—the one I created in my mind. The one my generation dreams about and swears on a stack of pancakes they will find someday before they are too old to look. No, I'm going back to have an apple cider in Bullers Arms. To say hello to Gwen and Keith and Bob. To try to see "Captain" again—I've brought her a Bulls T-shirt, and a Notre Dame T-shirt with a fighting Irishman on it for her daughter, Joanne. (She's part Reilly, right?) I'll look for Chirpy, for Mr. Pipe & Pits, for Crafty Cool and Mr. Sloppy. For Mr. and Mrs. Properly Attired, who undoubtedly will be. For Hugh Griffith, cap on head, eyebrows jumping off his forehead. For Miss Short Blonde, chatting away with the P.A.s. Perhaps for Young Blonde and Young Brunette, if they haven't moved on to another pub, another part of Devon, maybe a big city, like Exeter.

And yes, I might even run into Nick. The dart tournament is over for 1993, but I wouldn't be surprised to see him firing away at the dart board in Bullers Arms with the precision of a diamond cutter. I will watch, from a discreet distance.

I know I remain the outsider. That even if I moved to Chagford, and people were as friendly to Mark the Resident as they are now to Mark the Visitor, I will always be The American Living in Chagford. *I had a conversation with Bob—co-proprietor of Bullers Arms—about his desire to one day retire to France, a country he loves to venture through, much as I do with England. Yet he has no illusions about such a move: he will always be* The Englishman *when he and his wife settle into that quaint French village. He accepts that. I would have to wonder the wisdom of such a move, the costs and the benefits, what I was gaining and what I was losing. All those thoughts Americans think because that's our culture. It's just not that simple.*

But I look to the immediate future now. I will rent a car at Heathrow and drive to Winchester, to visit the cathedral and snoop around the North Transept until I find a memorial to General Sir Redvers Buller, V.C. I will move on to Glendarah House, just outside Chagford before the calming effects of the speed bumps make themselves known. I will walk round the Market House, and sit in the porch of the Three Crowns Inn where Little Sidney Godolphin groaned his last groan, probably in iambic pentameter. I will venture out on the Dartmoor to look for the remnant traces of ancient lives—lives that were simple in their harshness and precariousness for survival.

A simple life in Chagford? Not really. A fulfilling, contented life? Yes. And when I sit in the pub sipping my cider, and I slowly turn to the portrait on the wall of the General, I will be reminded that ghosts never go away. That they haunt a village and a nation, much as my generation is haunted by its ghosts in America. You can't escape ghosts. That's why they're still in business.

Time to turn off the overhead light, put back the tray, close my new note pad and dream the life that never was and always will be. And the dream will focus on a pair of old hiking boots and a bicycle tire. It will zoom out, slowly, to show them next to a building. A doorway. A sign. The sign says Bullers Arms.

Fade to black.

Appendix
The Bankrupt 90s

The start of the 1990s in America was the beginning of the *Bankrupt Decade*—bankrupt in many ways despite a roaring economy in the second half. On the business side, the profligate spending (and not a little embezzling and corporate raiding) of the Reagan years had suddenly turned up **Payment Overdue**. Bloated corporations like General Motors and IBM and AT&T and Sears, Roebuck were now discovering why Olympic high jumpers, pole vaulters and long jumpers cannot compete when they are overweight: they don't move very quickly, and they come in last every time. The 1990s corporate solution? Downsize, Rightsize, Streamline, Merge & Acquire, Re-engineer, Lean-And-Mean...catchy euphemisms for "let's fire as many people as we can and still get the product into the marketplace." Or as one general manager once told me when considering what to do with a long-time employee, "Let's *lose* him."

And let's not forget Kodak's rationale for laying off 10,000 employees in the mid-1990s amid *earnings of $1 billion*: "We owe it to our stockholders to make more profit."[*]

The rich, of course, including those large stockholders, will never be lost. Although corporate boards are beginning to clamp down on

---

[*] On Income Tax day, 1998, Ameritech announced layoffs of 7,000 workers, or 7% of its work force, amid record operating profits. Downsizing can go hand-in-hand with a booming economy, and not just in a recession. The same is true with mergers and acquisitions: the Chemical Bank-Chase Manhattan merger in 1995 resulted in 12,000 job cuts worldwide.

outrageous salaries and bonus packages for corporate executives, especially those heading financially-strapped companies, the rich did just fine in the 1980s and continued to do so into the next century.* The richest one percent of all Americans account for 37 percent of all the private net worth in the U.S., up about 20 percent since 1980. Their net worth of almost $6 trillion is more than the net worth of the bottom 90 percent. Bill Gates of Microsoft, all by himself, is worth more than numerous countries combined, or at least he was until the April, 2000 "correction." Are those that made a killing during the 90s any happier than before their windfalls? No, and not just in America. An international study determined that money did not buy happiness: "neither increasing income at the individual level nor country level were accompanied by increases in subjective well-being," it noted. In fact, "rapid increases in wealth resulted in less, not more, happiness."

At the same time, sadly, the U.S. acquired a higher rate of children living in poverty—1 in 5—than any rich country on earth, double that of the industrialized world and four times that of Western Europe.

Corporate America began steering a course that could not take people's lives much further away from a simple one—let alone a stable, secure one. The downsizing directive from the corporate office reached new highs the year after *Time's* cover story hit the newsstands in 1991, and it has continued unabated: General Motors cut its work force 32 percent; Ford Motor, 24 percent; General Electric (worldwide), 33 percent; IBM (worldwide), 26 percent; Amoco, 22 percent. These, of course, are percentages, which on the surface are easier on the conscience and less annoying to read than numbers about *real people*. People? From 1992 to 1996 alone, for IBM we are talking 122,000 *people*; 50,000 for Sears; 83,000 for AT&T; 74,000 for GM. Numbers that are larger than whole towns or cities. And merger-mania will have a

---

* In the second quarter, 2000, profit-anemic Mattel—the makers of the Barbie doll—gave their 46-year-old female CEO $40 million dollars to leave, on top of a $700,000 a year check. Barbie has come a long way. Unfortunately, Mattel employees have not.

huge forward effect on layoffs and firings: in 1998, more than 7,200 mergers occurred (a record) worth well over $1 trillion. How many people will those merged companies *lose*?

Remember when the computer started invading offices and factories, and "the experts" told Americans that, no, their jobs were secure and that, behold!, the computer would actually create *more* jobs? I don't think so. In just the banking industry, from 1994 to 2000 some 450,000 jobs simply *disappeared*, along with half the U.S. bank branches. Who will take their places? Computers, in the form of automatic teller machines and PCs using telephone and cable lines and remote connections. Wonder if "the experts" whose predictions went amiss are still gainfully employed, or if their desks are now occupied by, well, you know....

Simple life? In the first half of the 1990s, more than 3,000,000 Americans lost their jobs. If you take the period 1987–92, 6,000,000 Americans were sacked, and the Bureau of Labor Statistics reports that a full 85 percent of those who were laid off believed they will never be rehired. In fact, a survey of executives from America's 1,000 largest companies noted that *one-third* of all U.S. workers will lose their jobs during the course of their employment. What about the *new* jobs being created that politicians like to tout? They are lower paying, and many are temporary. The only "big bucks" sector, the internet companies, saw their stock values plunge in April, 2000—all stocks lost $2 trillion on paper in just five days—signaling the beginning of more layoffs.

It is rather telling to point out that the largest private sector employer in the United States today is Manpower, Inc. (600,000 and rising), a *temporary employment service.* Indeed, almost 60 percent of all college teachers are part-time or temporary instructors! Americans at all levels—blue collar, white collar, senior executive—have been cut loose from the umbilical cord of lifetime employment, or even full-time employment. No, life is drifting further away from being even a slice of simplicity in America, and at a time when a "simple life" seems more and more desirable…and less attainable.

Baby Boomers are becoming financially bankrupt, mirroring the economic woes of the entire work force. Personal bankruptcies have now reached more than one million for the first time in history. Boomers are also in for a tough retirement. Despite a booming economy through much of the last decade of the 20th century, 40 percent of all Boomers have saved *less than $10,000* for their retirements. Why? Many Boomers have never met a nickel they didn't want to spend: ask VISA and MASTERCARD, the twin Boomer gods of debt facilitation. And many more simply cannot afford to save. Add to that being caught in the middle—having to take care of children and aging parents—and the Boomers are in for a rough, complicated ride for the rest of their lives.

More frightening still were the results of a recent survey asking future retirees where they thought they would get enough money to live in a manner similar to their current lifestyle. The number one answer: win the lottery.

Our neighborhoods have also become bankrupt in meaning and even in physical appearance. A December, 1998, cover story in *PARADE* asked the question "Where Have All The Small Towns gone?" *Time* magazine thought Americans might have had enough when, in a March 1999 article, "The Brawl Over Sprawl," it was suggested that "before America turns into one giant paved-over subdivision, people are fighting back." But then the story asked the unanswerable question "Is there hope?"

Americans have also begun to face a society where it has become dangerous just to set up that quaint food market in St. Paul described earlier. My own city of Chicago has been approaching 1,000 murders a year—with one out of every 10 of those victims children—and other cities large and small are witnessing their populations solving problems, irritations and jealousies by ending life at a rapid pace. Since 1960, the U.S. population grew 41 percent while the violent crime rate exploded 500 percent! And every 15 seconds, a house is broken into in America;

every two minutes a murder committed. And from 1985 to 1995, the number of juveniles murdered by firearms rose 153 percent. Kids, of course, are familiar with guns. More than 40 percent of U.S. households with children ages three to 17 have guns; in about one-quarter of those homes, the guns are kept loaded at least some of the time. And in 43% of them, the guns are not locked up or fitted with trigger locks.

We need not dwell on the 1999 Columbine High School shootings and the ones occurring before and after. They will continue and they will increase as long as families remain bankrupt in ethical teaching, in moral and parental responsibility and in a willingness to "make time" to find out what children are doing, and why.

Here are some more uglies: every school day in America, at least 100,000 students tote guns in schools, and *1 out of 5* carry some form of weapon; 160,000 skip classes because they fear physical harm; 40 are wounded or killed by firearms; 6,250 teachers are threatened with bodily injury; and 260 are physically assaulted. And that's just in the quiet confines in and around our schools! Lots of hate, lots of fear—and all this going on in spite of the fact that *1 out of every 150 Americans is in jail*—men, women and children! Other symptoms of a bankrupt family unit and lack of moral values and caring for our youth: the number of criminals under 18 serving time in adult prisons has doubled between 1985 and 1997, and teen heroin use is rising, with 12th graders doubling their intake between 1990 and 1996.

It should therefore not be surprising that *stress* has become the single-most invasive malady in our lives, and not just from fear of personal safety. Americans now work longer hours, thanks in part to the "losing" of employees. Morale in the workplace is down: 75 percent of companies surveyed who cut their work force said "employee morale had collapsed." And 3 out of every 4 visits to the doctor involve stress-related complaints. Women have also discovered stress on their long road to employment equality. When 250,000 women were surveyed about their jobs, 60 percent mentioned stress as their number one problem; nearly 75 percent of Baby Boom women in managerial or professional jobs said the same thing. Even when Americans go on vacation to "relax" from the stress, 40 percent bring a pager or cell phone along. Is it really surprising that the word *simple* often pops up, even long after the 1991 *Time* cover story? A December, 1999, *Associated Press* article, entitled "Stressed-out consumers willing to pay for simpler life," noted that "the ubiquity of the word 'simple' in advertising may not be new but marketers say it is becoming more prominent as Americans try to restore some calm to frenetic lifestyles." Small wonder. A government survey found that 40 million American adults "often find themselves in a bad mood—bored, restless, lonely, upset or depressed."

The phenomenon of stress is not confined to our shores. The United Nations International Labor Union observed that "job stress is increasing to the point of a worldwide epidemic." (Actually, that would make it a *pandemic*.) In Japan, for example, death by overworking has a word, *karoshi*, and 40 percent of all Japanese workers fear they will suffer it.[*]

The kids, of course, are under enormous stress from the breakup of the nuclear family—barely 50 percent live with both their parents—and the economic woes that have beset most Americans. This undoubtedly has led to some of the school activities previously listed. Some 13 percent of all children are on welfare, up 268 percent since 1960. (One out of 10 Americans receives food stamps.) Teen suicides are up 300 percent over the same period—in 1998, 10 percent of all teens said they had tried or considered suicide—and one-third of all babies born in the U.S. are to unwed mothers, many of them teens.

---

[*] In 1994, Japanese companies chopped the recruitment of new graduates by 17 percent and the trend continues. The land of the Rising Sun seems to be setting its corporate hiring agenda along the lines of U.S. companies: the world was shocked at the end of the decade when giant Nippon Telegraph and Telephone Corp., second largest worldwide telecommunications company, announced it would cut 21,000 jobs over 36 months. Europe does not have shiny, happy people either. European Community statistics point to a 10 percent unemployment rate in the EC countries, with a steady rise in sight. Spain currently holds the dubious unemployment honors: 19.5 percent. And the 1998 global economic collapse in the Pacific Rim region promises a worsening employment condition for the near term.

America also "discovered" in the last decade of the 20th century that they lived in a morally bankrupt society. Graft has become as common as the cold—speaking of which, even health care giant Blue Cross-Blue Shield of Illinois felt no pain in bilking Medicare out of $144 million in phony charges. The same was true of payoffs and favors, whether through government contracts or favors obtained for favors granted— "Doesn't everybody do it?"

There is no need to belabor the President Clinton-Monica Lewinsky affair or the hypocritical behavior of those critics calling for his head, although a sidebar at the end will make note of both the comedy and tragedy of it all. Suffice it to say that private problems and indiscretions are now fodder for public review, rebuke and revelry, and the "best and the brightest" will wisely—although sadly for the republic—eschew running for office in order to preserve their personal lives. The ancient Romans were into 'bread and circuses' before their fall as a society. An American collapse may come from 'bed and perquisites'. Same results.

Finally, Americans are also lonely—millions of them. According to the 1990 Census, there are 72 million single people over 18 years of age in the United States, a 53 percent jump from the 47 million lonelies in 1975. In this millennial year, fully half the U.S. population is single— from the death of a spouse, divorce or never being married. That's a very lonely nation on the horizon, and coupled with what is taking place in the workplace, the streets, the schools and the home perhaps explains why during the last decade people have turned inward towards being with oneself, rather than with one another. Lots of videotape rentals, computer games and surfing the internet—the latter activity, according to a recent study, resulting in "higher levels of depression and loneliness than they would have if they used the internet less frequently."

No, it is not simple in America. Never was, never will be.

* * * *

HYPOCRISY AND HONOR

When impeachment became a rallying cry for the Republicans in 1998, it centered as much on President Clinton's deplorable extramarital affair as his lying to the courts and the public. The "man-in-charge" of the impeachment proceedings was the Honorable Henry Hyde of Illinois, Republican Chairman of the House of Representative's Judiciary Committee. As it turned out, the Honorable Chairman had an adulterous affair himself in the 1960s. Did he feel just a little funny about prosecuting a politician for the same behavior he himself had exhibited? Not at all. His response when the truth came out, which of course he had been hiding: "The statute of limitations has long since passed on my youthful indiscretions." Excuse me? Does this mean that President Clinton's behavior would have been acceptable to the Honorable Chairman if he were "youthful"—although the Honorable Chairman was *41* at the time of his "indiscretion?" Did Bill Clinton just miss Chairman Henry Hyde's morally-reasonable Adultery Deadline by just a few years? What an unlucky fellow, President Clinton was. And how fortunate for the Honorable Congressman that he is comfortable in subscribing to the belief that one of the Ten Commandments does not apply if you are "youthful" enough, say, 41 years old. Apparently the Honorable Congressman discovered that only nine commandments cover one's entire life—an interpretation both Moses and Charleton Heston clearly missed.

The hypocrisy scale added a new reading from virulent Clinton basher Congressman Dan Burton—he called the president a "scumbag" (a rude street term for a condom). The Honorable Republican Congressman from Indiana "forgot" to mention that he as well had an adulterous affair, a decade ago, which ended in his fathering a child— apparently through an oversight in failing to utilize one of those scumbags. To hush it up, the Honorable Congressman lied about it (is that legal?) and sent money to support the child and silence the mother (is *that* legal?) so he could protect his career. President Clinton simply lied (that's not legal), foregoing cash payments to anyone. The Honorable Congressman Dan Burton is still in office.

More readings. Another politician calling for Clinton's resignation, the Honorable Republican Congresswoman Helen Chenowith of Idaho, was forced to confess, after word leaked out, that she once had an affair *with a married man*. Chenowith perhaps forgot about it—at least long enough to run for office on a "family values" platform in 1994 while disclosing to the public that her opponent had been involved in, if one can imagine, *an affair*! When she finally "remembered" what she had done—during the investigation of Clinton—she said "I've asked for God's forgiveness, and I received it." It was fortunate for Honorable Congresswoman Chenowith that God deemed her affair a forgiving one, although not a few people would like to see in writing what exactly she received from the Almighty in the way of a moral parole.

President Clinton, for all his political acumen, obviously failed to cultivate an advantageous relationship with the Ultimate Politician Himself. Otherwise, he might have avoided moral condemnation, as his honorable Republican colleagues managed to do.

About the Author

Mark R. Horowitz is a well-known writer, historian and marketing consultant. The author of *Stonehenge to Star Wars: Discovering the Present by Exploring the Past*, described as "Fascinating Reading!" by Paul Harvey, Mark was a syndicated UPI columnist, a WMAQ radio commentator, and penned Guest Columns for USA TODAY.

His commentaries, articles, quotes, and notes have appeared in the *New York Times, Wall Street Journal, Chicago Tribune, Time Magazine, Houston Chronicle, Sacramento Bee, San Francisco Chronicle, Birmingham News, Baltimore Sun, Rocky Mountain News, Cedar Rapids Gazette, Chicago Sun-Times*, among others. Mark has been a Lecturer in the University of Chicago's Publishing Program, and he is a former editor of the University's *Social Science Reports*. He is a consultant to, and founding board member of, the IADC Institute, coordinating the *National Jury Trial Innovations Project* to improve the jury system of justice in America. Mark's video, "Order in the Classroom," depicting a college class conducted as a jury trial, has received high marks from thousands of judges and attorneys across the U. S. He holds degrees from Tulane University, the University of Illinois and the University of Chicago, was affiliated with the *Institute of Historical Research* (University of London) and has published scholarly articles and given papers at academic conferences. Mark enjoys creating stories, travel, tennis, climbing, photography, historical research and writing, and snooping around old churches, castles and Neolithic ruins. His photo-essay on the place-name origins for Conan Doyle's *Hound of the Baskervilles* is in the Sherlock Holmes Collection at Benedictine College. His English Brass Rubbing Collection has toured the United States and accompanied the *Magna Carta* when it made an appearance in America; it now resides at the Spurlock Museum of the University of Illinois (Urbana). Mark was sponsored for *Pulitzer Prizes* in Explanatory Journalism, and News Commentary.